EYEWITNESS VIETNAM

EYEWITNESS VIETNAM

Firsthand Accounts from Operation Rolling Thunder to the Fall of Saigon

DONALD L. GILMORE with D.M. GIANGRECO
Foreword by Lester W. Grau

Sterling Publishing Co., Inc.
New York

Published by Sterling Publishing Co, Inc.
387 Park Avenue South, New York, NY 10016

©2006 by Sterling Publishing Co, Inc.

Distributed in Canada by Sterling Publishing
c/o Canadian Manda Group, 165 Dufferin Street
Toronto, Ontario, Canada M6K 3H6

Distributed in the United Kingdom by GMC
Distribution Services, Castle Place, 166 High
Street, East Sussex, England BN7 1XU

Distributed in Australia by Capricorn Link
(Australia) Pty. Ltd.
P.O. Box 704, Windsor, NSW 2756, Australia

ISBN-10: 1-4027-2852-2
ISBN-13: 978-14027-2852-5

Printed in Belgium

10 9 8 7 6 5 4 3 2 1

For information on custom editions, special
sales, premium and corporate purchases, please
contact Sterling Special Sales Department at
800-805-5489 or specialsales@sterlingpub.com.

Cover designed by Kevin McGuinness.

FRONT AND BACK ENDPAPERS: UH-1D Hueys of the 25th Aviation Battalion land at the Filhol Rubber Plantation, northeast of Cu Chi, to extract 25th Infantry Division troops of the 2d Battalion, 14th Infantry, during Operation WAHIAWA, May 16, 1966.

HALF-TITLE PAGE: A U.S. Navy A-7A Corsair II prepares to launch from a carrier off the coast of Vietnam. Based on the design of the Crusader, the Corsair was armed with half the number of 20-mm cannons but carried a prodigious bomb load of fifteen thousand pounds—more than twice that of a World War II–era B-17 bomber. The later A-7E in Vietnam service mounted a Vulcan multi-barrel cannon in place of the two 20-mms.

HALF-TITLE PAGE, INSET: Following a hard day during Operation YELLOWSTONE in War Zone C, 25th Infantry Division soldiers relax with a guitar, Tay Ninh Province, January 18, 1968.

TITLE PAGES: Marines of a signals or headquarters unit near the Demilitarized Zone hug the earth as incoming rounds explode nearby during 1968. Fire bases established as much as two years earlier by the 3d Marine division along Route 9 (which generally paralleled the DMZ separating North and South Vietnam) extended from Khe Sanh in the west through The Rockpile, Ca Lu, Camp Carrol, Cam Lo, Guo Linh, and Cua Viet in the east. Often the scenes of fierce fighting, these bases were well within the range of heavy artillery situated in North Vietnam and Laos.

COPYRIGHT PAGES: Marines of 1st Division's P Company, 2d Battalion, 5th Regiment, fire at maneuvering Viet Cong during Operation NEW CASTLE, Quang Nam Province, March 26, 1967.

CONTENTS PAGES: Soldiers "pop smoke" to guide in a medevac helicopter picking up wounded troopers during 1st Cavalry Division operations in the A Shau Valley, April 30, 1968.

Acknowledgments

The authors would like to thank the many veterans who lent their assistance during the production of *Eyewitness Vietnam*, in particular: Dr. Jerold E. Brown; Colonel Jerry D. Morelock, Ph.D. (U.S. Army, Retired); Major Terry A. Griswold (U.S. Army, Retired); Lieutenant Colonel James H. Willbanks, Ph.D. (U.S. Army, Retired); Joe Galloway; Colonel J.D. Coleman (U.S. Army, Retired); Lieutenant Colonel Lester W. Grau (U.S. Army, Retired); Major John L. Plaster (U.S. Army, Retired); and especially Captain Shelby L. Stanton (U.S. Army, Retired), who gave generously of his time throughout the production of *Eyewitness Vietnam*.

The publisher also wishes to acknowledge the help of the following for making this book possible:

At First Person Productions, LLC: Marc Honorof, Robert Kirk, and Robert Lihani; on behalf of First Person Productions: David Connelly, Michael Dolan, Harlan Glenn, Mike Grove, and Nat Wieczorek.

At Sterling: Janice Ackerman, Betsy Beier, Karen Matsu Greenberg, Erikka Haa, Nathaniel Marunas, Jacqueline Rossi, Daniel Rutkowski, Michele L. Trombley, and Kevin Ullrich.

This book is dedicated to the Americans missing in action during the Vietnam War. They have not been forgotten by their families or by those who appreciate their sacrifice. Many of their bodies lie in foreign soil an ocean away from the United States, but the memory of them lives on.

Contents

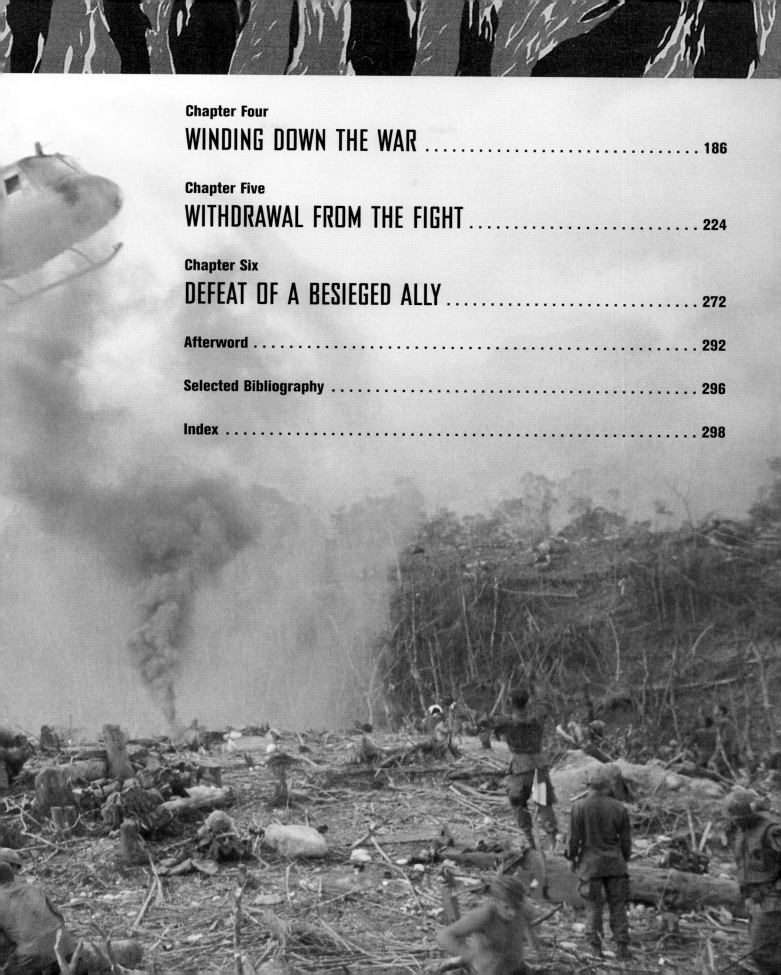

Foreword

The Vietnam War was a long time ago—and just yesterday. It certainly was long enough ago for the U.S. Army to evolve full circle from a guerrilla-fighting force to a premier maneuver-warfare force to a guerrilla-fighting force once again. And yet, for the participants, the Vietnam War happened only yesterday. It was a time of youth in an exotic land amid a mostly welcoming people. And what an experience it was—the sights, the smells, the heat, the damp, the leeches, the boredom, the heady excitement, and the occasional terror. We grew up there—fast—and generally for the better. Yet when we returned home, it was to a different country than the one we had left behind.

Most of our fellow citizens tolerated our return, but were a little embarrassed about approaching or acknowledging us. Many American leftists and anti-establishment types openly denigrated us and, in some cases, just as openly supported the Communists. Some American youth condemned us for fighting in an "immoral war," though this moral indignation quickly dissolved in many quarters once President Nixon abolished the draft. With little fanfare, we were left to pick up our lives and move on. The vast majority of servicemen shifted easily back into society. Some unfortunate veterans had severe adjustment problems and their struggles became the media's reflexive image for all Vietnam vets. Others of us could not stomach civilian community and stayed in the military.

Initially, few veterans wrote about their experiences. Back then, few people were really interested in what we had to say. A few, however, produced brilliant histories of the conflict. Dave R. Palmer's *Summons of the Trumpet: U.S.–Vietnam in Perspective,* Harry G. Summers Jr.'s *On Strategy: A Critical Analysis of the Vietnam War,* Harold G. Moore and Joseph L. Galloway's *We Were Soldiers Once...and Young: Ia Drang–The Battle that Changed the War in Vietnam,* and James H. Willbanks's *Abandoning Vietnam: How America Left and South Vietnam Lost Its War* are my personal favorites.

Today, there is widespread interest in the Vietnam War as history and as a defining time in American social development. Don Gilmore's and D.M. Giangreco's *Eyewitness Vietnam: Firsthand Accounts from Operation Rolling Thunder to the Fall of Saigon* addresses this growing interest nicely. Although neither man is a veteran of the conflict, their long association with the Army and its soldiers is displayed through their balanced account of the war as seen through the fighting man's eyes. *Eyewitness Vietnam* contains a first-rate collection of photographs and first-hand reminiscences that bring it all back: the creaking squeal of the tracks on a M113 personnel carrier; the dank, dark smell of the jungle; the warning grunts of always-hostile water buffalo; the off-putting stench of *nuoc mam* (a ubiquitous fermented fish sauce used as a condiment in the local cuisine); the boisterous yells of children and their tireless interest in Americans' hairy arms; and the sharp crack of a bullet flying way too close. But this book is more than nostalgia for aging warriors. It successfully re-creates the entire experience.

Vietnam was a war of maneuver. Vietnam was a positional war. Vietnam was a war fought on flooded rice paddies and rivers. Vietnam was a war fought over rugged mountain ranges. Vietnam was a guerrilla war. Vietnam was a war conducted in the jungle. Vietnam was a futuristic war fought with modern air power, innovative electronics, and air assault forces. Vietnam was a conventional war fought by slow-moving infantrymen slogging through mud and muck. Vietnam was a civil war. Vietnam was an ideological war fought out on the streets and television sets of Europe and America. Vietnam was all of these things, and what one experienced depended where you were and what your job was. When I was there, most of my contemporaries were fighting a conventional North Vietnamese force in the jungles. My personal war was fighting the Viet Cong guerrilla and, with the South Vietnamese army, trying to bring security to the locals— the kind of tasks that the U.S. Army and Marine Corps have always done.

Part of *Eyewitness Vietnam* reflects the much larger population involved in the war—the Vietnamese people. The war was about their land and their future, after all. South Vietnam was made up of a mix of ethnic Vietnamese, Chinese, Cambodians, Montagnards, Eurasians, and home to a diverse mixture of religions, including Buddhism, Hoa Hao, Catholicism, Cao Dai, and animism. Many South Vietnamese were, in fact, refugees from North Vietnam. Not surprisingly, a good number tied their identity, their fate, and their future to the United States' defense of their country. Of course, other nations also aided the South Vietnamese in their struggle.

Australia, New Zealand, South Korea, and the Philippines sent forces, while numerous other nations provided aid, relief workers, staging areas, and rest-and-recreation sites. Despite the efforts of the United States and the other nations that had come to South Vietnam's side, of course, the battle-field was lost. Those South Vietnamese who could not flee were left to endure the horrors of the Communist "re-edu-cation camps," penury, and subservience to their new masters from the north.

At home, the Vietnam War was and remains divisive. Many of the children of the "Greatest Generation" followed in the footsteps of their parents and served in the Armed Forces. Others avoided service, and some even cheered when the nation's flag was burned. Those who served included a high percentage of volunteers from a broad spectrum of society. Those who avoided service were generally children of privi-lege, some of whom later pretended they had actually been there. Likewise, as has happened since time immem-orial, some men who saw little action or who performed non-combat roles that are nonetheless critical to the functioning of any army, "upgraded" their service to include intensive combat. Some soldiers who served honorably are falsely accused of lying about their experiences. Some objec-tors, who avoided combat or who participated in anti-war activities, refuse to accept that the people who served in Vietnam were generally men of honor and decency and that their intentions were good.

Nowadays, there are plenty of books on the Vietnam war—biographies, autobiographies, histories, coffee-table books, exposes, apologia, and more. So what is the purpose of this book?

At first, it appears to be just another photo book. But these pictures are not the stuff of the photojournalists who periodically choppered out for a few days in the "boonies" from their hotels in Saigon. The bulk of these images were shot by military photographers in the course of daily duties that placed them all over Vietnam, from the DMZ to the Mekong Delta and everywhere in between. Living in the base camps and in the field, they were a part of the experience, not occasional observers recording fleeting aspects of it. Further, *Eyewitness Vietnam* is loaded with interviews and recollections of the sol-diers, Marines, and airmen themselves that will bring it all back for those who were actually there and give those who weren't a unique look at that long, complex war. Bringing balance to the mix are the reminiscences of Vietnamese military and civilian personnel.

Don Gilmore and D.M. Giangreco are particularly well equipped to write *Eyewitness Vietnam*. Gilmore is the author of *Civil War on the Missouri-Kansas Border*, a thoroughly researched history of the brutal 1854-to-1865 guerrilla war in America's heartland that documents the mass deportations, summary executions of civilians, and terror perpetuated by both sides of this little-known and poorly understood conflict. Prize-winning historian Giangreco has published eight books, including *Eyewitness D-DAY: Firsthand Accounts from the Landing at Normandy to the Liberation of Paris*, co-written with Kathryn Moore. Giangreco has also written numerous studies and articles dealing with a wide range of subjects, including Special Forces, military operations during World War II, and the evolution

of fire support doctrine. Together, Gilmore and Giangreco bring a welcome professionalism and even-handedness to *Eyewitness Vietnam*.

Once again America is battling guerrillas. Neither Iraq nor Afghanistan is the same as Vietnam, but much of the job of soldiering remains the same. The locale, the people, and the geography are different, but the troops on the ground and in the air are still faced with the tedious, uncomfortable, and dangerous job of dealing with combatants who dress like civilians and avoid direct battle whenever possible. Hopefully there will one day be books about Iraq and Afghanistan that will offer, like this one does about an earlier war, an honest look at the many challenges faced by our men and women in uniform.

—Les Grau,
author of *The Bear Went Over the Mountain: Soviet Combat Tactics in Afghanistan, The Other Side of the Mountain: Mujahideen Tactics in the Soviet-Afghan War,* (with Ali Jalali), and *The Soviet-Afghan War: How a Superpower Fought and Lost*

Introduction

"Vietnam veterans believe . . . ," "Vietnam veterans maintain . . . ," "Vietnam veterans feel. . . ." At times, particularly during election years, it seems there is no shortage of confident assertions as to just what is in the hearts and minds of those who served in Southeast Asia during America's longest war. These men, however, have proven to be a hard lot to quantify, categorize, or pigeonhole, particularly since theirs was the last great conflict to see hundreds of thousands of young conscripts sent halfway around the world to a strange, alien land.

Yet this popularly held image of the Army during the 1960s (that is, an army of draftees) is less accurate than it seems. The cold, impersonal statistics of the U.S. Department of Veteran Affairs tell us that of the 2,594,000 personnel who served within the Republic of Vietnam's—South Vietnam's—borders, just less than 25 percent were draftees, a figure far below the 66 percent of World War II. In all, some 3,403,100 Americans served in the Southeast Asian theater of operations, from the air bases and intelligence facilities in Thailand to the Seventh Fleet ships in Yankee Station on the South China Sea, between 1965 and 1975.

Much of the raw data from the war are not surprising: for instance,

that 10 percent of the 47,400 combat and 10,800 noncombat deaths in Vietnam were among helicopter crews. Other data defy the common media myths or are, at least, counterintuitive, such as that fully 23 percent

of the soldiers in Vietnam came from "privileged" families, in which the fathers held professional, managerial, or technical occupations.

Of the men who actually served in "Nam," 88.4 percent were Caucasian, 1.0 percent, "other," and 10.6 percent were African American, even though black Americans of military age made up 13.5 percent of the U.S. population. Black soldiers, nevertheless, represented 12.1 percent of those killed in action because of their higher representation in infantry units. It also turns out that 79 percent of the servicemen sent to Vietnam had completed high school or at least some college—16 percent more than those who had fought in the Korean War.

But what do such statistics really tell us? Certainly nothing about the fear of finding yourself ambushed by an unseen enemy as you push your way through a chest-deep, stinking stream or while flying through a hail of anti-aircraft fire over North Vietnam's "Thud Ridge."

Eyewitness Vietnam documents two such first-person reminiscences, and many more besides, from the men who participated in America's longest war, a war that remains just as unsettled and troubling for some Americans today as it was more than three decades ago, and whose legacy is still playing itself out today.

ABOVE: Above a photograph of President John F. Kennedy, Secretary of Defense Robert McNamara, and General Maxwell D. Taylor, a 1963 edition of the U.S. Army newspaper *Pacific Stars and Stripes* confidently announces that the American advisory effort in South Vietnam will be concluded within two years. The war, in fact, dragged on a decade beyond the optimistic estimate.

OPPOSITE: Carbine in hand, Captain Robert Bacon pauses to scan the far treeline while leading a Vietnamese Army patrol in Long An Province, southwest of Saigon, May 1964.

The biggest shock was coming out of the airplane and being in Vietnam for the first time. The heat and the humidity were just stifling. The smell was overwhelming.

—Specialist Fourth Class Ken Cory,
2d Battalion, 14th Infantry Regiment, 25th Infantry Division

Chapter One

A NEW KIND OF WAR

In August 1945, immediately after the close of World War II, in an almost bloodless revolution, the Communists under General Vo Nguyen Giap seized control of North Vietnam. Shortly thereafter, when French general Jacques Leclerc arrived in the country to stabilize the situation in the South, he was met at the airport by General Giap, who had been ordered to make this conciliatory move by Ho Chi Minh, the leader of the North Vietnamese Communist Party, as a ruse to cover up their violent intentions to seize power over the entire country. To prod his general into this show of false friendship, Ho was reported to have said, "Cry your eyes out, Giap, but be at the airport in two hours." Not long after this meeting, Ho and Giap began a protracted, bloody war with the French that culminated in the crushing defeat of the French Army at Dien Bien Phu on May 7, 1954. The war was characterized by atrocities and a bitter guerrilla struggle.

The War's Background

The Geneva Convention of 1954, convened to resolve the Indochina War, split Vietnam into two parts, with the Communist Viet Minh ruling

PAGES 12–13: Vietnamese soldiers and U.S. Marine advisors scramble to move supplies as their landing zone comes under small-arms fire, April 16, 1964.

TOP: Some of the eighty thousand mostly Catholic Vietnamese evacuated from the North by the U.S. Navy after the Geneva Conference found temporary refuge in camps like this one, named New Cana by its occupants.

BOTTOM: President Ngo Dinh Diem, his aides, and local officials visit a shop in Long An Province near Saigon, July 1960. Photo ops did little to halt the decline of Diem's fortunes as he persecuted South Vietnam's Buddhist majority, refused efforts at political reform, and concentrated on building a conventional military instead of one structured to counter the expanding guerrilla activities.

OPPOSITE, TOP: Viet Minh commander Vo Nguyen Giap (left) and Vietnamese chief of state Ho Chi Minh, circa 1946.

the country north of the 17th parallel and the French controlling the country south of that line. Many Vietnamese, particularly Catholics, fled south. Some South Vietnamese were Communists and Marxists, while others were nationalists who either supported or opposed the Viet Minh. The convention stipulated that an election be held in July 1956, in which the reunited country would decide its political affiliation. In the interim, the conflict raged on between Ho Chi Minh, Communist Party leader in the North, and the Vietnamese led by Ngo Dinh Diem in the South. Hampered by their inadequate industrial infrastructure, the North Vietnamese increasingly relied on Russian and Chinese armaments and war supplies to continue the conflict. The South Vietnamese, on their part, looked to the United States for advisors, military hardware, and support. Earlier during the war, the United States, under

President Harry S. Truman, had backed the French by providing a small Military Assistance and Advisory Group (MAAG). President Eisenhower had continued that policy.

In 1955, Diem was elected president of South Vietnam by a plurality of votes in a contest among ten candidates. After taking office he refused to consider any concessions to the local peasants in the way of land reform, since this would have alienated the political power brokers. This cost Diem badly needed support in the countryside. In addition, he angered and marginalized the country's Buddhists, a powerful group, by favoring South Vietnam's Catholics. Diem was himself a Catholic, and it was they who controlled the political process. He strengthened his position by enlarging the army and naming his brother, Ngo Dinh Nhu, to lead a secret spy organization that monitored and attempted to suppress his many opponents. In 1956, Diem refused to allow the scheduled reunification election to take place, realizing that the Communists in the North, with the support of their allies in the South, would carry the vote.

Senior General Vo Nguyen Giap

Vo Nguyen Giap was born in 1912 in central Vietnam, the son of an ardent nationalist. Giap attended the Lycée Nationale in Hue, as did Ho Chi Minh and Pham Van Dong, one of the founders of the Indochinese Communist Party and eventually prime minister of North Vietnam. Poor and sickly as a child, Giap became a revolutionary at the age of fourteen. By the time he was eighteen, he was imprisoned for his subversive activities. Later, he ingratiated himself with the French and was allowed to earn a Bachelor of Laws degree, but he never pursued law as a career. In 1937, Giap joined the Communists, and in 1938 began a short career in teaching at the Lycée Thang-Long, a private high school in Hanoi. Giap's students referred to him as the General because of his mastery of the campaigns of Napoleon, whom Giap obviously admired.

Upon his introduction to Ho Chi Minh, Giap became an important Communist operative and later assumed the presidency of the Vietnamese Supreme Council of National Defense. After World War II, when the French returned to Vietnam to reassert their authority, Giap commanded the Viet Minh in the First Indochina War. In 1954, Giap defeated the French at the Battle of Dien Bien Phu, which drove them out of Indochina and earned him a high reputation as a military leader and strategist.

ABOVE: Vo Nguyen Giap, circa 1962.

When the United States entered the Vietnam War (the Second Indochina War), Giap led North Vietnamese Army/Viet Cong forces against it. After the Third Indochina War—the war between North and South Vietnam, 1973–1975—Giap lost influence in the Communist Party and the People's Army of Vietnam until, in 1980, he relinquished his last Vietnamese post, that of defense minister.

17th Parallel

THAILAND

LAOS

CAMBODIA

Mekong River

TONLE SAP

PHNOM PENH

Quang Tri
Quang Tri

Hue
Thua Thien

Da Nang
Hoi An
Quang Nam

Quang Ngai
Quang Ngai

Kontum

Kontum

Binh Dinh

Pleiku
Qui Nhon

Pleiku
Song Cau

Phu Yen

Darlac
Ban Me Thuot

Khanh Hoa
Nha Trang

Quang Duc
Gia Nghia
Tuyen Duc

Phuoc Long
Song Be
Lam Dong
Da Lat
Ninh Thuan

Binh Long
An Loc
Phuoc Thanh
Phuoc Vinh
Djiring
Phan Rang

Tay Ninh
Tay Ninh
Binh Duong
Phu Cuong
Long Khanh
Binh Tuy
Binh Thuan

Kien Tuong
Long An
Gia Dinh
Gia Dinh
Xuan Loc
Phan Thiet

Kien Phong
Go Bac Chien
SAIGON
Bien Hoa
Bien Hoa
Phuoc Tuy
Ham Tan

An Giang
Cao Lanh
Tan An
Phuoc Le

Kien Giang
Long Xuyen
Vinh Long
Dinh Tuong
My Tho

Rach Gia
Vinh Long
Ben Tre
Kien Hoa

Phong Dinh
Can Tho
Phu Vinh
Vinh Binh

GULF OF THAILAND

Khanh Hung (Soc Trang)
Ba Xuyen

Quan Long (Ca Mau)
An Xuyen

SOUTH CHINA SEA

Con Son

SOUTH VIETNAM
1959

0   100 MILES

0   100 KILOMETERS

At the same time that Diem was attempting to consolidate a viable government in the South, the Communists in both the North and the South were striving for complete control of Vietnam. John F. Kennedy was confronted with this volatile situation when he became president on January 21, 1961. He responded by raising the number of U.S. advisors in South Vietnam over the next three years from nine hundred to seventeen thousand and committing U.S. helicopters in support of the Army of the Republic of Vietnam (ARVN). By December 1961, the ARVN was conducting air assaults fifteen miles west of Saigon using American helicopters. During the next two years, the United States integrated the new UH-1B "Huey" helicopters into ARVN operations, and Kennedy expanded the use of Special Forces (the Green Berets) in an attempt to counteract Communist insurgencies around the globe. In February 1962, the U.S. Military Assistance Command, Vietnam (MACV), was formed. The MACV, commanded by General Paul D. Harkins, vigorously supported Diem.

In May 1963, however, a revolt by Buddhists in the old imperial city of Hue caused Kennedy and his advisors to have serious doubts about Diem. When a military clique within South Vietnam moved to oust Diem, the plot was backed, in part, by the United States. During the successful coup, Diem was killed. Unexpectedly, the removal of the unpopular

Diem, instead of stabilizing the situation in South Vietnam, caused greater chaos. The continuity was lost in U.S.-backed programs as well as those instituted by Diem. Because of the political spoils system prevalent in the South Vietnamese government, Diem's death resulted in a purge of leadership at every level of government down to the district chief. Within three weeks of Diem's death, President Kennedy was assassinated, further exacerbating the situation.

ABOVE: Saigon, 1948. French military strategy concentrated on holding the cities and surrounding rural areas while maintaining key cities as islands of industry, government, and modernity.

BELOW: Vietnamese laborers groom the airfield at Da Nang as a U.S. Army CH-21 helicopter takes off on a training mission.

Growth of the Viet Cong

In 1963, the ranks of the Communist resistance in South Vietnam—the Viet Cong (VC) and the National Liberation Front (NLF)—began to grow. The VC were guerrillas trained by North Vietnamese advisors and given material support by Russia and China. The Russian and Chinese supplies were trucked in from China, unloaded in North Vietnamese ports, then distributed southward. At about this time, Ho Chi Minh, president of North Vietnam (the Democratic Republic of Vietnam), and the Northern leadership began supplying the VC with improved weapons: Chinese 75-mm recoilless rifles, heavy machine guns, American-made .50-caliber machine guns on Chinese mounts, and 90-mm rocket launchers and mortars.

General Vo Nguyen Giap, commander in chief of the Viet Minh when they defeated the French in 1954, was now minister of defense in North Vietnam. In this role, he devised the logistical and administrative support for the Viet Cong. Giap strengthened the VC by pouring a steady stream of North Vietnamese advisors into the South, as many as twelve thousand by 1963, where they operated as a well-trained and dedicated cadre. By 1964, Giap had formed the 9th VC Division out of the 271st and 272d VC regiments plus support units. He also upgraded other VC formations into larger units, and instituted training programs to transform them into effective combat forces. From 1963 to 1965, the Viet Cong increased in strength from 30,000 to 150,000 men. A common military rule of thumb at the time postulated that containing (not defeating) a guerrilla insurgency required a ten-to-one advantage in manpower. This suggests the enormity of the problem facing the South Vietnamese as they struggled to prevent a Communist overthrow.

Upon Diem's death on November 1, 1963, a disconcerting succession of governments followed in South Vietnam, starting with General Than Van Minh ("Big Minh"), who was soon

TOP: A Vietnamese father, Pham Tong, grieves for his slain daughter, Pham Thi Hai, the victim of Viet Cong guerrillas in Binh Dinh Province, in the Central Highlands of South Vietnam. On September 4, 1964, the girl was shot and killed while returning home from school in the little hamlet of An Trinh, My Hiep Village. Disregarding her presence, VC guerrillas fired on a local militia patrol and caught her in their crossfire. When U.S. advisors arrived at the scene, they discovered that Pham Thi Hai had still-wet finger paint on her hands from a recent art class. On September 18, in the same province, the Viet Cong deliberately fired on two other children, wounding both. They were taken to the Qui Nhon provincial hospital for treatment.

deposed by a coup led by General Nguyen Khanh. The atmosphere of confusion encouraged the Viet Cong to increase their attacks. In February 1964, they assaulted Tay Ninh Province, the Mekong Delta area, and Kontum City's U.S. advisory compound. On February 7, the VC raided Saigon's Kinh Do Theater, killing three Americans and wounding forty-nine. None of these incursions provoked a significant American response—which the Viet Cong may have interpreted as U.S. weakness.

On March 16, 1964, U.S. secretary of defense Robert McNamara sent now-president Lyndon B. Johnson a memo reporting that "40 percent of the territory is under Viet Cong control or predominant influence.… In twenty-two of the forty-three provinces, the Viet Cong control 50 percent or more of the land area." The secretary concluded by saying, "In the last ninety days the weakening of the government's position has been particularly noticeable." Obviously, South Vietnam was unraveling. McNamara suggested twelve actions, eight of which entailed further financial support to South Vietnam. Direct military action was recommended but rejected by President Johnson.

In mid-April, the VC captured Kien Long, a district capital in the Mekong Delta, killing

BOTTOM: A Viet Cong suspect being questioned by South Vietnamese military authorities. Because the Viet Cong operated in and out of military garb, it was difficult to determine who they were unless they were captured in the process of committing terrorist acts or were shot or captured in military operations. To protect themselves, allied soldiers considered any armed civilian as hostile.

three hundred South Vietnamese troops. The following month, VC frogmen sank the helicopter transport USS *Card* in Saigon harbor. In July, the Viet Cong attacked a Special Forces camp at Nam Dong, where fifty South Vietnamese and two Special Forces soldiers were killed. Still, there was no military response from the United States.

Airborne Special Forces

ABOVE: Green Berets Frederick Paulson (left) and Thomas Hanaway of U.S. Army Special Forces prepare medications at a Buddhist temple as part of the ongoing effort to win the allegiance of rural Vietnamese, December 1962. Special Forces personnel and other Army advisors trained the ARVN in counterinsurgency tactics and worked hard to deny the Viet Cong guerrillas free movement in the countryside by quickly forging Vietnam's many disparate groups and outlying tribes into competent anti-Communist forces.

RIGHT: U.S. Army Chief of Staff General George H. Decker (right) and MACV commander General Paul D. Harkins (center) watch members of the Civil Defense Guard in Hao Cain conduct a firing exercise utilizing a makeshift bamboo stand during Decker's 1962 inspection tour. During this period of the war, the United States limited its involvement to advising and instructing South Vietnamese soldiers in combat, logistics, communications, and transportation skills.

Gulf of Tonkin Incident

On August 2, 1964, a reported engagement between North Vietnamese torpedo boats and a U.S. Navy destroyer in the Gulf of Tonkin led to a heightened state of hostility between the United States and North Vietnam. Several events combined to cause this escalation. On August 2, the USS *Maddox*, a destroyer on an intelligence-gathering mission, cruised in international waters some twenty-eight miles off the coast of North Vietnam. At 1630 hours, three North Vietnamese torpedo boats attacked the ship, blasting away at it with their 12.7-mm machine guns and firing torpedoes. The *Maddox* returned fire with its 5-inch guns, scoring a direct hit on one of the torpedo boats. Within an hour, four U.S. Navy F-8E

fighter aircraft, flying off the USS *Ticonderoga*, joined the fight. They assailed and damaged the remaining two torpedo boats, which raced northward seeking refuge along the coast.

The motivation for the attack was unclear at the time because the *Maddox* was merely collecting data on North Vietnamese radar and other electronic capabilities and monitoring the movement of enemy ships supporting operations in the South. This mission had been going on for some time as part of operations referred to as DeSoto. Some analysts attempting to determine a cause for the attack have noted that the United States was also conducting Operation Plan (OPLAN) 34A at the time. That operation had included raids on North Vietnamese coastal installations. Only two days earlier, as part of that plan, South Vietnamese commandos had raided two

islands near the port of Vinh. The attack on the *Maddox*, from this perspective, might have been the result of the North Vietnamese confusing the DeSoto mission with OPLAN 34A, or it may have been in retaliation for OPLAN 34A raids. Another possible explanation for the attack may be that the United States' passivity in the face of serious North Vietnamese Army (NVA, sometimes called the PAVN, People's Army of Vietnam) attacks earlier in 1964 had encouraged the attack on the *Maddox*.

The *Maddox* continued on its way after sending the remaining torpedo boats scurrying. In the United States, President Johnson, after learning of the attack, ordered no reprisal. Involved in a presidential campaign, he had been emphasizing a peaceful posture. Johnson's only response to the torpedo attack was to order another destroyer, the USS *C. Turner Joy*, to accompany the *Maddox* on its mission. On August 4 at 2035 hours, sonar and radar men on the ships received enemy contacts indicating that three torpedo boats some thirty miles distant were approaching the American ships. The sky was dark and cloudy, so perfect identification was impossible. Soon, sonar detected

some twenty torpedoes approaching the destroyers. Some American commentators have claimed that the attack never happened, nor was one imminent; however, an examination of North Vietnamese radio communications later verified that there had been hostile movement toward the destroyers. In fact, after the war, the North Vietnamese admitted to attacking the ships.

As a result of the attack, Johnson convened the National Security Council on August 4 and ordered U.S. forces to assault Vinh, the torpedo boats' base. On August 5, a U.S. air strike destroyed eight torpedo boats and damaged twenty-one, leaving the port with black smoke billowing into the sky from burning oil tanks. Just two days after the attack on Vinh, the U.S. Congress passed the Tonkin Gulf Resolution by a vote of 416 to 0, authorizing the president "to take all necessary measures to repel any armed attack against the forces of the United States and to prevent further aggression." Clearly, the attack on the *Maddox*, followed by the U.S. naval and congressional responses, marked a radical change in American policy toward Vietnam.

> [The Tonkin Gulf Resolution was] like Grandma's nightshirt—
> it covered everything.
>
> —President Lyndon Baines Johnson,
> in *Vietnam: A History*

LEFT: South Vietnamese paratroopers receiving training in airmobile-assault techniques, August 1962. Although the CH-21 Shawnee, generally known as the Flying Banana, was highly vulnerable to small-arms fire, it provided ARVN forces with a solid edge during counterguerrilla operations.

RIGHT: A U.S. Army advisor shows ARVN rangers various types of explosives, cords, and fuses during a demolition class at the Ranger Training Station, October 1962. The rangers at this point in the conflict were using World War II–era M1 Garand rifles.

BELOW: UH-1B and UH-1D helicopters form a queue as troops of the 2d Regiment, 101st Airborne Division, load up before moving to an assault area, August 23, 1965.

LEFT: Phosphorous explosives dropped by a U.S. A-37 Skyraider cascade over a Viet Cong target, January 1966.

BELOW: An Air Force crew chief takes extra precautions to keep out any Viet Cong intruders who might try to harm his F-102 Delta Dagger aircraft at Da Nang air base, spring 1965.

ROLLING THUNDER

By the end of 1964, Saigon, the seat of the South Vietnamese government, was in chaos. Catholics and Buddhists were at each other's throats, and students rioted in the streets. The government appeared to be collapsing. Meanwhile, to step up the pressure, Viet Cong units attacked ARVN troops in Tay Ninh Province on October 11; killed four Americans and destroyed five B-57 bombers at the Bien Hoa air base on November 1; and seized virtually all of Binh Dinh Province on the coast. After the U.S. presidential election in November, Johnson called in his advisors and attempted to stave off the collapse of South Vietnam. Secretary of Defense Robert McNamara admitted that the situation was "going to hell." In late December, the 9th VC Division seized Binh Gia, east of Saigon, destroying two elite South Vietnamese units, the 33d Ranger Battalion and the 4th Marine Battalion. On top of this calamity, the 325th NVA Division invaded South Vietnam by moving into the Central Highlands. The North Vietnamese seemed convinced that the Americans were unwilling to bring their military power to bear in Southeast Asia and were acting accordingly. They were wrong.

By late 1964, President Johnson and his advisors realized the seriousness of the situation and recognized the NVA invasion as the beginning of what the Communists called phase three of the revolutionary process— the general, final offensive. This entailed the introduction of regular "main force" units into what previously had been a guerrilla struggle. The Communists believed that this would result in the imminent destruction of the South Vietnamese Army and government.

On February 7, 1965, the North Vietnamese struck another violent blow, attacking the U.S. airfield at Pleiku, where they killed 9 Americans, wounded 137, and destroyed 16 helicopters and other aircraft. This time, Johnson ordered a reprisal attack, named FLAMING DART. Three aircraft carriers, the USS *Ranger, Hancock*, and *Coral Sea*, conducted the operation. Bad weather and inappropriate targets, however, led to minimal results. The U.S. government nonetheless referred to the actions as an appropriate reprisal, a warning to the Communists of what was to come. After the Viet Cong attacked Qui Nhon on February 10, killing 23 soldiers and wounding 21, Johnson authorized an air strike on an NVA base at Vit Thu.

On February 13, Johnson announced an operation called ROLLING THUNDER, a graduated aerial response to continued NVA actions in the South. These bombardments would continue for three and a half years. From the start, ROLLING THUNDER was a civilian-initiated example of "limited war," a type of warfare characterized by increasing the tempo of violence "one screw at a time" in the hope of causing the enemy to cease hostile operations in favor of the negotiating table. The limited-war process was also called gradualism, wherein targets were chosen selectively and with appropriate restraint. Gradualism had its drawbacks. Its measured, "gradual" violence allowed

the enemy to make fairly accurate predictions concerning where and when the United States would attack and to initiate step-by-step corrections in their defenses, adapting them to the escalating American actions. Many U.S. military leaders objected to this policy, favoring widespread, unrelenting attacks on North Vietnamese industry, gas storage depots, and airfields, administered with utmost surprise and ferocity to gain the maximum effect. But Johnson and his advisors repeatedly vetoed such operations, fearing an expanded war involving China and an adverse reaction from the American public.

Jerry Hoblit had close calls with the Soviet-manufactured SA-2 surface-to-air missile (SAM) while part of a bombing mission in ROLLING THUNDER.

Well, I had expected the moment. I had been told what it was like. But I really wasn't expecting it that soon. We were on our first mission into a high-threat area, and we had actually reached the high-threat area. So I was terribly surprised. And just like a quarterback in a broken play, you don't want to be surprised. It's one thing to be sacked, but to be surprised because you're sacked from behind is quite another thing. There was a very large warhead in that missile, and it had a lot of energy. You have a forty-thousand-pound airplane at combat weight, and it's going nearly

ABOVE: North Vietnamese air defense personnel operating a Chinese Type 55 37-mm anti-aircraft gun based on the Russian towed M1939. Although obsolescent and based on the same Swedish Bofors design as the famous 40-mm gun used principally by the U.S. Navy, both the Chinese and the Soviet varieties of this weapon were used with some effectiveness against U.S. aircraft forced to attack fixed targets like bridges from predictable angles. They also proved effective against piston-driven aircraft and helicopters along the Ho Chi Minh Trail and in the tri-border region of South Vietnam, Laos, and Cambodia.

ABOVE: A pilot flying an F-8E Crusader from Fighter Squadron VF-162 based on the USS *Oriskany* fires a salvo of 2.75-inch rockets in support of ground operations in South Vietnam in July 1966. The *Oriskany* and its air wing were in their first month of operations in the South China Sea since returning from San Diego.

RIGHT: A North Vietnamese 57-mm anti-aircraft battery, March 1967. Three of the eight gun positions are unoccupied, and the site includes related electronic and radar equipment.

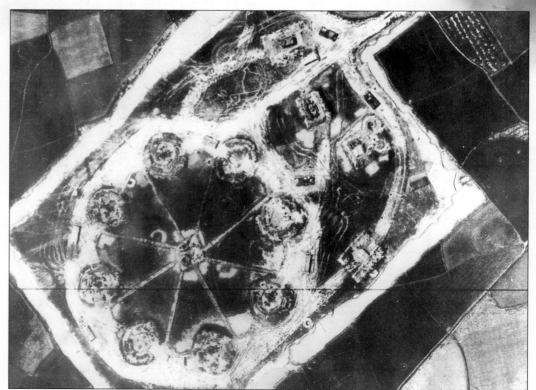

the speed of sound. But the missile is so powerful that a near miss can actually roll you over, and we had that experience several times.

Well, the first SAM site that we killed really increased my confidence. Up until that time, I was daily more and more frustrated. But I never got to that moment that I got it under control, for the simple reason that I knew that there was a very smart enemy on the other side of the fence that was looking for control. And I knew that it's like a sports game, like a football game. The minute that you think you know how to trap-block the guy next to you, he's going to pull, and you're going to get trap-blocked yourself. So, yes, there was a lot more confidence, and I felt a lot better about it after we made our first SAM kill. But I never got to the point where I felt I had all the answers.

Well, we hadn't gotten to the point where we'd split our elements, that is, where we started off as a flight of four, then split off into two flights of two. We hadn't quite got to that point. We were about ready to do it, when Leo Thorsness, who was leading, called a SAM that was pinging him. And it just so happened that I was so positioned in the flight that when the missile fired at Leo, I was looking straight at him. As a matter of fact, I could look right under the camouflage netting and actually see his entire site, which is very unusual that you're that close in. It was very vivid. I saw the missile leave the pad, and it was not a very difficult tactic for me to climb to bombing altitude, drop into my dive, and deliver my weapons on him.

The second good thing about it was that the CBU, this cluster bomb unit, what we called a broken-back weapon, had to be delivered under very tight conditions in order to be effective. Probably more by luck than anything else, I got a perfect delivery, and my CBU absolutely blanketed his [SAM] site perfectly. There were a lot of secondary explosions. A secondary is when a missile goes off on the ground. It went off, and it was obviously a kill right off the bat. Of course, Leo was pretty happy about it. The missile that was shooting was aimed at him. That missile site was aimed at him. When we got back on

the ground, I can still kind of, after thirty years, close my eyes and remember that.

But on one occasion, one missile didn't seem to want to be dodged. No matter what I did, it just seemed like he was coming right at me and seemed as though he was alive. The last thing that I did, when he was close enough in that I could see his canards move [the control surfaces on the forward part of the missile], was just yank for all I had, and he went off under me and turned me over and put a few dents in the bottom of me. But that's about it. That made me kind of nervous because I was wondering: how come, all at once, this one missile seemed to be so much better than the others.

—Colonel (then Captain) Jerry Hoblit,
U.S. Air Force pilot,
357th Tactical Fighter "Wild Weasel" Squadron

JERRY HOBLIT

🎙 *Electronic Warfare Officer Tom B. Wilson, Jerry Hoblit's Wild Weasel mate, describes how the two "trolled" for opportunities to destroy SAM sites during Operation ROLLING THUNDER.*

To find a site, you had to see it. But the North Vietnamese were masters of camouflage. The world was green over there. They hid their sites very well, and they had dummies set up so we would attack the wrong site. So we had to know where it was and how to find it: the only way you could find it was to have him launch missiles. You could very successfully get him to launch his missiles at you if you flew up high, throttled back a little, and presented a great target, which is what we did. Once he launched missiles at you, you might have another site launch at you, also. But all the while, Jerry had to keep his eyes on the missile site. While he was dodging the missile and everything, he had to keep his eyes on the smoke from the site. Keep it in view.

Then, we would do our dive-bomb maneuver. It was extremely difficult to do all of the execution phases and then to successfully hit the site, but we did it.

—Colonel (then Captain) Tom B. Wilson,
U.S. Air Force electronic warfare officer,
357th Tactical Fighter "Wild Weasel" Squadron

Above: A 750-pound bomb falls from an F-100 Super Sabre toward its target in the Mekong Delta, forty-seven miles southwest of Saigon. Although the F-100 was to be replaced by the F-105 Thunderchief in the late 1960s, four F-100 squadrons were still flying close air support missions in 1971. This August 1965 strike was carried out by Super Sabres of the 35th Tactical Fighter Wing based at Phan Rang.

Major Leo Thorsness was instructed to protect bombers from the SAM sites around Hanoi during Operation ROLLING THUNDER. *To protect the bombers, however, he had to become a target himself. He describes how this felt.*

There was a challenge. Most fighter pilots like to have a challenge, and you're sort of out there on the edge. But there were times when, if someone didn't have high anxiety, they were abnormal. But if you'd go a little bit further, then it's fear, and fear starts controlling you. There were times when we got very close to that; I don't know if you would say we were close to losing it. It was a very high level of anxiety, but the joke was you'd tell the first pilot when he came in on a first mission, "Your mouth's going to get real dry, so chew gum." Well, your mouth does get dry, and the gum starts sticking to your teeth. And then that's the big joke, you know, when you're back that night. But the odds of coming out alive were not great, so you went in and stumbled on.

I think the way that you dealt with it is, you were just so busy, and there was so much activity going on, that you didn't really have time to dwell on it, like wondering, is this my last mission; I wonder if I'll get shot down. You're in there, and you've got all these signals coming at you. You've got a back-seater, your electronic warfare officer [EWO], and you're talking between yourselves, and you're listening to all these different strike flights [bomber's radiomen], and you're listening to the electronic people warning that MiGs are taking off in a certain area. I got to a point where, instead of keeping a flight of four, I'd split us up. We'd go two airplanes on each side, kind of a pincer movement. There was just more to do and more going on than you could just about keep up with. You were just so busy, time went by, and all of a sudden that last flight of bombers was in, and you were very aware of who that last flight would be, and you were out of there as fast as you could get out of there.

I've never used drugs, but they talk about the highs and being addicted to it. Well, I was not addicted to the high that you got coming out, but I can tell you, it was a very high feeling when you crossed the Mekong River coming out of Laos. You're over Thailand, you're safe, you're over the good guy territory, and it really was an exhilaration to beat death that day. Many days, you saw people get shot down. So it's there in your mind, all the time, the possibility. But it's usually: it won't happen to me; it's the other guy who will get it.

The next day, you go home, and after you get back, you look on the schedule for tomorrow, and if you're on it, you start getting your target out, and you start studying the photographs of it. And when you go home, you're dead tired, and you sleep. The alarm goes off, it's right by your ear, and you get on your bicycle, you ride back down, and you're in another briefing, and you're ready to go. Then, you get your hat out, and you put another tick on there. You're looking for one hundred of them [missions]. You went from one high to the other, so to speak. And maybe I'm overplaying that, but it was an exhilarating feeling to have cheated death.

As a Wild Weasel pilot [one of the protectors of the strike/bomber pilots], I didn't consider it a suicide mission, but I knew the odds of my finishing one hundred missions were significantly less than a strike pilot, where he was over the target area so much less. We used a lot of tough slang in the military, us pilots, that I don't use now, but an example of the respect or reputation that we had is illustrated in this story. My back-seater, Harry Johnson, and I were R&R [on rest and recreation] one day in the Philippines for a couple of days, and we were getting back on a tanker on our way back to go flying the next day. Harry, an EWO, was talking to a B-52 EWO, talking their EWO language, I guess. So my back-seater said, "Well, I'm a Weasel; we're a Weasel crew." And the B-52 guy, he's kind of big, and he said, "Well, where's your extra bag?" Harry said, "What do you mean?" The B-52 EWO said, "Where do you carry your balls?"

Kind of a very indirect way, a slang way, of saying, "I have a very high regard for you guys that'll hang it out like that day after day, you know, knowing what the odds are."

We found out the best way to find a SAM site, after we'd been there a little while and they got used to what we were doing, you'd turn into them and get ready to launch a strike at them with our missile. They'd turn their site off [radar] and back up. There were enough of them where, they kept you going; you were bouncing between them, and eventually they pulled you in; they sucked you in to the strike, and they had you. So the way we decided to do it was, we would just figure out how to evade the missiles, let them shoot at us. We'd troll somewhere between fifteen thousand to eighteen thousand feet, somewhere in that range, and we just kind of trolled around while these guys [our bombers] were coming in, hitting the targets, and leaving. Eventually, the North Vietnamese thought

they had us in a position to launch a missile and get us, and they'd launch a missile. As soon as we'd hear the launch—we had the equipment to know that they'd launched, and so I'd immediately turn so that missile was either on my one side or the other—I'd roll the airplane, invert it, and just say, "Take her down!"

That became the common statement, "Take it down; take it down." And you'd point that airplane toward the ground and plug it, burn it, and go as fast as you could. And you'd pull out before you hit the ground, with not a lot to spare. You'd start pulling, and you'd pull a lot of Gs, and you had all this airspeed so that you could. The missiles, they would swing down, they'd arc down, trying to get you, and they couldn't make the corner with you. So the first one, you'd start pulling, and you'd wait till the last minute, and they were traveling a mile every two seconds, three thousand feet per second. So you'd pull, and they couldn't quite make it. You'd pull, and then the next one would be there. They usually fired [them] at three- to six-second intervals. You knew what to expect. Had they figured out and delayed the last one eighteen or twenty seconds, they'd have gotten a lot of us, because with that last one you're running out of airspeed. We didn't have the airplanes of today. We'd go fast, but they didn't have that much thrust.

And you're up here, not very maneuverable. We'd just troll around, back and forth, and we'd sucker them into firing at us, and then we got good enough to dodge them. Then, we could go kill the SAM site. Because when the SAMs fired, they kicked up all that dust on the ground. So we'd go down with our CBUs or bombs or guns, and we could

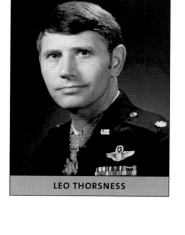

LEO THORSNESS

Most fighter pilots like to have a challenge, and you're sort of out there on the edge. But there were times when, if someone didn't have high anxiety, they were abnormal. But if you'd go a little bit further, then it's fear, and fear starts controlling you.

—Major Leo Thorsness,
Wild Weasel pilot and Medal of Honor recipient

MIKE GILROY

BELOW: The Soviet-made SA-2 surface-to-air missile, code-named GUIDELINE, rocketed toward its target at a blinding speed of Mach 3.5. The Soviets supplied large quantities of SA-2s to the North Vietnamese Communists. Its two-thousand-pound warhead was so large and deadly that when the SA-2 brought down its first U.S. aircraft, an F-4C Phantom, in July 1965, the other three jets in its formation were peppered with flying shrapnel. Fortunately, the telephone pole–size missile let off such a fiery discharge and smoke plume that it could often be spotted in time for pilots to make radical evasive maneuvers. It took an average of thirty missiles to bring down a single U.S. aircraft.

destroy all that radar equipment. If there were any SAM sites or SAMs still stored there, they're thin skinned, and the type of ordnance we had destroyed a lot of SAM sites that way. But it was a touch-and-go game to coax them, coax them into firing at you, and then go destroy them.

—Lieutenant Colonel (then Major) Leo Thorsness, U.S. Air Force pilot, 357th Tactical Fighter "Wild Weasel" Squadron, Medal of Honor recipient

Not everything occurring in a combat aircraft happens like clockwork, as EWO Mike Gilroy, recipient of the Air Force Cross, discovered on his seventh mission, when he and his pilot, Ed Larson, were shot down over the Hanoi area during Operation ROLLING THUNDER.

Ed Larson and I were tasked to protect a strike force on the Northeast Railway. The Northeast Railway is the main rail line that goes from Hanoi up into China. It is an extremely heavily defended area because it's one of the main sources for their supplies for MiGs, interceptors, surface-to-air missiles, ammunition, food, and everything else.

The weather was terrible. There were towering cumulus clouds, thunderclouds, and there was a haze below that, so your visibility was really pretty poor. A month

later we wouldn't have flown that mission, we would have known it was too dangerous. We would've known better; known to be a little more cautious, to hold ourselves back a little farther.

Ed successfully dodged the first two missiles. Then, the third missile came at us, but it came right out of a bank of clouds. We were right up against this cloud, and the missile was right there. It seemed right in front of the aircraft, and it blew up—a tremendous explosion just pitched the aircraft probably about five or six feet up in the air. The cockpit was full of black smoke, and all that I could see through the smoke were two fire-warning lights, right in front of me, at eye level. They were glowing and said, "FIRE." I could hardly breathe because the missile had hit the front of the aircraft and blown up the ammunition drum for our 20-mm cannon. So all that burning cordite smoke was flowing back into the cockpit.

I thought this was a pretty serious situation. I couldn't breathe because of all the cordite smoke, and I was almost asphyxiated. There was a handle in the back you could pull to jettison your canopy. I tried to find the handle, and I'd only had probably a dozen missions in the airplane. I knew where it was, but I couldn't reach back and put my hand on it. I reached back and couldn't find it, and I was just about on my last gasp of air. I thought I'd rather take my chances in the parachute, so I gave up trying to find the handle, and I rotated the ejection seat handles that blow the canopy. I had every intention of getting out of the airplane because if I didn't get out, I was going to die there. So I rotated the ejection seat handles, and the canopy blew. At the same time, the fire blew out.

Just like that, you know, that rush of air blew the fire out. As it so happened, Ed Larson, the pilot, blew his canopy at exactly the same time. So the combination of both canopies going at the same time blew the fire out. In order to eject you, once you raise the handles to blow the canopy off, it arms the seat and a trigger falls down. So you have to open your hand again and grab the trigger and squeeze it. I had every intention of doing

that, and my hands were opening to get around the trigger. And then I thought, "No, let's think about this a minute."

So I just waited, and it was beautiful. The smoke was all gone, the fire was out, there's a patch of blue sky over here. Things weren't nearly as stressful as they were fifteen seconds before when I was not able to breathe. Of course, we're in an open-cockpit airplane going about four hundred miles an hour. So we had to sit sort of straight up. I called Ed on command—there's a command position on the uniphone box that boosts the volume— and I said, "Ed, are you there!" He says, "Yeah, I'm here!" And I think he said something bright, like, "Mike, are you there?"

I replied, "I had to rotate the ejection seat handles to blow my canopy off." He said, "Me too." He couldn't find the handle either. He had been trying to do exactly the same thing I had been doing. [Their plane's tail was gone and shrapnel had blown a big hole in one wing. As they limped along hoping to reach the South China Sea and avoid capture, they were fired on by NVA artillery. Finally, their controls failed, and they bailed out over the ocean, where they were rescued.]

—Mike Gilroy,
U.S. Air Force electronic warfare officer,
"Wild Weasel" squadron

🎙 *In a duel the Wild Weasels described as dancin' with missiles, the pilots and their EWOs attempted to outsmart the computer-driven SA-2 to clear the way for the waves of bombers in Operation* ROLLING THUNDER.

We were going toward Haiphong, just south of Haiphong, and just looking at a site there, when the site came up and fired at us. They all fired in threes, so we had three missiles coming at us. We knew about those. By that time, we'd been there forty or fifty missions, and we knew what we were doing.

Jerry [the pilot] turned and went after that site, and another SAM site fired at us. Okay, that's six missiles in the air after us. That's okay; we're still concentrated on that

ABOVE: Captain Thales A. Derrick, of the 481st Tactical Fighter Squadron, fires an AGM-12 Bullpup missile at camouflaged Viet Cong defenses near a canal twenty-nine miles southwest of Saigon. The air-to-ground missile was launched from an F-100 Super Sabre.

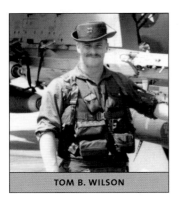

TOM B. WILSON

first guy. Then, I announced a third site, which fired at us. So we had nine missiles in the air, all pointed at our little rosy bodies. Our wingmen and the rest of the flight just kind of pulled back, and here we were facing all these SAMs. Jerry astutely dodged the first one, and, normally, if you dodge the first one, the other two will go by you on that covey, then they reversed their course in response to whatever you did. But anyway, all nine SAMs were going by the wayside when he was in the pop delivering the weapons on the first SAM site. There's a camera that comes on when you release your weapons; it's a 70-mm camera, and it goes from fore to aft, and it picked up three more missiles coming in from the rear.

So we had twelve missiles in the air at that one moment in time after our butts!

—Tom B. Wilson

 Tom B. Wilson, Jerry Hoblit's EWO, describes their first duel with a SAM.

We were going out to protect the force and had no bloody idea what we were doing. So we drew our route out in front of the force, and we went to a place called Yen Bay, which was a crossing point for the Red River. We didn't know that you should avoid Yen Bay, but as we approached it, we had these three other airplanes out there relying on our astuteness. There was an undercast, a very heavy undercast. They launched missiles. I picked it all up on my instruments. They launched, and we'd been told these looked like great big telephone poles. Well, this missile is going Mach 3.5, if you can imagine it— three-and-a-half times the speed of sound.

We're going about three-quarters the speed of sound, so closure is at well over Mach 4. That gives you an idea how fast this thing is coming. It's a blur. It's just a blur, and we can't see the ground. Jerry couldn't see it to dodge it. So we're looking and we're yammering, and the rest of the force very astutely said heck with you guys and went back across the Red River and waited for us. I guess they knew what would happen. I guess they'd been there a while.

The SAM came darting out of the clouds, blew up just beneath us. By the way, all the sound effects you hear on television and movies, the boom: there's no boom. High explosives go *crack*. Just like that. It's a great, huge, orange explosion with black shooting out the top and bottom of it, and that's all shrapnel and deadly stuff. It just knocked our airplane upside down. So we're kind of feeling ourselves, you know, and saying, "Are we still alive? Are we still here?" We were alive all right, and I finally said, "I'm okay." Or probably something like that in a very high-pitched voice. And Jerry said, "I'm okay."

We assumed they [the SAM site] had a visual system. In other words, they were not just using the radar, but they were also looking at us visually and adjusting. It was almost impossible to dodge that SAM under those conditions. We were sort of in shock. You know, we'd dodged all kinds of missiles, but couldn't dodge this one. We finally did, though, and poor Jerry went berserk.

He [Jerry] started strafing, sixty-degree strafes, sixty-degree strafes, and he just shot the guys [SAM site operators] to bits. But it was another hairy mission.

—Tom B. Wilson

The SAM came darting out of the clouds, blew up just beneath us . . . a great, huge, orange explosion with black shooting out the top and bottom of it, and that's all shrapnel and deadly stuff.

—Tom B. Wilson

 Major Leo Thorsness meditated on the loss of fellow pilots and crews in the fighting.

At first it was very tough to see a friend of yours and his airplane just blow apart or, even worse, to see him floating down in his parachute, knowing he's going to be captured. I'd say that was the biggest fear of all of us, being captured, being taken a prisoner of war. If the airplane took a direct hit and just blew apart, it was over like that. That's easier to contemplate than spending years in a prison camp. The way you dealt with it was you just did the best job you could. My goal was not to lose a wingman. I made it through fifty missions before one of my wingmen was shot down.

And that was a devastating night, to think that there were two guys from a Weasel plane sitting in a prison camp, if they lived. You didn't dwell on it. Again, maybe it was because we were so busy and our mission was so challenging that we didn't have time to dwell on those types of things. You had another mission to fly tomorrow, and there were twenty guys, if there were five flights of four, one guy per airplane; that's twenty guys who were depending on you to eliminate that surface-to-air missile threat and hope somebody else took care of the MiGs and the flak.

—Leo Thorsness

EWO Tom B. Wilson describes how he felt about the worthiness of his mission.

Inside my heart I said, yeah, it's worth it to go up and protect these guys [the strike bombers]. I would do it again today if they said, "Listen, you're old and crotchety, but you can go out, fly an airplane, and protect probably the bravest people that have ever faced combat." Army guys are very brave folks, too. I don't mean any slight there. But I've never seen people go and face death like these bomber pilots did. And to protect them, yeah, I'd do it today. So it was worth it. I just came to that conclusion.

—Tom B. Wilson

Search and Destroy

Because ROLLING THUNDER was directed at North Vietnamese territory and not at enemy forces in the South, which were dispersed, it had little positive impact on ground operations in the South, and was ineffectual even in the North. For that reason, the United States was forced to introduce ground forces into South Vietnam in 1965 to stabilize the crumbling situation. The first American troops were U.S. Marines, sent to Da Nang to defend the airfield from attacks by main force NVA and Viet Cong units. The Air Force used Da Nang as its point of departure for ROLLING THUNDER raids into North Vietnam, so that base was a prime enemy target. After much debate, Johnson ordered two Marine battalions to guard the airfield perimeter. On April 6, the president, in National Security Action Memorandum (NSAM) 328, authorized the deployment of two more Marine battalions and one air squadron and gave General William C. Westmoreland, Commander in Chief, MACV, discretionary control of the units, which implied their use in an aggressive combat role—a new departure in the war.

In May, the Viet Cong began its summer offensive, striking an outpost at Ba Gia, in Quang Ngai Province, where it destroyed two battalions of the ARVN 51st Regiment. U.S. military intelligence detected signs that the 325th as well as the 304th NVA divisions were in the South. On June 10, two regiments of the Viet Cong assaulted the Dong Xoai Special Forces camp and defeated ARVN units. Following up on this victory, on June 25 a regular NVA regiment captured a district headquarters in Kontum Province in the Central Highlands, and Westmoreland complained in late June to General Earle Wheeler, Chairman, Joint Chiefs of Staff, that the situation was becoming critical. Wheeler promised forty-four combat battalions as soon as they could be routed to Vietnam.

Encouraged by this commitment, General Westmoreland ordered the 173d Airborne Brigade and five battalions of ARVN infantry to

173D AIRBORNE BRIGADE

The 173d Airborne Brigade, known as the Sky Soldiers, was activated in 1965 at Okinawa and assigned to Vietnam on May 7 to provide infantry security for the Bien Hoa air base complex. The first major ground combat unit in Vietnam, the 173d was soon deployed in Operation ATTLEBORO, September–November 1966; Operation JUNCTION CITY, in War Zone C, February 22, 1967; and at Dak To in November 1967, where it uprooted an NVA regiment from Hill 875 in fierce fighting. In 1968, the brigade operated in Binh Thuan and Binh Dinh provinces and in 1969 performed pacification missions and ensured highway security along Highway QL 1 in Binh Dinh Province in the An Loa valley. The unit performed similar missions over the next two years in the II Corps Tactical Zone, finally leaving Vietnam on August 25, 1971.

attack the Viet Cong in War Zone D, north of Saigon. This was one of the earliest examples of "search and destroy," a type of operation that would be conducted for the next three years. General Westmoreland characterized the search-and-destroy strategy as a "war of attrition," which enflamed his critics, who insisted that war could be waged in a more bloodless fashion. Some military analysts believed that the proper response to the Viet Cong and NVA was to organize armed enclaves, creating well-defended areas along the populated coast of Vietnam from which attacks could be launched into the backcountry. But Westmoreland believed the best policy was to take the fight to the enemy wherever you found him, destroy his installations, capture his war materiel, decimate him, and convince him of the futility of continuing the fight.

Search-and-destroy operations were inherently hazardous and precarious, more so than other types of military operations. Essentially offensive in purpose, they involved soldiers entering a hostile area where the enemy's location was uncertain. While searching an area, soldiers became vulnerable to booby traps, handmade traps, mines, and ambushes. Many men were killed without ever seeing an enemy soldier. Soldiers in these operations were ferried by helicopters into a landing zone (LZ) in the middle of enemy territory, where they became the target of small-arms fire, mortars, and artillery. After a while, U.S. officers adapted to these dangers, clearing their drop zones as much as possible with heavy preparatory fire: helicopter gunship barrages, artillery, and air strikes. On the ground, before nightfall, U.S. soldiers built up defenses with whatever was available, registered their artillery, and dug in.

BELOW: In one of the first U.S. Army "ground force" deployments in Vietnam, paratroopers of the 173d Airborne Brigade march toward Vung Tau Airfield. Two soldiers in the foreground carry a box of bazooka rounds. The 173d was composed of three battalions and support troops, including armor and engineers. The paratroopers were used to provide security for the air bases at Binh Hoa and Vung Tau.

and some weren't. Some wore khakis. I was. We boarded toward the rear of the plane, and there were the stewardesses there, and they were crying. They knew what we were headed for.

They opened the door, and you could feel the heat just enter that doorway. All of a sudden we had instant humidity. The heat, the stench: it was mind-boggling. It was nothing like I'd ever experienced, and, needless to say, welcome to South Vietnam. So there it was.

—Sergeant Art Tejeda,
Headquarters, 25th Infantry Division,
423d Mechanized Tomahawks

 Gerry Schooler also found Vietnam different from what he had expected.

I know my first impression after I got off the plane and walked straight to a bus was that it had chain link on all the windows. It came across pretty fast to me that it was to keep grenades from flying through the windows as we went through town. That was supposed to be a town filled with people we were trying to save? So there was this dichotomy right after I was off the plane. You see it's dangerous, not just out there in the jungle; there were people here in the towns that wanted to kill us, too. That kind of went against what we'd been told in our training back in the States. I remember seeing films that they showed us where we were trying to help these people defend their freedom. And so to get on that bus and see those grenade screens made you realize maybe there's a little bit more to this war than we were told.

—Gerry Schooler,
A Company, 2d Battalion,
27th Infantry Regiment (Wolfhounds)

ABOVE: U.S. troops leap from their helicopter and sprint toward cover. Operating in the jungle, soldiers had to respond instinctively to danger. One moment of inattention, a failure to note a nearby mine or booby trap, or an unexpected movement in the wall of green around them, and their lives were in jeopardy.

 Sergeant Art Tejeda recalls his arrival in Vietnam from the United States.

Being in the air, you could see all this smoke. I thought maybe they were bombing the airfield or something was going on. It was sort of a jittery feeling. So we're going to land down there? They might be shooting. But we landed, and after we taxied off the runway, we all got up. We were in fatigues, some were

My first impression after I got off the plane and walked straight to a bus was that it had chain link on all the windows. It came across pretty fast to me that it was to keep grenades from flying through the windows as we went through town.

—Gerry Schooler

LEFT: The commander of a Vietnamese ranger battalion listens closely as Captain Robert W. Butler, of Frederick, Maryland, explains his concept of an upcoming operation, February 1967. Butler, a specialist in jungle combat and survival techniques, was the senior U.S. advisor to the battalion.

Ken Cory was nineteen years old when he arrived in Vietnam as a private first class in August 1968. He had been training at Fort Lewis, Washington, for action in Vietnam, but when he got there, the situation was a surprise.

It was a shock when we got there. I can remember landing at Tan Son Nhut Air Force Base, and the first thing that struck us was how we landed. The pilot had indicated that previous jets had taken fire and that he was going to do a very fast landing. So it was almost like coming straight down. So we were scared already before we had landed. We were taking shots before we even got down on the ground.

But the biggest shock was coming out of the airplane and being in Vietnam for the first time. The heat and the humidity were just stifling. The smell was overwhelming. It was just something that you'd never forget once you smelled it.

It was funny, because when we had practiced in advanced infantry school, the enemy forces would always run around in black silk pajamas with rice helmets on—Lon Nols: that's what we expected. When we got off the plane, the first thing that comes running at the plane are all these people dressed up in black pajamas wearing rice hats. It took us by surprise. All of a sudden, this preconception of what the enemy is going to look like was blown right there. So the first impression was that what we had learned wasn't going to matter over here, which turned out to be the case. We just didn't know exactly what a guerrilla war was going to be like. We had thought that you would be able to tell who was who. One of the roughest things over there was never being able to distinguish the enemy unless he had a uniform on. It made it tough on us.

—Specialist Fourth Class Ken Cory,
2d Battalion, 14th Infantry Regiment,
25th Infantry Division

GERRY SCHOOLER

 Gerry Schooler discovered that the enemy was closer to him than he might have imagined.

Base camps were interesting in that they were really small cities. They had their own water systems, their own electrical generators. Cu Chi was one of the bigger camps. The 25th Division at one point had sixteen thousand or seventeen thousand troops there. That's a lot of people. Plus, they were bringing in people from the outside, civilians, many of whom were Viet Cong, I'm sure, to the tune of three thousand or four thousand. There would be huge masses of them at the gates every day coming to work.

And they'd do all the KP and all the cleaning and everything. So they hired Vietnamese to do these kinds of things, which was very dangerous when you think about it. It became evident that Saigon was becoming endangered by these creeping [covert] Viet Cong regiments and so forth. They were allowed to mix with us and work with us during the day. Then, at night, we had to sort them out. Frequent ambush patrols were sent out from Cu Chi base camp at night to try to stem the flow of guerrillas. One night, they sprang an ambush, and one of the men they killed was a lieutenant. When they identified him [he had his U.S. division ID on him], he was a barber who had worked at the Cu Chi barbershop by day. By night, he was a lieutenant in the 9th Viet Cong Division.

When we talked about the guy, we kind of laughed because he had given several of us shaves, and he'd had his razor at our throats, and you can imagine what was going through his mind at the time.

—Gerry Schooler

 Sergeant Art Tejeda, after fighting in search-and-destroy operations, found the experience of being shot at difficult to describe.

Yeah, it's not like a firecracker or the backfire of a car. When you hear a round go off, you can hear the rat-tat-tat or the crack. But when they get close to you, these hypervelocity shells from a Kalashnikov AK-47 [a Soviet-manufactured assault rifle], which is 7.62-mm and going just about double the speed of sound, when it goes by your ears or close to you, it goes *crack*. It's not a popping sound. It sounds real sharp, and you know it's close. So that's what it feels like.

—Art Tejeda

 When Sergeant C.W. Bowen arrived in Vietnam, he became his unit's forward or point man, the soldier the farthest advanced when the unit moved forward and usually the first to make contact with the enemy, his booby traps, and mines.

I felt more secure on point than I did back in the squad, the platoon. Over a period of time, I developed a good sixth sense about things like booby traps or whatever. I just felt more secure on point. I guess maybe it was a control thing. I felt more in control, and a lot of times, you weren't always up there by yourself. You had what they called a slack man [the man directly behind the point man on patrol], and he would count paces, so you'd know how far you had gone. They'd say, well, you need to go one or two klicks [kilometers].

And they'd give you an azimuth [a bearing from north] or whatever, and the slack man would count when it was one klick. So he would count it off and tie a knot in a piece of string or something like that and keep count of how far you went on that certain azimuth you shot with the compass. Gary Heeter walked slack for me a lot of times, and Tom Curly, who was from Chicago. It could get kind of hairy up there on point.

One of the favorite tricks of the enemy was to let the point man walk by so that they could ambush the main body of troops behind him. Then, the point man was just kind of stuck out there by himself. If they didn't kill you in the end, you had to fight your way back to the main body to survive. So a lot of point men got just completely blown away out there because they were the first guys that ran into the enemy.

Everything could break loose at one time. You never knew. You were always wound up

TOP AND BOTTOM: VC or NVA? An ARVN lieutenant points to a suspected enemy position during a search-and-clear mission (top), November 1969. German shepherd scout dogs (bottom) help two members of the 199th Light Infantry Brigade search a hut in Long Trung, a VC-infested village some five miles northeast of Saigon. A Vietnamese ranger, on the left, operates as a guard and lookout in case of trouble.

No training would ever prepare you for the sound and smell of battle. The odor of battle is an entirely different thing. . . . It reeks of sweat and gun oil. It smells of gunpowder, foliage, and cut leaves.

—Major Dennis Ayoub, Australian Army

tight as a spring. One of the big things in the Ho Bo Woods [inside the Iron Triangle] where we fought was booby traps. That place was just completely covered with booby traps. You could go in there and go fifteen or twenty or fifty meters and find five, six, seven, maybe ten booby traps. You'd disarm them, come back the next day, and find more there again.

In most of the areas where we operated, there were some NVA troops, but the majority were VC. They were farmers by day, fighters by night. The VC were not as well trained as the NVA, but they were trained well enough. They had good weapons and everything. But the thing you noticed about the VC was that they would disperse and just blend in with the general populace, be mixed in with the civilians.

When they were needed, they would organize out in the jungle somewhere and either set up an ambush or we'd do battle with them. Once the battle was over, they'd disperse again, hide their weapons, and go back to the village and act as farmers or whatever. But they were still damned good fighters. I had a lot of respect for them. They kicked our butts a couple of times. If it wasn't for artillery and air strikes, we'd have just never got out of there.

We fought one, two days, out there on the Saigon River, called the horseshoe of the river. We fought all day, probably didn't move fifty or sixty feet. You couldn't stick your head up; snipers were all over the place, picking our guys off. We bombed them all day, brought in artillery all day and all night. They would just put a ring of steel around us, and they had us. Choppers had come in and dropped us in the middle of one of their bunker complexes, and that's where we ended up all day. So they were good fighters, and walking point, you just never knew what to expect.

You were always tight and wound up, and if something broke loose, you just opened up and tried to fall back to where your men were, whether it was crawling, running, or hollering. We'd holler, "Manchu! Manchu!" [Bowen's unit], so that when we got back to our company, they wouldn't shoot us. They were shooting at anything that moved. So

you always alerted them that you were coming back. Sometimes, you couldn't make it back, and you just had to ride it out. You hoped that the platoon or the company beat back the attack, so that you could get out of there. Otherwise, you were gone. You weren't going to survive. That was it.

—Sergeant C.W. Bowen,
4th Battalion, 9th Infantry Regiment,
25th Infantry Division

C.W. Bowen

 Major Dennis Ayoub of the Australian Army found the sound and smell of battle surprising.

I think the thing that no training would ever prepare you for is the sound and the smell of battle. The odor of battle is an entirely different thing. It is a mechanical-type thing. It reeks of sweat and gun oil. It smells of gunpowder, foliage, and cut leaves. There's lots of dust around, and the noise is indescribable: it's a huge din.

The other thing is that time elongates. What might be a three- to five-minute engagement or skirmish seems as though it was twelve, fifteen minutes or so. Time stands still for you, and things become very vivid whilst you are in action.

—Major Dennis Ayoub,
Australian Army

 Sergeant C.W. Bowen described his GI comrades as just "average citizen soldiers."

The majority of the guys [fellow soldiers], you could count on. I mean, they were just average citizen soldiers, like us. The majority of us were poor whites, blacks, Chicanos, and when we got out in the jungle, everybody was equal, the same. Everybody depended on each other. Sure, we got scared as hell sometimes, and, occasionally, we'd get so damned scared we couldn't move. But when it got down to brass tacks, everybody supported each other. If somebody was out there, and we had to get them, we went for them.

Most of the time, we had no problem as far as guys supporting us and backing us up, but later on they had the "McNamara 100,000."

These guys were a lot of the guys that originally didn't pass the [entrance] test when they originally drafted them. Then, [after they lowered the standards] they started drafting them. And there were some problems with them. I saw one guy blow his legs off with a claymore [mine] because he just didn't understand that when you tightened the fuse down on a claymore, you just cinched it, and that was it.

He just kept forcing it, forcing it, and it only takes thirty-five pounds' pressure to set a blasting cap off. When he put that pressure on, it blew the claymore, and it was in his lap. It blew his hands and legs off and killed him right there. That was a needless death. There were some guys like that. They just didn't make it.

—C.W. Bowen

 Reaching a battle zone could be a "sticky affair," even when a soldier was transported by helicopter.

The first time I'd gone up in a helicopter, it was on an Eagle; we called them Eagle flights. We landed in the Iron Triangle, not in the rice paddies but in a swamp, in knee-deep mud and waist-deep water. There was also a sort of seaweed-type plant that bound to your legs. It took an incredible amount of energy just to get to the shore, where the danger was supposed to be.

We'd land that far out just in case there were snipers, to be more secure. In those kinds of landings, the choppers didn't actually touch down. They hovered and you jumped out of the chopper, dropped maybe six feet. The weight you were carrying, your gear, maybe fifty pounds or so, all that drove your legs down into the mud, so that the first two or three steps were quite difficult.

I remember some of the new guys having a lot of trouble, especially if they were bigger, a bit overweight or something. I know we had a couple of guys that bogged down so much they had to be pulled out with ropes. By the way, after a while out there, nobody was overweight. It's a great diet plan. But some of them would get to the bank and just

Helicopters

Rapid, aggressive movement and massive concentration of firepower on the modern battlefield was the dream of forward-thinking World War II and Korean War–era cavalry soldiers—by now colonels and generals—who experimented with heliborne troop movements throughout the late 1950s and early 1960s. However, it was the technological and tactical leap made possible by the rugged Bell Company UH-1 Huey and Boeing Vertol CH-47 Chinook helicopters that really made airmobile tactics possible. Yet even before these "fast movers" arrived in Vietnam, less capable machines were already proving their worth. Ultimately, the war lasted so long that virtually every helicopter type that began the conflict was superseded and replaced by Hueys, Chinooks, and other modern machines by the middle of the conflict.

TOP: An AH-1 Cobra gunship from Troop D, 3d Squadron, 4th Cavalry, operating in support of the 25th Infantry Division in 1968. Add-on armaments enabled Hueys—and even Chinooks—to direct suppressive fire on VC and NVA units. The Cobra was a purpose-built gunship of remarkable ability that entered service in August 1967. In addition to one or more Gatling-type miniguns or 40-mm grenade launchers in a power-operated chin turret, the Cobra also had short, detachable wing stubs capable of handling a wide range of direct-fire machine guns and rocket pods. By positioning the pilot behind the gunner, the Cobra could be constructed with a much narrower silhouette than the Huey's, thus offering a smaller target to Communist gunners and providing a degree of armor protection.

CENTER: OH-13 Sioux scout helicopters, like these 1st Cavalry Division machines awaiting shipment to Vietnam, flew more than five hundred thousand sorties before they were completely replaced by the OH-6A Cayuse "Loach."

BOTTOM: A crew member of an Americal Division Huey connects a sling that will allow a disabled Loach to be airlifted from LZ Siberia to Chu Lai, May 1970.

ABOVE: The HH-3E/CH-3E "Jolly Green Giant" was able to fly great distances and had a large cargo capacity. Mounting an external, variable-speed hoist and with a special "jungle penetrator" attached to the end of the 250-foot cable, the Jolly Greens could pluck Special Forces personnel and downed airmen from even the densest jungle. The follow-on HH-53B, although nearly identical in appearance, had an even greater range and payload capacity.

ABOVE: A Flying Crane ferries a crippled CV-2 Caribou from An Khe to Qui Nhon, February 1970.

BELOW: Both the highly distinctive CH-37 Mojave, known as Duce, Cross-Eye, and Cross-Eyed Monster, as well as its equally distinctive replacement, the CH-54 Flying Crane, or "Skycrane," were highly valued because of their ability to lift and transport extremely heavy loads in one operation—like downed Chinooks from enemy territory and intact artillery pieces to new firebases.

RIGHT: Crew chief Frank Head surveys the Mekong Delta area from his CH-21 Shawnee "Flying Banana," based at Tan Son Nhut Airfield, July 1962. The CH-21, some pilots said, was "a lot of helicopter with not a lot of lift." Consequently, crews had a standard list of items (i.e., cabin doors, heaters, seats, insulation, soundproofing) to be removed that would lighten the helo by three hundred pounds, the weight of two combat-loaded ARVN soldiers. In 1964, the CH-21's missions were taken up by the UH-1 Iroquois Huey, designed to accommodate eight passengers, and the CH-47 Chinook "Shithook," which could transport as many as forty troops.

BOTTOM LEFT: A CH-34D Sea Horse "Huss" evacuates Marine casualties south of Cu Chi in Quang Ngai Province as an M48 tank with an amphibious exhaust stack stands guard, August 1965. The CH-34 could handle up to twelve passengers and was replaced in the mid-1960s by a slightly smaller, naval version of the CH-47, the CH-46 Sea Knight.

BOTTOM RIGHT: Troops of the 101st Airborne Division await airlift by a CH-47A Chinook, which will take them to Bao Loc.

LEFT: UH-1 Hueys of the Army Support Command, Vietnam, descend to pick up ARVN troops at Song Be who will engage Viet Cong elements near the Cambodian border, April 19, 1956.

BACKGROUND: A USS *Guadalcanal* CH-46D Sea Knight banks into its glide path to the carrier's deck in 1967. The Sea Knight had "tricycle" landing gear—featuring widely spaced rear wheels—that was more suitable for carrier operations than a Chinook's wheel system.

BERNARD JONES

have to sit down because they were exhausted. Of course, that's very dangerous, to group up, sit down bunched together. So there was a lot of yelling: "Get up and go that way! Spread out!"—that kind of thing. It's not good to be standing together, sitting together.

—Gerry Schooler

🎙 *Search-and-destroy operations, even successful ones, could be bloody affairs. In Operation RIO BLANCO, U.S. Marines carried the day, but only through valor and perseverance.*

It was Thanksgiving Day in 1966. We were on a battalion-size sweep, part of Operation RIO BLANCO. The whole battalion had just sat down to have lunch, when we were ambushed. We could see the enemy out in the open, across a rice paddy. Artillery was called in, and our unit began moving to push them back. They were running from us, and then they stopped, turned around, and decided to fight it out. I was on a dike in front of our main line with about fifteen or twenty other guys. We were lined up on the wall of a paddy, firing. I noticed the guy next to me slump over, and I turned to my right to see how he was. At that moment, I was hit in the chin. I fell down on the guy, and when a medic came over, he told me the soldier was dead.

The medic patched me up, put a clip in my rifle, and sent me back to the main line. On my way back, an exploding shell hit in front of me and blew me into the air. I saw a small portion of my M14 [wood-stock rifle used early in the war] sticking straight out of the ground; the rest was buried. I was really banged up, dazed, hurt pretty bad. I lost the index finger on my left hand, lost partial

sight in my left eye, and suffered wounds to my legs and arms. I saw the gunnery sergeant underneath a tree motioning me to come over to him, and I went over and lay down in his lap. To this day, I don't remember the guy's name. I had been there [in Vietnam] three months and served with him, but we just referred to him as Gunny. The "Gunny" was a Korean War veteran and was also wounded. He was missing part of his nose. He really knew his stuff and was the enlisted man in charge.

I was sent over to the hospital ship *Repose*, and they started to cut off my clothes. This may sound silly, but I had just been issued new combat boots, the kind with canvas on the sides. They were really comfortable, not like the leather ones. I told the doctors not to cut them up because I still needed them. That was the last thing I remember. General Victor Krulak came into the hospital to see me. He came to see everybody. He asked me if there was anything that he could do. I told him I wanted to make E-3. Two weeks later, his representative came over and gave me the promotion.

—Bernard Jones,
U.S. Marine Corps

🎙️ *Some soldiers, like Marine scout sniper Charles "Chuck" Mawhinney, acted as the "eyes and ears" of their units in after-dark maneuvers. Sometimes, in this role, they were called upon to kill the enemy, aided by a rifle sight and a see-in-the-dark "Starlight" scope.*

They taught us [in our sniper training] how to move through an area without setting off booby traps, which was one of the key things to know. First, you stayed off trails, especially if you were traveling at night. Charlie [the VC] didn't want to spend all the time booby-trapping the ground over there. Normally, they booby-trapped trails because that's where the Americans walked. So we learned early, as soon as we got over there, that if you stayed off the trails, the chances of hitting booby traps were pretty slim. At night, it's

LEFT: Marines stop for a break in their forced march along the road to Highway 1 south of Quang Ngai City during Operation RIO BLANCO, November 24, 1966.

ABOVE: A Marine mortar team prepares for action during Operation RIO BLANCO, a joint operation incorporating the 1st Marine Division; ARVN regular, Regional Forces, and rangers; South Korean marines; and Special Forces elements, November 21, 1966.

The medic patched me up, put a clip in my rifle, and sent me back to the main line. On my way back, an exploding shell hit in front of me and blew me into the air.

—Bernard Jones

hard to detect booby traps because you don't have a light; you don't have anything. You're trying to move quietly.

So we learned that by staying in the thick vegetation, we were pretty much out of the area that they booby-trapped. For natural camouflage, and what was used varied by sniper teams, we'd cut tire inner tubes into strips. We used [them] on our weapons, on our arms, on our legs, and on our packs. We also [tied] parachute cord to whatever we could tie it on. The idea is to just use anything to break up your outline. You also wanted to try to match the color of the area that you were in.

The big key is, when you get to your final firing position, you don't want to use up the vegetation around the area that you're going to, because that makes it fairly obvious somebody has done something around that position. So what we tried to do was get close to the final position where we were going and pick up vegetation along the way. I didn't stay out for days and days, so it wasn't a problem

as far as things wilting. We'd usually set up before daylight, and by evening we'd be exiting the area.

We used camouflage paint and also some of the leaves over there that were green. You could actually rub the leaves onto your skin, and it would give a green color to it. But the main thing was to break up your outline.

Most of our movement was at night, just a command team. The trick is that you don't let the villagers see you, because you don't know who's friendly and who's not. So you don't let the villagers see you. You stay in the heavy brush when you're moving. You stay off the trails, out of the rice paddies.

Normally, before I went into an area, I would pick my route to and from the target area. I'd find an area that I thought was going to be advantageous to us. I would look and see what kind of vegetation was going to be in the area I wanted to set up in. I picked my routes from the previous patrols we were out on, and that's how we'd work our way into it.

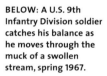

BELOW: A U.S. 9th Infantry Division soldier catches his balance as he moves through the muck of a swollen stream, spring 1967.

Sometimes, during the daytime, village people noticed me. Then I would abort the mission because I didn't know if they were going to get the word back to the VC, or maybe the people were VC.

The longer you spend with somebody [Mawhinney refers to his assistant, his spotter], of course, the more risks you end up taking, because you feel a little more comfortable going a little farther out with them. About the time you get somebody that's outstanding, that's excellent, then you can travel all night; you can go all day. You don't have to talk; you know what's going on with each other. About that time, they would rotate the fellow back, and you'd get a brand-new guy, with his little white head, going "Hi! I'm your new spotter."

We'd do night ambushes with them [Mawhinney refers to his unit]. They'd set up a night ambush; we'd take our Starlight scope [to view objects in darkness], mount it on our M14. [Mawhinney usually used a Remington Model 700, with a practical range up to one thousand meters.]

During the day, the scope stayed in the pack because it was ineffective during the day. At night, we'd mount the Starlight scope on the M14, and we'd go out. We'd stand the perimeter lines, go out on night ambushes with them. For us, the rules of engagement were simple. When we were out there, if the people we encountered were enemies that were identifiable, say they had on NVA uniforms or were carrying weapons, or if they were farmers carrying weapons, they were the enemy. So the rules of engagement in Vietnam were pretty basic.

—Charles "Chuck" Mawhinney,
U.S. Marine Corps scout sniper

The heat, the humidity, the torrential rains—even the flora and fauna—seemed to conspire against soldiers in Vietnam, as medic Clarence E. Sasser notes.

Probably the most common problem that I treated was plain old jungle rot. We were down in the Mekong Delta, which was down south in the rice paddy area. Movement

ABOVE: A sniper of the 3d Battalion, 26th Marines, on Hill 881 South, near Khe Sanh, takes careful aim at suspicious movement on the "India" and "Mike" companies' perimeter, February 1968.

CLARENCE E. SASSER

down there almost always involved water, water on the skin. In this area, a permeable area such as this, the moistness always produces very virulent, fungus-type problems. The biggest thing was the fungus infection. It was preventable to a certain extent, but over time it became almost unpreventable. Almost everyone had it, and it may seem at first glance to be a minor problem, but once an area becomes macerated, in other words raw and everything, it produced tremendous pain [and] impairs soldiers.

First off, rice paddies [in Vietnam] were not like the rice fields I was used to in the United States. I grew up in a rice-farming area and had farmed rice and had worked in rice fields growing up. But these were different from ours. We rotated our fields. Their fields were perpetual rice fields. So, consequently, there was always a lot of stinky mud—and I'm sure that people are aware how mud gets when it is continually covered with water. So it was fairly stinky, hence the fungus. The leeches were there, too.

[Sasser describes the situation during a firefight with the VC.] Probably the most striking remembrance of that day was the leeches. When we went into the rice paddy, you couldn't stand up; you had to lie in the water. The only protection that was available was the levies or dikes, and to utilize them, you couldn't stand up. You couldn't stand up anyway because of the incoming fire and the snipers. I remember lying in the water and fighting leeches all night. It was just terrible, but one of those things.

—Specialist 5 (then Private First Class)
Clarence E. Sasser, medic,
Medal of Honor recipient

 Gerry Schooler, of A Company, was lucky to be trained early on the threat posed by mines and booby traps.

When we got to Cu Chi we were sent to a unit out in the field, and what we did was fill sandbags and go to school. They had a mines and booby traps school there. It was probably the best thing they did for us because it made us aware of the dangers. I thought the school was kind of stupid in a way because they used, unlike out in the jungle, a very obvious example of a bright-green wire over here or a very obvious grenade tied to a tree over there as part of the training. They were just trying to make a point, I think.

When you got out in the real deal, booby traps and mines weren't so visible. But it did get us to start thinking about the fact that there are more dangers out there than just riflemen. You can get hurt other ways. By the time I got there, the unit had been there since 1966. When I got there at the end of 1967, they'd had quite a few experiences with mines and booby traps. Those first guys, those poor guys that showed up in 1966 with the division, they'd never seen one or even heard the term *booby trap*.

—Gerry Schooler

 Corporal Gary Heeter was operating in the Iron triangle with his unit when he encountered a mine.

I had like three days left in-country [Vietnam], and I had already gotten my new uniform ready to go home. But the guy who took my place, a radio operator, got wounded, so the captain asked me to go out on one more

1ST MARINE DIVISION

The 1st Marine Division arrived in Vietnam in February 1966 and was headquartered at Chu Lai. The division participated in Operations STARLITE and PIRANHA, the first major engagements of American ground troops in South Vietnam. From March 1966 to May 1967, the division conducted forty-four named operations, including HASTINGS and UNION I and II. It defeated the enemy in all of its engagements. By June, the entire division was operating in its zone in the two southernmost I Corps provinces. During Tet, in 1968, the division threw back NVA and Viet Cong offensives in its sector. The 1st Marine Division returned to Camp Pendleton, California, in April 1971, and in 1975, the division supported the evacuation of Saigon by furnishing temporary shelter and food to Vietnamese refugees at Camp Pendleton.

mission. I wasn't crazy about it, but he was a friend, and I had worked with him for four or five months. His name was Captain Baker. I said, "Okay, I'll go out." I was short [had almost completed my service], but you're still scared. I've heard guys brag that they were short, and it bothered me. I was proud; I'd do anything for the captain; he was a good man. But the first day out, we saw some bicycles. I used to use explosives when I was with C.W. Bowen, so I blew up these bicycles, like ten bicycles; it was a known VC area we were in. So, about 3:30 in the afternoon, the VC opened up on us. They were the best snipers I'd seen as long as I'd been over there.

We lost eight men in one platoon, shot between the eyes. We were all scared, but the captain had left, and we didn't know where he went. So some fifteen or twenty minutes went by, and these snipers were shooting at us, and we were all lying down as close to the ground as we could get. Meanwhile, I took three guys and went looking for the captain. I knew about where he was. Soon, I heard the captain, or I hoped to God it was the captain. I heard some limbs break on the ground and sure enough, the captain came out and

ABOVE: A U.S. Army M48 tank pauses while the road ahead is swept for mines. Roads and highways had to be examined continuously for VC and NVA mines, which were emplaced and replaced night and day.

LEFT: Wounded soldiers are rushed from a medevac helicopter to a nearby hospital. Prompt treatment was critical to the men's survival.

addressed me as "Skeeter." I never knew why. My name was Heeter, but he called me Skeeter all the time.

He says, "Skeeter, what are you doing out here?" I said, "Well, we were looking for you." He says, "What are you doing here by yourself?" I turned around. The guys who had been with me, when they heard the captain's voice, I guess not knowing whose voice it was, they ran. But I was listening for the captain and waiting to see if he would come back. So the captain and I went back and got the platoon. We had to get behind the VC, and the captain found a way. When we got to the side where the VC was, we spotted a minefield. The captain said, "We've got to go through it." A little lieutenant said, "Well, I'm not going through it." But the captain wouldn't ask you to do anything that he wouldn't do himself. A lot of people said he was gung ho, and he was, kind of. So he took point, and I carried his radio, so I had to go behind him.

As soon as I stepped on a mine, I knew it. We'd seen these mines before. I knew it was a "Bouncing Betty" because I heard the spring. We were running through this minefield, and it went off. It didn't knock me unconscious. I was awake until I got to the hospital. But I couldn't see my leg. I couldn't feel much because experiencing a mine is like smashing your thumb with a hammer; it numbs you for a few minutes. A medic came up and gave me a shot in the leg. You're in shock. You know what's going on, yet you don't really understand it all.

Of course, when he gets shot, John Wayne always lights a cigarette and smokes. I said, "Captain, give me a cigarette." They calm you down when you're getting shot at or whatever. So I was smoking a cigarette and, of course, [I was] in shock. It took fifteen or twenty minutes before the morphine started working. But even though the morphine starts working, that numbness is going to wear off. I was lying there, and I was talking to the captain and looking at the guys behind me. I knew I was in shock because I couldn't see colors. Everything was black and white.

A friend of mine, nearby, had blood running down his face, and it was just black.

I had lost all my colored vision. I couldn't see my leg, and the captain pointed up over my shoulder. My foot was up there, and my shoe was facing down here, where I could tie it if I could have. My leg, the doctor told me, was broken, like in eight places.

Earlier, my brother soldiers had gotten bamboo poles and made litters out of their shirts and came up through that minefield for me. They didn't know if that was the only mine, the one that struck me. We could've been in the middle of a minefield. But friends do that for you. When they picked me up and put me on the litter, my leg fell through the two shirts.

When the chopper came in, the VC opened up on it, so it had to leave. They had to carry me even farther out. I think they had to carry me over one hundred yards before they could get me aboard a chopper, because the VC kept opening up on the chopper. Finally, they put me on the chopper and got me back to the hospital in Cu Chi. The medic was there and also the chaplain. I said, "Chaplain, I'm not going to need you. I think I'm just going home."

I knew I was going home. Lots of times, the chaplain comes up and gives you the last rites and stuff. I told him, "I don't need that." God was with me. He was going to send me home. But they were wonderful. I had five or six people on both sides of me cutting my clothes off. I had had my new uniform on. And the front of it looked good. The back of it was blown away. But I yelled at them, "Don't cut that uniform. That's new." I stayed awake until they put me on that cold X-ray table, and then I passed out.

I was in the hospital for two years, and my friends were the most important thing to me. I mean, I'm proud I fought for my country. They didn't treat us too good when we got home. But we still had our friends.

—Corporal Gary Heeter,
4th Battalion,
25th Infantry Division

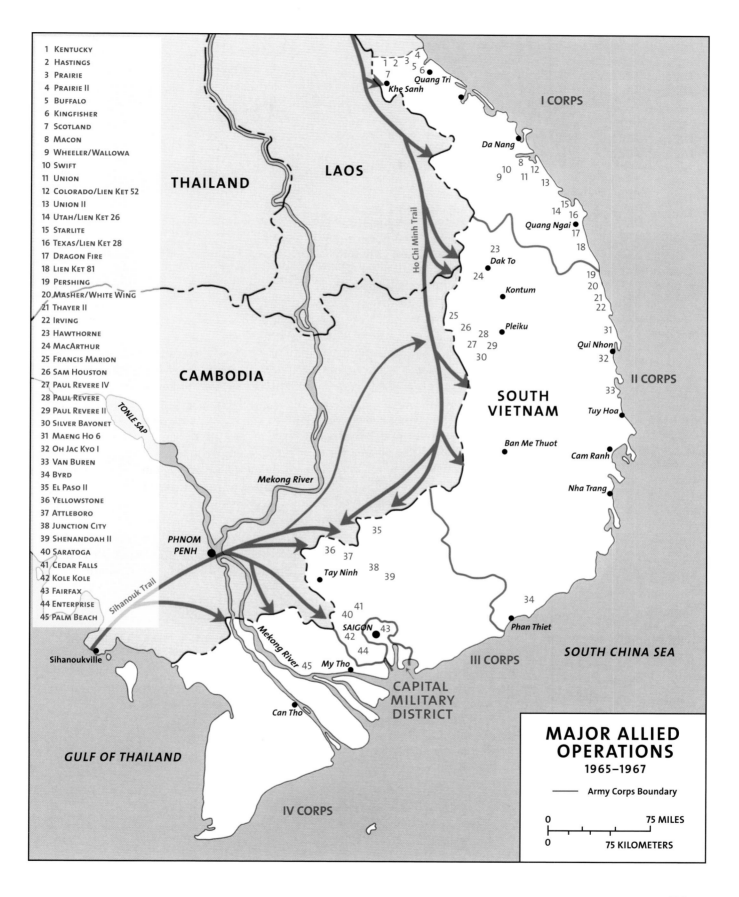

1 KENTUCKY
2 HASTINGS
3 PRAIRIE
4 PRAIRIE II
5 BUFFALO
6 KINGFISHER
7 SCOTLAND
8 MACON
9 WHEELER/WALLOWA
10 SWIFT
11 UNION
12 COLORADO/LIEN KET 52
13 UNION II
14 UTAH/LIEN KET 26
15 STARLITE
16 TEXAS/LIEN KET 28
17 DRAGON FIRE
18 LIEN KET 81
19 PERSHING
20 MASHER/WHITE WING
21 THAYER II
22 IRVING
23 HAWTHORNE
24 MACARTHUR
25 FRANCIS MARION
26 SAM HOUSTON
27 PAUL REVERE IV
28 PAUL REVERE
29 PAUL REVERE II
30 SILVER BAYONET
31 MAENG HO 6
32 OH JAC KYO I
33 VAN BUREN
34 BYRD
35 EL PASO II
36 YELLOWSTONE
37 ATTLEBORO
38 JUNCTION CITY
39 SHENANDOAH II
40 SARATOGA
41 CEDAR FALLS
42 KOLE KOLE
43 FAIRFAX
44 ENTERPRISE
45 PALM BEACH

THAILAND

LAOS

Quang Tri
Khe Sanh

I CORPS

Da Nang

Ho Chi Minh Trail

Quang Ngai

Dak To

Kontum

Pleiku

Qui Nhon

CAMBODIA

TONLE SAP

Mekong River

SOUTH
VIETNAM

II CORPS

Tuy Hoa

Ban Me Thuot

Cam Ranh

Nha Trang

PHNOM
PENH

Sihanouk Trail

Tay Ninh

SAIGON

Phan Thiet

SOUTH CHINA SEA

III CORPS

Sihanoukville

Mekong River

My Tho

CAPITAL
MILITARY
DISTRICT

Can Tho

GULF OF THAILAND

IV CORPS

MAJOR ALLIED OPERATIONS
1965–1967

—— Army Corps Boundary

0   75 MILES
0   75 KILOMETERS

I heard it another time, I remember, when a grenade went off on a guy's belt; his own grenade. It was the same thing. It wasn't him, he was killed immediately, but the person behind him screamed. So you always knew it was a booby trap when you heard that—that *bam*—and then that high-pitched screaming.
—Gerry Schooler

A Company's Gerry Schooler felt that booby traps and mines evoked a larger emotional and psychological response from the soldiers who fell victim to them.

It's significant when men get shot. They fall down, they say "Medic!," or they groan. But there's something about an explosion, booby traps, that just sets off soldiers' nervous systems, and so you hear this high-pitched screaming. It's not really any intelligible words necessarily. You can hear it through the whole valley. It's ear piercing. When you hear that sound, you don't forget it. You know that it was a booby trap.

When someone was wounded, especially by mines or booby traps, the medics were the difference between life and death. Treating the wounded, however, was a dangerous task, as Medal of Honor recipient Clarence Sasser recalls.

The most difficult thing I found involved isolated injuries, injuries from booby traps. There were a lot of booby traps set in Vietnam. Some were command-detonated ones [set off by a VC from an over-watch position]. If somebody hit a booby trap, it was usually either a point man or one of the first men in the line of movement. Invariably,

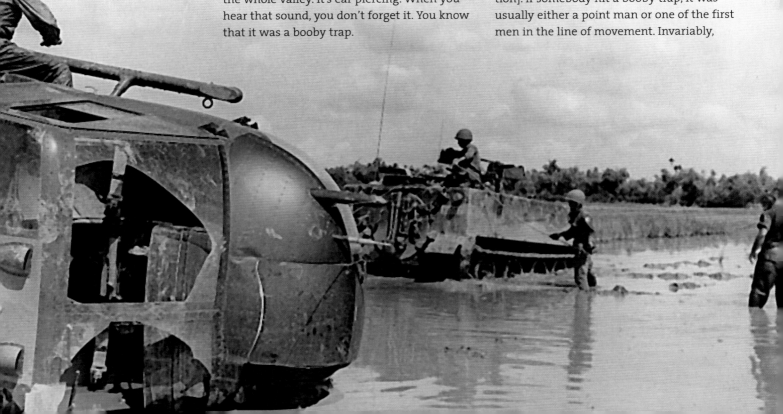

when someone was hit by a booby trap, the medic had to treat him. If it was a command-detonated booby trap, that meant that somebody might be sitting there that pushed the button or threw the lever that detonated it.

If the VC set two booby traps there, one that got the injured person, when the medic came to see about it a VC might detonate the other one. That was always the scariest, most difficult thing to deal with when you went up to treat someone wounded by a booby trap: there might be another command-detonated booby trap ready to blow up.

We had the whole range of wounds: sniper-type ones, ordinary gunshot wounds, firefight-type injuries, and various booby trap–type wounds. There were also the *punji* pits that had sharpened, bamboo-charred spikes that were made sort of like tiger traps. The traps were covered over so that the ground would collapse before the soldiers, and they'd fall in on the spikes, causing them severe injuries. A lot of times, they covered the spikes with excrement in an effort to produce infection.

You looked out for your people. It's part of the job. The medic's job is the welfare, the care, and the health of the entire platoon. If one has a problem, the medic is just like a mother hen. You go get him and square it away. The medic did whatever he had to do, even go to the CO [commanding officer] about it. Whatever the guys came to you about, you tried to work with it. Of course, there's also that little point about being a confidant in the equation, too. You listened to

ABOVE: The South Vietnamese landscape as seen over the shoulder of a machine gunner. The soldier is perched in the door of an H-21 Shawnee helicopter of the 57th Transportation Company. Two more H-21s are flying in the same formation, all carrying troops of the ARVN 1st Airborne Brigade from Tan Hiep airstrip to operations in the Plain of Reeds.

VC Mines and Booby Traps

Booby traps were the Viet Cong's stock-in-trade. Cheap to produce and made from easily acquired materials, these devices were nonetheless capable of killing or maiming unwary American and South Vietnamese troops. The VC worked diligently and meticulously to fashion and camouflage them so that they were virtually impossible to detect until triggered.

Grenades were often used to make booby traps. Easy to carry and simple to conceal, they could be placed at gates, tied to trees or fences, or hidden in bushes along trails, where a simple trip wire, anchored to a bush at one end and connected to a friction-type fuse in the grenade, triggered an explosion that sent sprays of deadly shrapnel in every direction. Explosives from discarded, captured, or unexploded U.S. artillery shells were made into larger bombs with more deadly charges. Grenades were fixed at the top of a bamboo arch, with a trip wire extending vertically to the ground where it was anchored. Soldiers approaching a VC position in the darkness would stumble into these wires, setting off the overhead grenades. Another VC tactic was to drive numerous short stakes into the ground at sites suitable for helicopter landings. Grenades fastened atop the stakes and connected to a network of wires were set off when a helicopter made contact with any of the wires. In addition, daisy chains of grenades were fashioned of fish line or wire strung around the handles of a series of grenades with their firing pins removed. When a trip wire attached to the first grenade was triggered, it detonated that grenade, releasing the pressure on the wires strung around

ABOVE: Improvised traps and fortifications were also used by pro-government Vietnamese peasants. Here, Self Defense Corps militiamen pound sharpened bamboo stakes into the ground to form a defensive belt around their village in the autumn of 1965. Almost useless against NVA or "main force" Viet Cong attacks, embedded stakes, together with moats and tough bamboo screens, did greatly hinder infiltration, however. They also slowed and channeled attacks by local Viet Cong, who frequently went barefoot or wore only light rubber sandals. Note that about midway down each stake is a notch that provides a flat surface for the hammer to strike while leaving the razor-sharp point intact.

the handles of the other grenades, which set off a string of explosions.

Early in the war, ARVN soldiers frequently rode on the backs of tanks, so guerrillas would drive two fifteen-foot-tall bamboo trunks into the ground, with a drooping wire leading from the top of one pole to the other. Two grenades dangled from the wire at equal distances. When tanks moving through the jungle passed between the poles, the grenades exploded, killing or maiming the infantrymen riding atop the armor. Another ploy practiced by the VC was to hide a string of grenades along a well-traveled trail. Long fish cords or wires were attached to the grenade fuses. The wires led to hidden guerrillas, crouched in over-watch positions. At the appropriate moment, they triggered the grenades.

"Man traps" were one- to two-foot-deep pits camouflaged with a mat of bamboo slats and a thin layer of dirt that would collapse under pressure, sending a soldier's leg plummeting in to sharpened bamboo stakes (punji) or nails fixed in boards that gave way, then pivoted, pinning the soldier's legs in a vise of spikes. Far sides of gullies were often embedded with sharp stakes—called gully traps—hidden in the grass so that when allied soldiers leaped across a ditch, they became impaled. Bamboo whips affixed with spikes were positioned along roadways, where they were placed under tension. When they were triggered, they slammed into the faces and bodies of passing soldiers, seriously wounding or killing them. Small bridges were covered with mud, hiding where they had been nearly cut in two.

When crossed, they collapsed, sending soldiers reeling into punji stakes. Mortar rounds were hung in trees along roads and paths and set off by nearby VC using battery-powered detonators.

Low-tech mines were created from coconuts filled with black powder and furnished with friction-type fuses connected to trip wires. Larger mines, constructed of large bamboo tubes filled with steel nuts, bolts, and scrap metal, were primed with plastic explosives or black powder and detonated by a friction-type pull-fuse. One of the most feared mines was the "Bouncing Betty," used by both the allies

and the Communists, in varying varieties. The mine was sometimes conical in shape, with three detonating prongs hidden below the surface of the ground. When the mine was stepped on, it set off an arming mechanism, heard by the soldiers immediately before the mine shot into the air and exploded at chest height, hurling shrapnel in all directions and blowing off arms and legs and killing soldiers. The existence of these sinister weapons had a chilling effect on soldiers.

their cares, their troubles, and their fears. And even if the problem wasn't the result of action, it was your job to try to resolve it. You looked out for your people.

Medics have been special persons throughout all warfare. It's genuinely recognized that some injuries in war may not be totally disabling to a soldier, and that with sufficient treatment you can regain the use of that soldier. Plus, there's the psychological advantage for the soldier of knowing that if he gets hurt, someone's going to take care of him. They won't just leave him behind to die. That, in my estimation, has a bearing on the temperament of a fighting soldier. It's a tradition, medics, that goes way back to the Civil War and Dr. Mary Walker, back to the Revolutionary War and medics during those times. So again, medics have a long and glorious history, and I'm especially proud that I fit in as one.

—Clarence E. Sasser

ABOVE: Sergeant First Class Floyd R. Adkins, 2d Battalion, 7th Cavalry, disarms a Viet Cong booby trap found during the search of a village. The trap was made from a 41-mm artillery round filled with explosives.

LEFT: An NVA soldier carefully aligns the top of a large Chinese-made antitank mine with ground level during a 1966 training exercise.

Booby traps and mines struck in an instant, and a solder's life could be changed forever—if he survived.

We were doing pretty good, got about an hour into our movement, and I said to myself, we're doing good, nobody's shooting, and we're covering some ground. We took a break, stopped. This is the first time I saw anybody killed. My first day out some guy sat down on what we called a stick mine. It's a vertical bamboo stick of some type, runs down on a shaft, and it's really a sort of tilted rod. You don't even have to step on it, just tilt it and it goes off. It's like an antitank mine.

It's huge, about thirty pounds of explosive. Well, it killed the soldier and the guy next to

him and wounded a third guy. We were all spread out, like we should have been, or it would have killed a lot of people. But I still remember hearing the explosion, and people calling for a medic. It happened maybe a hundred, two hundred feet from me, behind me. Then I saw the "Dustoff" come in, the chopper. I saw the company commander walk up. I didn't know any of these people's names [the wounded and killed]; I didn't even know how long they had been there [in Vietnam].

I heard on the radio, spoken nonchalantly, it struck me: "We got two kilos and a whiskey." The radioman gave the coordinates to bring in the chopper, and of course, I figured out pretty fast what kilo and whiskey meant. That was it. Then they picked the bodies up and took them out. We finished our smoke break, and we got up and started walking again.

—Gerry Schooler

Many times, the Viet Cong obtained American munitions and made booby traps out of it.

As far as the munitions are concerned, I think the failure in Vietnam was the 4 percent of dud rounds that were everywhere. You're talking about millions and millions of tons of bombs, that's a lot of ordnance that didn't explode. They're still finding it today. The VC would take that, break it apart, and take the powder out of it. Then, they'd take a 155 [mm] round and make ten booby traps with the powder from that thing.

But if you think about it, that's kind of a tricky job. You have to get the thing open and get the powder out without blowing yourself to bits. A lot of VC were killed doing that. They had a way of accepting that kind of death as being part of the overall fight. They would just put up with it. But I've learned from recent trips over there that some Viet Cong would talk about those kinds of hardships. But they were taught from an early age that they had to put up with it.

—Gerry Schooler

Battle of the Ia Drang Valley

By the fall of 1965, the U.S. Army had assembled a force in Vietnam that was more than 180,000 men strong, composed of two Army brigades, a U.S. Marine regiment, and a Republic of Korea (ROK) division. In addition, the entire 1st Cavalry Division (Airmobile), one of the Army's premier units, was deployed to the Central Highlands, a prime trouble spot infested with enemy troops from the 32d, 33d, and 66th NVA Army Regiments. On November 14, units of the U.S. 1st Cavalry locked horns with the NVA in the Ia Drang Valley. The ensuing fight lasted for more than a month.

The NVA opened up the campaign on October 19 by attacking Special Forces troops at Plei Me, a camp twenty-five miles from Pleiku. When units from the 1st Cavalry reinforced Plei Me, the NVA melted into the jungle. But Captain William P. Gillette, an intelligence officer from the squadron relieving the camp, detected suspicious signs of the NVA's continued presence some eight kilometers to the west. Units from the 1st Brigade followed up on Gillette's report by pursuing the NVA aggressively with rifle and gunship platoons. Charging into the area in a skirmish role, they soon killed some seventy-eight NVA soldiers and captured fifty-seven—all carrying Hanoi-issued IDs. The U.S. cavalry lost five men killed and seventeen wounded in the encounter. In this fight, the NVA initiated "hugging," a tactic that later became routine for them. To avoid the horrendous American aerial and ground artillery fire, NVA soldiers fought the Americans at the closest proximity possible, making it difficult for U.S. fire support to zero in on and destroy them without injuring Americans with friendly fire.

On October 20, Brigadier General Richard T. Knowles, assistant division commander, sent the 1st Squadron, 9th Cavalry, to pursue the NVA troops. They found them in an area along the Ia Drang River beneath the Chu Pong Mountains. Knowles ordered the 1st Squadron to LZ Mary, where they landed and engaged the enemy. General Chu Huy Man, the NVA regional commander, responded by sending three of his battalions into the fight in an attempt to annihilate the Americans. By November 4, the U.S. 1st Squadron had inflicted 150 casualties on the North Vietnamese, then turned over its position to two follow-on infantry battalions commanded by Colonel Thomas W. Brown, who sent his men searching for the enemy in the area south and southeast of Plei Me.

As part of the continuing operation, Lieutenant Colonel Harold G. "Hal" Moore, 1st Battalion, 7th Cavalry, on November 14 chose LZ X-Ray for his air assault drop into the area. The LZ itself was barely large enough to hold ten UH-1Ds (Hueys). X-Ray was also bordered by hundred-foot-tall trees and bristled with neck-high elephant grass and eight-foot-tall anthills—all of which afforded the enemy good cover. At 1017 hours, helicopter gunships pounded the position around X-Ray, using up half their ammunition in a blistering, thirty-second barrage. Then, Moore's men were brought to the ground. The aerial artillery

1ST CAVALRY DIVISION (AIRMOBILE)

The 1st Cavalry Division was sent to Vietnam in September 1965, the first complete American fighting division deployed in the country. In a fierce engagement with NVA forces in the Ia Drang Valley, October–November 1965, the division earned the Presidential Unit Citation. The division continued to engage enemy troops in the II Corps area throughout 1966 and 1967, distinguishing itself in battles against the 610th NVA Division and VC units in Operations MASHER/WHITE WING, PAUL REVERE, IRVING, THAYER II, and PERSHING I and II. During NVA attacks on U.S. Marines at Khe Sanh in April 1968, the 1st Cavalry Division valiantly supported the defenders. During its tour in Vietnam, the 1st Cavalry Division clearly demonstrated the effectiveness of airmobile operations. In spring 1971, the division returned to Fort Hood, Texas.

hovered overhead in case they were needed.

As A, B, C, and D companies were landed, the air became thick with dust and smoke. By mid-afternoon, the Americans were fighting for their lives. Incoming supply and reinforcement helicopters were being riddled by enemy fire, and one pilot and his gunner were wounded and a radioman was killed. Division artillery fired phosphorus rounds, and by their lurid glare, the killed and wounded were retrieved from the defensive perimeter. Moore yelled over the din into his radio for reinforcements, and Company B, 2d Battalion, 7th Infantry, was sent in. During their landing, two helicopters were hit on the ground, and another, still in the air, spun helplessly out of control, its main rotor clipping leaves from the treetops before it crashed in a resounding heap. Meanwhile, a platoon from Company B was cut off from the rest of the forces and suffered twenty casualties, leaving it with only seven fighting men.

In the early morning hours of November 15, hand-to-hand fighting ensued, but by that afternoon, the enemy had retired from the battlefield. It had been a brutal, relentless battle. When U.S. troops emerged from their defenses, they found a dead American in a nearby foxhole surrounded by the remains of five NVA soldiers. Another U.S. trooper was found with his hands clasped around the throat of one of his enemies, both men dead. The area was littered with bodies, and NVA weapons and equipment were strewn across a wide area. Bloody trails left by the NVA soldiers led into the jungle. The U.S. soldiers dug in for the night, but the battle was over.

U.S. leaders had found an enemy that was well trained and aggressive, and that fought fanatically with the latest automatic weapons and abundant ammunition. Nonetheless, some 1,200–1,800 NVA were killed and more were wounded in their encounter with the 1st Cavalry.

BELOW: Clad in "Tiger Stripe" battle dress, members of the Delta Team that reinforced the Plei Me Special Forces camp watch as air strikes pound NVA positions on the Chu Ho Hill mass south of the camp. The NVA opened up the 1965 Ia Drang Valley campaign with an October 19 attack on the Special Forces troops at Plei Me, twenty-five miles from Pleiku, but troopers from the 1st Cavalry Division (Airmobile) arrived in time to repulse the Communists.

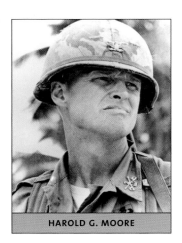

HAROLD G. MOORE

The Americans lost 79 killed and 121 wounded, only a fraction of the enemy's casualties, but nevertheless the greatest U.S. losses up to this point in the war. The NVA was prepared for its bloodletting. In the United States, however, the news media bewailed what they called the appalling American losses, and for some time the battle was described in dire terms. Because there were no front lines in the Vietnam War, and therefore no ordinary measurements quantifying military success, "body counts" became that measure. The military used this method to point to successes or improvements in the campaign to "attrit" (kill) the enemy; the news media, on the other hand, often used body counts to demonstrate the barbarism of the president and the military. Some Americans thought warfare could—or should—be a more civilized event. But the Battle of Ia Drang Valley was an exceedingly bloody encounter, the first of many, in what was to become a long, bitter war, brought, for the first time, into American living rooms via television.

Lieutenant Colonel Harold G. Moore approached LZ X-Ray and watched the helicopters of the aerial artillery slam the area around the landing zone with rockets, grenades, and machine-gun fire. Moore knew, however, that the enemy was likely hidden nearby.

The door gunners on the lift ships were firing into the tree line as we dropped into the clearing. I unhooked my seat belt, switched the selector switch on my M16 to full automatic—rock 'n' roll—and fired bursts into the brush to the left, toward the mountain, as [A Company commander Major Bruce] Crandall came in hot and flared over the dry, five-foot-tall elephant grass. As the chopper skids touched the ground, I yelled, "Let's go!" and jumped out, running for the trees on the western edge of the clearing, firing my rifle. It was 10:48 AM.

[Later, on the defensive perimeter.] The small bloody hole in the ground that was Captain Bob Edwards's Charlie Company command post was crowded with men.

THE IA DRANG
November 1965

Air Assault
National Highway

0   10 MILES
0   10 KILOMETERS

Pleiku

QL-19

ARVN
Relief
Force

QL-19

QL-14

Duc Co
Special Forces
Camp

CAMBODIA

Enemy Retreat

Ia Drang   River

Special Forces
Camp   *Plei Me*

LZ Albany

Enemy Retreat

LZ X-Ray

1st Cavalry
Division Forces

Chu Pong Mt.

Sergeant Hermon R. Hostuttler, twenty-five, from Terra Alta, West Virginia, lay crumpled in the red dirt, dead from an AK-47 round through his throat. Specialist 4 Ernest E. Paolone of Chicago, the radio operator, crouched low, bleeding from a shrapnel wound in his left forearm. Sergeant James P. Castleberrry, the artillery forward observer, and his radio operator, Private First Class Ervin L. Brown, Jr., hunkered down beside Paolone. Captain Edwards had a bullet hole in his left shoulder and armpit, and was slumped in a contorted sitting position, unable to move and losing blood. He was holding his radio handset to his ear with his one good arm. A North Vietnamese machine gunner atop a huge termite hill no more than thirty feet away had them all in his sights.

"We lay there watching bullets kick dirt off the small parapet around the edge of the hole," Edwards recalls. "I didn't know how badly I had been hurt, only that I couldn't stand up, couldn't do very much. The two platoon leaders I had radio contact with, Lieutenant William W. Franklin on my right and Lieutenant James L. Lane on Franklin's right, continued to report receiving fire, but

had not been penetrated. I knew that my other two platoons were in bad shape and the enemy had penetrated to within hand-grenade range of my command post."

One of Captain Edwards's men, Specialist 4 Arthur Viera, remembers every second of Charlie Company's agony that morning. "The gunfire was very loud. We were getting over-run on the right side. The lieutenant [Neil Kroger, twenty-four, a native of Oak Park, Illinois] came up in the open in all this. I thought that was pretty good. He yelled at me. I got up to hear him. He hollered at me to help cover the left sector."

Viera adds, "I ran over to him and by the time I got there he was dead. He had lasted a half-hour. I knelt beside him, took off his dog tags, and put them in my shirt pocket. I went back to firing my M-79 grenade launcher and got shot in my right elbow. The M-79 went flying and I was knocked down and fell back over the lieutenant. I had my .45 and fired it with my left hand. Then I got hit in the neck and the bullet went right through. Now I couldn't talk or make a sound."

"I got up and tried to take charge and was shot a third time. That one blew up my right leg and put me down. It went in my leg above the ankle, traveled up, came back out, then went into my groin and ended up in my back, close to my spine. Just then two stick grenades blew up right over me and tore up both my legs. I reached down with my left hand and touched grenade fragments on my left leg and it felt like I had touched a red-hot poker. My hand just sizzled." [Despite the violence and chaos, however, Edwards's Charlie Company eventually obtained the upper hand and blunted the main NVA attack on LZ X-Ray.]

—Lieutenant General (then Lieutenant Colonel) Harold G. Moore, U.S. Army, Retired, in *We Were Soldiers Once… and Young*

On another perimeter of the Ia Drang battlefield, an equally violent struggle ensued. Lieutenant Henry T. Herrick's 2d Platoon had become isolated and was surrounded by the North Vietnamese. Bravo Company's 1st and 3d platoons, led by Captain John Herren, were sent in to rescue them.

BELOW: The approved caption text on this 1st Cavalry Division photograph, not previously identified as taken during the fighting at LZ X-Ray, states only that the men are attempting to "relieve other units under heavy attack by VC near the Cambodian border." However, bearing a date of November 15, 1965, and picturing terrain appropriate for X-Ray, the photo likely depicts troopers of the division's 1st Battalion, 7th Cavalry, sweeping the area beyond their perimeter to recover American wounded, search NVA dead for documents and letters, and discourage enemy movement to their front.

At that moment, Lieutenant Bob Taft and his 3d Platoon of Alpha Company collided head-on with the enemy force of about 150 men charging down and along both sides of the dry creek. A savage fight now broke out over ownership of the creekbed. Captain Nadal, who had spent a year in South Vietnam with the Special Forces, looked across the creekbed at the enemy boiling out of the trees and knew these were not Viet Cong guerrillas but North Vietnamese regulars. He got on the battalion net radio and yelled: "They're PAVN! They're PAVN!"

Specialist 4 Carmen Miceli, a native of North Bergen, New Jersey, remembers, "We were told to drop our packs. We got on line and moved forward in the attack. I saw Specialist 4 Bill Beck on an M-60 machine gun out to my left. Captain Nadal was right there with us. We took fire, and the guys started going down. We could see the enemy very plainly. We were assaulting. A lot of our guys were hit right away."

Sergeant Steve Hansen was behind and to the right of Lieutenant Taft. He says, "We moved at a trot across the open grass toward the tree line and heard fire up on the finger to the west where we were headed. My radio operator friend, Specialist 4 Ray Tanner, and I crossed the streambed. Captain Nadal's party and the two other platoons were off to the right. Lieutenant Taft was well forward as we crossed over into the trees. Sergeant First Class Lorenzo Nathan, Ray Tanner, and I were close, maybe ten yards behind. We were moving fast. Specialist 4 Pete Winter was near me.

"We ran into a wall of lead. Every man in the lead squad was shot. From the time we got the order to move, to the time where men were dying, was only five minutes. The enemy was very close to us and overran some of our dead. The firing was heavy. Sergeant Nathan pulled us back out of the woods to the streambed."

Bob Hazen, Bob Taft's radio operator, recalls: "Lieutenant Taft got out in front of

ABOVE: One the first NVA soldiers captured by the 1st Cavalry Division is interrogated as the division's 1st Brigade deputy commander, Lieutenant Colonel Harlow W. Clark, listens in, November 2, 1965. The prisoner was probably among the forty-three North Vietnamese seized when elements of the 9th Cavalry overran an NVA field hospital the day before.

me. I was off to his left. He had the radio handset in his left hand, connected to the radio on my back with that flexible rubber wire. It got tight and I pulled back on the lieutenant and hollered: "We're getting off line." He glanced back at me, turned back to his front, and took four more steps. Then he fired two shots at something. I couldn't see what."

"Then he dropped face down on the ground. Lieutenant Taft was hit. I didn't realize how bad till I rolled him over. He was shot in the throat and the round had ricocheted down and came out his left side. He was dead and it was difficult to roll him over, even though he was a slightly built man."

In the center of that fury, Bob Hazen struggled and rolled his dead platoon leader over. "He was gone and there was nothing I could do. The first thing I thought of was what they taught me: Never let the enemy get his hands on a map or the signals codebook. I got those from Lieutenant Taft and was kneeling over to try to pull his body back. That's when my radio was hit and the shrapnel from the radio hit me in the back of the head. It didn't really hurt; all of a sudden I was just laying face down on the ground

next to Lieutenant Taft. I felt something running down my neck, reached back, and came out with a handful of blood."

—Lieutenant General Harold G. Moore, in *We Were Soldiers Once … and Young*

The Battle of Ia Drang Valley was no picnic for the NVA forces, either. Pitted against tough and stubborn U.S. cavalrymen, they suffered unrelenting fire from ground and air artillery. U.S. riflemen and machine gunners chimed in.

Although they had been hit hard and had suffered several casualties, Taft's platoon, now led by Korean War veteran Sergeant Lorenzo Nathan, stood firm and stopped the momentum of the attack. The enemy recoiled and slowly drifted off to their left still trying to find a way to flank Bravo Company. This brought them directly in front of Joe Marm's troopers, who had been moving up to join Bravo. About eighty North Vietnamese soldiers were caught by surprise as Marm's troopers opened up with volley after volley of grazing, point-blank machine-gun and rifle fire and heaved hand grenades into their packed ranks on their exposed right flank. Marm's men mowed them down. Two enemy were taken prisoner.

Several of the men still remember the curious behavior of the North Vietnamese who came under this murderous fire. Captain Tony Nadal says, "It wasn't much of a fight; the 2d Platoon just mowed them down." Staff Sergeant Les Staley recalls, "Fifty NVA came right across my front and were cut down almost immediately and they did not turn and try to return our fire." The enemy survivors fell back to their right rear, toward the creekbed. That brought them back in front of Tony Nadal's 1st and 3d platoons, which were now in the four-foot-deep cover of the creekbed. Again the enemy was cut down by close-range flanking fire from their right. They just kept walking into the field of fire.

—Lieutenant General Harold G. Moore, in *We Were Soldiers Once … and Young*

BELOW: Lieutenant Colonel Harold G. "Hal" Moore, commander of the 1st Cavalry Division's 1st Battalion, 7th Cavalry, during the three-day fight at LZ X-Ray, examines a dead NVA soldier, November 16, 1965.

Fire Support

BELOW: A 1st Cavalry Division M102 105-mm howitzer battery pummels NVA forces during fighting in the Ia Drang Valley as a slingload of ammunition is gently lowered to the ground, November 1965. Unlike the M101A1's 25-degree field of fire, the M102 rotated on a wide steel pedestal, which allowed it to fire in any direction with a minimum of manhandling. Designed for airmobile and airborne units, the M102 was also nearly 1,900 pounds lighter than its predecessor, which allowed it to be easily airlifted by a variety of helicopters, including the comparatively small UH-1 Huey Iroquois. The M102 had a maximum range of nearly 12,580 yards (11,500 meters). Both howitzers were served by eight-man crews and fired a very wide variety of high-explosive, smoke, illumination, and antipersonnel ammunition, including the murderous XM546 "beehive" round containing 8,000 tiny steel darts.

TOP: U.S. Forces arriving in Vietnam quickly found that the sodden nature of the terrain, with its rice paddies, canals, and streams, frequently placed severe limitations on the emplacement of artillery. Because howitzers and field guns could respond to unanticipated requests for fire support much more quickly than either aircraft or helicopter gunships, it was imperative that means be developed to position weapons where they could do the most good. Shown here, a battery of 17th Artillery 105-mm howitzers is squeezed into the narrow space along a raised road between rice paddies and a canal southwest of Tuy Hoa. The artillerymen were forced to stack ammunition crates right up to the edge of the water, and an M60 machine gun has been placed to repel an attack from behind the position.

BOTTOM: Specialized fighting vehicles were frequently used in direct support of ground troops and as convoy protection despite their light armor and open configurations that often required crewmen to fight from partially exposed positions. Here, a Marine M50A1 Ontos antitank vehicle armed with a half-dozen 106-mm recoilless rifles escorts amphibious LVTP5s (landing vehicle, tracked, personnel, model 5) south of Quang Ngai, March 1965.

LEFT: M107 175-mm self-propelled guns, like this one of the 3d Battalion, 18th Artillery, seen looming over its gun-pit bunkers at Tien Phuoc, could reach out 41,570 yards (32,700 meters)—more than 23 miles—when propelled by the blast from a maximum power charge. As a practical matter, however, ranges exceeding 20 miles were rarely ordered except in dire emergencies, such as the imminent overrunning of a far-flung firebase, because of the extreme wear that firing at such distances inflicted on the gun tubes.

BELOW: An M110 8-inch self-propelled howitzer of the 7th Battalion, 8th Artillery, in action at Long Binh, March 1968. The 8-inch had a reputation for extreme accuracy largely because its massive 203-mm, 200-pound projectiles were little affected by winds as they flew toward targets up to 18,375 yards (16,800 meters) away. Note the huge hydraulically operated spade that helps hold the M110 in place when the howitzer fires.

RIGHT: The only unit to field M56 Scorpion self-propelled 90-mm antitank guns, like this one in Long Khan Province, was the 173d Airborne Brigade. Special canister rounds that cut a wide swath of destruction were provided to M56 crews, but because the vehicle offered minimal crew protection and could not easily be up-armored, it was withdrawn from Vietnam by the end of 1966.

BELOW, INSET: While the M108 tank's howitzer suffered from the same range limitations as the unarmored 105s, the 155-mm howitzer of the M109 could throw its rounds some 15,975 yards (14,600 meters). This 2d Battalion, 138th Artillery, system is parked at Firebase Tomahawk, 20 miles south of Phu Bai, shortly before the unit was redesignated the 1st Battalion, 32d Artillery, in October 1969. Unless caught in the open, crews in bunkered M108s and M109s were generally safe from all but a direct hit during Communist artillery and rocket attacks.

BELOW: Armed with twin 40-mm guns, the M42 "Duster" was principally intended to provide anti-aircraft protection for fast-moving armor units but proved to be devastating in the antipersonnel role.

LEFT AND BELOW: A CH-54 Flying Crane airlifts (left) a 34th Artillery, 9th Infantry Division, M102 to its Mekong River firebase (shown below).

TOP: The 1st Logistical Command's 1099th Transportation Company and the 1st Infantry Division's 1st Battalion, 7th Artillery, team up to convert an LCM (landing craft, medium) and an M101A1 105-mm howitzer into a floating battery. Unfortunately, if the craft isn't solidly grounded, even slight wave action can cause distant targets to be missed by hundreds of yards.

BOTTOM: Flat-bottomed barges provided a more stable gun platform but were still adversely affected by the motion of the water. These are the airmobile M102 155-mm howitzers with 360-degree traverse.

LEFT: An M108 105-mm self-propelled howitzer of the 3d Battalion, 6th Artillery, awaits a fire mission in its bunkered position. In addition to the kill marks visible on the port side of the turret are more marks, unseen on the face of the opened hatch cover.

BELOW: A 4th Infantry Division gunner casts aside a spent shell casing as his loader quickly feeds another round into "The Bandit," an M101A1 105-mm howitzer. This weapon is nearly identical to the ones used to great effect decades earlier in World War II and Korea. Because its barrel had a limited traverse and the ground in battery positions turned to an oozing muck after even a modest rain, a stable gun platform of disassembled ammunition crates has been built to ease the soldiers' task when they must manually turn the howitzer to acquire targets beyond its field of fire. Discarded brass shell casings have been pounded deep into the ground to help prevent the platform from coming apart during the constant pounding and monsoon downpours. Mathematical aiming designations like the one at right (5600) have been placed at set intervals around the interior of the gun pit for easy fire-direction reference, so that the artillerymen can quickly orient their weapon. The 105-mm howitzer had a maximum range of 12,325 yards (11,270 meters).

To put a rein on an able general while at the same time asking him to suppress a cunning enemy is like tying up the Black Hound of Han and then ordering him to catch elusive hares.

—Sun Tzu,
in *The Art of War*

Chapter Two

TAKING THE OFFENSIVE

For a year, the U.S. Air Force had bombarded North Vietnam with thousands of tons of bombs as part of Operation ROLLING THUNDER. On the ground, U.S. Army and Marine forces had taken the war to the enemy in the wild jungles of South Vietnam, where thousands of Viet Cong were killed and wounded as they fought off the overwhelming firepower of a major world power. But despite the decimation of the enemy, the fight continued unabated, with little sign of weariness or lagging spirits from the Communists. Something had to change. A winning combination had to be found.

The Opposing Strategies

By 1966, even though U.S. military forces were now taking the fight to the enemy, the dispute over the war's long-term strategy continued to simmer between military and civilian officials. President Johnson and his advisors chose to pursue a strategy of "limited war," which many military leaders believed would be ultimately unsuccessful. ROLLING THUNDER was an example of that strategy, whereby the enemy was supposedly punished in incremental doses until they decided to come to the conference table. Allowing the NVA to use Laos and Cambodia for sanctuary was another instance of the limited-war strategy. A fervent belief existed among Johnson's advisors that the United States' vast superiority in materiel and manpower would either intimidate the North Vietnamese into negotiating an end to the war or overpower them on the battlefield. In any case, Johnson's people recognized no compelling need for a more innovative U.S. strategy.

The White House's position was influenced by the conviction that if the United States applied too much military pressure in Vietnam, China might feel so threatened that it would intervene in the conflict, as it had in the Korean War. The Soviet Union, for its part, might then feel compelled to offer security guarantees to the Chinese, thus escalating the conflict into what could become a nuclear war. Lyndon Johnson and his advisors wished to avoid that eventuality at all costs. This gradual approach, however, allowed the North Vietnamese time to adapt to American attacks rather than be overwhelmed by them, as would have been the case in an all-out war. While a number of military leaders from the start urged the president to attack airfields, industry, and petroleum storage facilities in the North with maximum, unrelenting force, Johnson's advisors believed that the Communists would come to terms as the tempo and severity of the air strikes increased. While the effects of this strategy made North Vietnam's situation increasingly difficult, it failed to create enough pressure on Ho Chi Minh or the North Vietnamese people to prevent them from prosecuting the war, and it had little effect on their will to fight.

On the ground, the U.S. strategy during 1964 to 1965 was one of attrition, in hopes of teaching the North Vietnamese an object lesson concerning the high cost of fighting a superior army in the field. But while U.S. forces won battle after battle, killing the enemy in ever-greater numbers, the contest for the hearts and minds of the South Vietnamese in the hinterlands was being won early in the war

by the Communists of the National Liberation Front, the Viet Cong's shadow government, through force and terror. Meanwhile, Ho Chi Minh and the North Vietnamese leaders cynically shrugged off Viet Cong and NVA losses, at the same time relishing the sanctuary afforded their forces in Cambodia and Laos. From these havens, the NVA channeled their supplies and men and assembled their troops for strikes into the heart of South Vietnam. Ironically, those who concocted the American "attrition strategy" assumed that the American people would stand by while the requisite number of American casualties were suffered to ensure success.

General Dave R. Palmer, who fought in Vietnam, added his own critique: "Attrition is not a strategy. It is, in fact, irrefutable proof of the absence of any strategy. A commander who resorts to attrition admits his failure to conceive of an alternative. He rejects warfare as an art. He uses blood in lieu of brains. To be sure, political considerations left military commanders no choice other than attrition warfare, but that does not alter the hard truth that the United States was strategically bankrupt in Vietnam in 1966."

But to the North Vietnamese Communists, the war was about willpower, not manpower and sophisticated armaments. Time was an important ingredient in their calculations. Despite their horrendous losses, the North Vietnamese were convinced that if they stayed in the struggle long enough, the American and South Vietnamese people would lose their will to resist, would shrink from the cost of the war in treasure and lives, and would capitulate. Meanwhile, the North Vietnamese occupied the moral high ground by proposing in their propaganda campaigns that the United States was imposing its will illegitimately upon a weak, downtrodden, Third World people.

At the same time, the Communists ensured that Saigon, the South Vietnamese capital, was made continually vulnerable to the NVA through the establishment of a virtually impregnable war zone in the "Iron Triangle," just northwest of the city, and the maintenance of high-speed avenues of advance from nearby Cambodia, along which attacking forces

RIGHT: A mortar squad of the 1st Battalion, 173d Airborne Brigade, trudges through a battlefield in Phuoc Tuy, December 1966. The battalion had just received a Presidential Unit Citation for operations against the Viet Cong near Bien Hoa Air Base.

BELOW: UH-1D Hueys of the 25th Aviation Battalion land at the Filhol Rubber Plantation, northeast of Cu Chi, to extract 25th Infantry Division troops of the 2d Battalion, 14th Infantry, during Operation WAHIAWA, May 16, 1966.

LEFT: An M101A1 105-mm howitzer is manhandled out of the cavernous bay of a CH-47A Chinook. During November 1965 operations in the Ia Drang Valley, artillery batteries were relocated sixty-seven times using Chinooks in order to be effectively positioned for immediate, twenty-four-hour support for the 1st Cavalry Division's wide-ranging airmobile operations. One six-gun battery was moved four times in a single day.

could charge upon the capital on short notice. Additional pressure was exerted on the Central Highlands, where the country could conceivably be split in two and the northern section of the country gobbled up by Communist forces. Another NVA pressure point was Quang Tri, the northernmost province in South Vietnam, which was along the Demilitarized Zone (DMZ) adjacent to North Vietnam and continually susceptible to quick NVA buildups and invasions.

While Ho Chi Minh and his advisors were aware of the impact of American casualties on morale in the United States and that this could influence the course of the war, their main thrust from the outset of the war was to pursue a doctrinaire, three-stage, revolutionary war strategy. In phase one, the Communists would oppose their enemies in a popular guerrilla insurgency that included raids, small attacks, even assassinations; in phase two, they would combine their main force NVA units with guerrilla operations; and in phase three, the climactic stage, the Communists would shift to large-scale operations and finally overthrow opposing government forces. The attempt to impose phase three in 1965 had been thwarted by the rapid intervention of

American ground forces, but the North Vietnamese firmly believed that this was only a temporary setback.

Fighter pilot Major General Thomas S. Swalm thought the U.S. leadership and strategy in Vietnam was faulty, especially as applied by "target masters" Lyndon Johnson and Robert McNamara.

I think that's well documented. I think that there are a number of books written on how that process took place, and if you want a long war, I guess that's a good way to do it. If you're trying to get a war over with, we've got a good model; the DESERT STORM model is a pretty good model.

Well, it was terrible [from the perspective of frustration]. It was terrible. I mean, we had a lot of airplanes, a lot of bombs, a lot of weapons. Clearly, if the generals in Vietnam had been given command of the war, as they were in DESERT STORM, I'm sure it would have ended entirely differently and a lot sooner.

—Major General Thomas S. Swalm,
U.S. Air Force fighter pilot, Retired

BELOW: An ARVN truck convoy on Highway QL1 between Saigon and Tay Ninh passes between a Buddhist cemetery and, at right, a small territorial outpost, in 1967. Hundreds of such circular strongpoints, built during the French colonial period, were scattered along highways in both North and South Vietnam, and at locations perceived by the French to have local or regional importance.

RIGHT: Unlike the strongpoint in the photo below, this one has loudspeakers mounted atop the simple frame structure that provides guards with some protection from the tropical sun. The walls were thick enough to ensure some small-arms and blast protection against the types of weapons most likely to be used by Viet Minh guerrillas of the 1950s and Viet Cong guerrillas of the early 1960s. The bunkered section underneath this tower was proof against larger weapons, but at many such outposts the tower sat atop a more vulnerable concrete pillbox. Close-in defenses, like the punji stakes and barbed-wire screens shown here, varied radically depending on the urgency perceived by local forces responsible for the strongpoint as well as their ability to acquire supplies from the central government or nearby villagers.

Even then, we knew it was a little shaky [U.S. objectives]. The Gulf of Tonkin incident: was that a good enough reason to get involved? But Kennedy and the arms people and Johnson built it up, and there we were. So I didn't really question if I should be there. I was following legal orders. I was performing the job I was asked to do and was somewhat proud to do it, even though I was totally disgusted with the fact that we fought with one arm tied behind our back.

Here are a couple of examples of what I mean. Ho Chi Minh had a summer palace in the mountains. We couldn't fly within ten miles of it. If a MiG was attacking us, and we got into a battle, and the MiG was within twenty-five miles of the Chinese border, we had to back off because of fear of inciting the Chinese to be more involved.

The most frustrating thing was, day after day, northwest of Hanoi, there was a base called Phu Kin. It was one of the major MiG bases. We could see them parked down there in the revetments. We could see them taxiing out, we could see them taking off, and we couldn't touch them till they were airborne. That was just ludicrous. It took me a week of briefing to find out what we couldn't do over North Vietnam in combat. It was a dumb, poorly run war.

No, I never had the thought that our mission wasn't worth it. I questioned the rules by which we had to operate. Those weren't

worth it. Those were dumb. Those cost lives. McNamara and Johnson were directly responsible for that. They dictated flight routes, day after day. After two days, [the enemy] knew your routes; they're naturally going to have their guns there. But our role, the job we were playing, we were saving our fellow pilots so they could do their jobs better, and that made our job very worthwhile.

—Leo Thorsness

ABOVE: A MiG-17 is shot down over North Vietnam by Major Ralph L. Kluster, of St. Louis, Missouri, June 3, 1968. A burst of 20-mm shells fired from Kluster's F-105D Thunderchief ripped into the left wing and exploded the MiG's drop tank.

Northwest of Hanoi, there was a base called Phu Kin. It was one of the major MiG bases. We could see them parked down there in the revetments, see them taxiing out, taking off, and we couldn't touch them till they were airborne.

—Leo Thorsness

BELOW: Troopers of the
1st Cavalry Division's 1st
Battalion, 12th Cavalry, slog
through a rain-sodden
valley in Qui Nhon Province
during Operation THAYER II,
January–February 1967.

Operation CEDAR FALLS

In early 1966, General Westmoreland began a serious campaign to decimate the VC and NVA forces through a series of search-and-destroy operations. In January, Operation MASHER was initiated by the U.S. 1st Cavalry Division (Airmobile), the largest operation up to that time. Under President Johnson's direction, the operation's name was softened to WHITE WING, to leave a milder impression on public opinion. Within six weeks, U.S. forces killed 1,342 enemy soldiers, captured 633 prisoners, and apprehended numerous suspected Communists. In October, MASHER/WHITE WING was succeeded by Operation THAYER/IRVING, during which another 1,000 enemy were killed. At about the same time, from September to November, U.S. forces in Operation ATTLEBORO engaged the enemy with some 22,000 U.S. and ARVN troops, killing 1,100 of the enemy.

But by 1967, the enemy was still not running out of soldiers. The North Vietnamese fielded some 280,000 men, and their ranks were growing. U.S. and allied forces by this time numbered some 1,173,800 men and women. This was an impressive number, but not against an elusive and cunning foe that fought only when it chose to fight and only where it had nearby sanctuaries preventing the full application of American power. With some of these forces, Westmoreland planned major operations in the Iron Triangle and War Zone C, northwest of Saigon, and in War Zone D, northeast of the capital. By attacking the enemy's base areas, Westmoreland hoped to cripple the VC's logistical capabilities, thin his ranks, and destroy the formidable tunnel system that lay under the Iron Triangle. Civilians living in the area were banished and all installations and military infrastructure destroyed.

Around January 8, 1966, Westmoreland ordered three U.S. divisions into the Iron Triangle in Operation CEDAR FALLS. Deemed a "clearing

operation," CEDAR FALLS was commanded by Lieutenant General Jonathan O. Seaman, commanding general of II Field Force. The site of the attack, the Iron Triangle, was a suspected longtime headquarters and base complex from which all political, military, and terrorist operations in the Saigon area were directed. Viet Cong occupation of the area, a mere twelve and a half kilometers from Saigon, allowed them control of most river and land accesses to Saigon and threatened the capital.

The Iron Triangle was a forty-square-mile natural fortress of jungle and bush undercut with a honeycomb of bunkers and tunnels. It was bordered on the southwest by the Saigon River and on the east by the Thi Tinh River. The northern border lay between the villages of Ben Cat and Ben Suc on the Saigon River. North of the triangle was the Thanh Dien Forest. The plan of attack would be a "hammer and anvil" operation, during which the area would be surrounded, covertly if possible using deceptive deployments, and attacked in force, sandwiching the enemy between major U.S. units and crushing them. Before the operation began, the area was sprayed with the defoliant chemical called Agent Orange, to clear the jungle.

On January 8, sixty UH-1 helicopters flying in two parallel lines dropped five hundred soldiers into Ben Suc. They seized control of the village, neutralized the enemy, and evacuated its citizens, some six thousand men, women, and children. Lieutenant Colonel Alexander M. Haig (the future U.S. secretary of state) commanded the force. Once the area was cleared, massed bulldozers ran through it, toppling houses and defensive positions and destroying as many of the tunnels that lay under the area as possible. Other 1st Division units, the 3d Brigade and Task Force Deane, spread out across the Iron Triangle searching for enemy soldiers, food, and war supplies.

On January 18, a report was received from the 1st Battalion, 5th Infantry, concerning the discovery of a tunnel complex that appeared to be the main headquarters of Military Region 3 or a considerable part of it. An entrance to the tunnel system, which sheltered thousands of VC, was found on some cleared land between the Ho Bo Woods and the Filhol Plantation. U.S.

soldiers referred to as the Tunnel Rats went in. Stripped to the waist and armed with flashlights and .38-caliber pistols—some of which were fixed with silencers to protect the "Rats'" eardrums from the loud underground bursts—these subterranean warriors crawled after the fleeing VC. After negotiating more than one thousand yards of tunnels, the Rats finally emerged at the surface with thousands of enemy documents as well as maps of Saigon, some detailing recent VC operations like the December 4 raid on the Tan Son Nhut Air Base. To conclude the operation, demolition experts dug a crater in the middle of Ben Suc Village, dropped ten thousand pounds of explosives and a thousand gallons of napalm in it, then lit a fuse and blew up the area.

Some five hundred Viet Cong surrendered to the Americans during CEDAR FALLS, largely as the result of PSYOP (psychological operations). Without food and shelter and exposed to the weather and the dangers posed by the U.S. soldiers operating in the area, little choice was left to the isolated VC but to surrender. But if attrition of the enemy was the purpose of CEDAR FALLS, the end result was not as

BELOW: U.S. soldiers shun the ovenlike interior of an M113 armored personnel carrier during a road movement. Even when temperatures were comparatively moderate and the troops were operating in a dangerous area, soldiers still preferred the vulnerability to bullets and shrapnel—and the ability to shoot back—over long rides in a metal box.

Agent Orange

After the United States began intensive military operations in South Vietnam, it became clear to commanders that the jungle overgrowth posed a major obstacle to uprooting the Viet Cong from their lairs. Some form of defoliant or plant suppressant was needed to clear guerrilla-infested areas, strip away their cover, so that successful operations could be effected.

During World War II, the U.S. Army had performed research that led to the formulation of 2, 4-D, and 2, 4, 5-T herbicides. At the time, they were believed to be relatively safe and less toxic than previously developed compounds. As early as 1960, President John F. Kennedy authorized the use of these chemicals in the form of Agents Blue, White, Green, Pink, and Purple, which were sprayed from C-123 planes onto the Vietnam landscape. The various agents were named after the colored stripes painted on their containers as identifiers. The spray was meant to kill crops and clear away overgrowth from roads and enemy lines of communication (routes of supply). After early 1965, Agent Orange, a combination of 2, 4-D, and 2, 4, 5-T, was employed with potent effect on large-leafed plants and trees. By 1969, more than 3 million gallons of Agent Orange had been sprayed on the country, much of it during Operation RANCH HAND.

By early 1970, use of the compound was discontinued, but the damage, say some experts, was already done. More than 11 million gallons of the toxic chemical had been sprayed over some 0 percent of the area of the country. As early as 1963, the President's Science Advisory Committee had warned of the toxicity of Agent Orange and its allied compounds. All of these compounds are dioxins, now considered to be quite dangerous when used at sufficient strength. Dioxins, in amounts as tiny as five parts per trillion, when placed in contact with animals or humans on a daily basis, have been shown to cause cancer.

During the 1960s, scientists in the United States and abroad, as well as opponents of the Vietnam War, denounced the use of Agent Orange. By 1967, petitions signed by prominent scientists were sent to President Johnson calling for a halt in the use of Agent Orange and other herbicides in South Vietnam. In addition, a United Nations resolution was passed accusing the United States of violating a 1925 Geneva Protocol prohibiting the use of chemical and biological weapons. After 1970, the U.S. military no longer authorized the use of Agent Orange, but it continued to employ Agents Blue, White, Green, Pink, and Purple.

After the war, when a considerable number of soldiers were diagnosed with cancer or discovered that their newly born children were deformed at birth, veterans attributed their health problems to the effects of Agent Orange, which they knew they had been exposed to in Vietnam. Several studies concluded that there was a possible connection between their conditions and earlier exposure to these chemicals. But because it was difficult to determine with certainty that there was a direct cause-and-effect relationship, lawyers for years aggressively pursued veterans' cases through the courts in class-action suits against stiff, equally spirited opposition, with few conclusive results.

favorable as U.S. commanders had hoped. Most of the VC availed themselves of spy reports and fled before the operation began, many of them likely underground into undiscovered tunnels. Two days after the operation ended, U.S. intelligence officers reported the Iron Triangle again crawling with Viet Cong. The importance and danger of the tunnels remained, for in 1968 the VC poured from the subterranean fortress to invade Saigon during the Tet Offensive.

 Agent Orange, with the aid of B-52 bombardments and napalm, often unmasked well-hidden caves.

There was more of the defoliation going on, again, in 1967. Tunnels were a lot easier to spot, like in the Iron Triangle, places like that. They would spray these areas, defoliate them, then they'd come in and burn them with napalm. Then the plows were sent in and leveled everything. By the time all that was done, all these holes would start popping up all over the place. There were a lot more holes than there were Tunnel Rats, I think. They figured, well, we can't wait for engineers to come from another sector, so they would just say, "Well, does anybody want to go down?" There were always a few of us that would.

—Gerry Schooler

LEFT: Three UC-123 Provider aircraft apply defoliant chemicals to the Vietnamese landscape to eliminate cover for the Viet Cong. These herbicides were considered safe for humans and animals during the early years of the war. Later, it was learned that the chemicals were highly toxic to humans and animals in contact with them on a daily basis. The chemicals were called Agents Blue, White, Green, Pink, Purple, and Orange (named for the colored stripes on their containers). Agent Orange, however, was given the most attention by those who opposed the use of defoliants in Vietnam.

ABOVE: A U.S. Air Force B-52 bomber flying in formation drops its load on a suspected enemy base north of Saigon. Carpet-bombing by flights of B-52s concentrated the destructiveness of an attack.

Cu Chi Tunnel Rats

Because of the proximity to Saigon of the seventy-five-mile-long tunnel system in the Iron Triangle, destroying it was considered of paramount importance by the U.S. military. CEDAR FALLS had made little impression on the labyrinthine system of tunnels, the complexity and extent of which resisted a simple fix. One of the offensive tools the U.S. Army devised was the pumping of acetylene gas into the tunnels using Sears and Roebuck orchard (air) blowers, nicknamed Mighty Mites. Once the tunnel was impregnated with the gas, it was ignited, causing passageways to implode. But the Army's primary weapons against the tunnels were the Tunnel Rats, who were given the chore of pursuing their own search-and-destroy mission in the dark passageways in and adjoining the Iron Triangle.

Most of the tunnels were in the Cu Chi district, just west of the triangle. The U.S. Army had been warned by an ARVN officer as early as 1963 that the tunnels existed and could be destroyed only by a "long-range operation" at a "dear price." ARVN soldiers had never been asked by their officers to enter the deadly tunnels and likely would have refused. Some American soldiers were bolder. When the

Tunnel Rats were first organized, they were called tunnel runners; the Australians called them ferrets. Later, there was an attempt to dub them tunnel exploration personnel, but the men relished the more macho sobriquet "tunnel rats," so that's what they were called. The name was a source of pride to them and a warning to their enemies.

These were bold men indeed. At any moment, they faced death from VC bullets, slit throats, garroting, trip wire–triggered booby traps, impalement by spears, or a false floor, through which soldiers fell onto poisoned or contaminated punji stakes. In addition, they had to be able to squirm through narrow passageways filled with foul air and sometimes infested with poisonous snakes, hordes of spiders, scorpions, rats, stinging fire ants, bats, and giant centipedes. Collapsing tunnels were also a threat. Wounded Tunnel Rats were often rescued by one of their brother "Rats," who would back out of the tunnel while pulling them by a rope attached from the wounded man's wrists to a loop around the back of the rescuer's neck—a hazardous exercise sometimes accomplished under enemy fire.

Captain Herbert Thornton, a Tunnel Rat officer, said that Tunnel Rats had to have "moxie" as well as "guts," and they had to have a special sense about what to touch and what

RIGHT: A U.S. Marine, his helmet removed, peers cautiously into a VC tunnel. The entrances to these subterranean passageways had to be carefully checked for booby traps.

You didn't have much of a feeling about the construction of the tunnel. . . . If you turned the light on, though, you risked all sorts of bad things . . . your eyes were screaming for light, and your ears were screaming for sound, and all you can hear is the thump, thump, thump of your heart in your ears.

—Major Dennis Ayoub, Australian Army

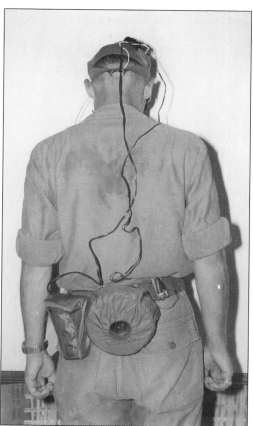

to avoid. Thornton said, "There were no bad days. They were all good days if you got through them [alive]." All the Tunnel Rats were volunteers, and they were removed from duty if they balked at performing a task. The Tunnel Rats' insignia showed a pistol-wielding rat holding a flashlight. Their motto was Non Gratum Anus Rodentum, crippled Latin for "Not worth a rat's ass." No matter how they referred to themselves, they were clearly extremely brave. Thornton, one of their leaders, became a marked man with a VC price on his head—one never collected. Tunnel Rat Peter Rojo, an enlisted man, said, "I loved it down there . . . when they told me they had a VC down there [in the tunnels], I came unglued." In most cases, the enemy combatants refused to surrender and had to be killed.

Today, ironically, a portion of the Cu Chi tunnel of horrors serves as a tourist attraction, a sort of poor man's Disney World for the cash-strapped Vietnamese Communists. For a dollar a bullet at an on-site range, sightseers can fire an AK-47 rifle. Or tourists may dress up in black "pajamas," pith helmets, and rubber sandals

TOP: The grim realities of tunnel warfare foiled the natural American tendency to develop technological enhancements. Here, a soldier models the Limited Warfare Laboratory's notion of the ideal Tunnel Rat equipment set, which includes a battery-operated spot lamp activated by a "bite switch" to free the hands; earphones for cave-to-surface communications; and a .38-caliber revolver with silencer to prevent eardrums from bursting during a firefight in the tight underground quarters. This equipment worked fine on a standing soldier or during short crawls on a stateside base, but 1966 field tests in captured VC tunnels demonstrated what the Tunnel Rats perceived as soon as they saw this getup. The headlamp continually slipped down over the eyes; the earpiece was easily dislodged; plus the holster, back-mounted battery, and assortment of wires were not only cumbersome, but also upped the chances that a booby trap might be snagged. Most subterranean searches for weapons and critically important intelligence were not conducted by specialized teams of Tunnel Rats, however, but by aggressive U.S. soldiers and Marines moving through their zones during search-and-destroy missions.

BOTTOM: A back view of a Tunnel Rat's uniform. Headlamp wires extend down the Rat's back to the battery fastened at his waist. The soldier's radio is attached to the right of the battery, where a wire extends to the earphone attached to one of his ears. A communications wire for the radio was reeled out behind the tunnel explorers, sometimes for as much as half a mile or more. Many Tunnel Rats carried no radio, believing it tied them down and that its communications wire was apt to snag on to trip wires or set off mines. If the Tunnel Rat had trouble, he usually settled his own scores. Many Tunnel Rats carried simple flashlights. Usually, but not always, they entered the caves with a partner. The second in line typically carried the team weapon. Sometimes, Tunnel Rats extended a small, quarter-inch cord or rope behind them so that they could find their way out of the labyrinthine passageways, which seemed endless and, in fact, extended for miles. One could easily get lost in the maze.

and crawl through dark, narrow, now-sanitized passageways to emulate VC underground guerrillas. For the less adventurous, T-shirts can be purchased declaring: "I've been to the Cu Chi Tunnel."

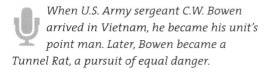 *Most American and Australian Tunnel Rats who ventured into the tunnels on their dangerous assignments found the small underground chambers tailored to the diminutive size of the Viet Cong. The tunnels were also foul-smelling and stifling.*

We were only armed with an automatic, and we had a torch [flashlight]. We had just enough string to leave behind us so that they could locate us in the dark, if they needed to do so. In the tunnels, it was dank, exceedingly dark, so dark that you strained trying to get your eyes to pierce through it, to find some light.

You didn't have much of a feeling about the construction of the tunnel, whether tree roots were there, for instance, unless you turned the light on. If you turned the light on, though, you risked all sorts of bad things. The idea was to go along in there very quietly, and what happened was that your eyes were screaming for light, and your ears were screaming for sound, and all you can hear is the thump, thump, thump of your heart in your ears, right?

That's the only sound you can hear, that heavy beating, and you tried to keep your breathing down so that others did not hear it. You tried to breathe shallowly. By doing that, of course, it caused all sorts of other problems. You started to rob yourself of the level of oxygen needed for the energy that you were expending in the tunnel.

—Major Dennis Ayoub,
Australian Army

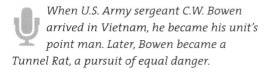 *When U.S. Army sergeant C.W. Bowen arrived in Vietnam, he became his unit's point man. Later, Bowen became a Tunnel Rat, a pursuit of equal danger.*

In our unit, you volunteered to do this. So once Gary Heeter and I went into the tunnels. If there was nobody else to volunteer to go in after you, if you didn't come back out, you were just gone. Nobody came looking for you. You were lost; that was it. Some guys tried to go into tunnels, and they'd crack, start shooting, come out hollering, screaming. It's a real spooky place in there. Claustrophobia can set in on you if you don't know you've got that and you're in there. Also, there are booby traps.

You either could do it, or you couldn't do it. There was no in between. There's no marginal response. If you tried to do it, and you couldn't, if you got partway in there and lost it, hopefully you made it back out. Then, that's it; you just didn't go in again. And you could stop anytime you wanted to. I mean, Gary and I ran tunnels for a long time, and if we wanted to stop, all we had to say was, "We're not doing it anymore," and nobody felt bad towards you. You had done your part, and that was it. Hopefully, some other new guys would come in full of rambunctiousness and step up to the challenge, but it was strictly voluntary.

[The caves] were so well concealed [that] normally you wouldn't find them unless you were in bunker complexes and stuff like that. Most of the time, you were going through the jungle, humping the jungles, breaking brush. You didn't run into that many tunnels, a few dozen, not that many over a year. We probably walked over thousands of them and never knew it, especially in the Cu Chi area. That's where the majority of the tunnels were in our area of operations. The laterite, the dirt or earth there, was easy to dig in, but once the air hit it, the walls almost set up like cement. So they didn't have to use shoring and all of that to prop up the walls and ceilings; they just dug the tunnel, and when the dirt dried out, it hardened. So they dug away. They had been digging since the French were there, and they'd fought a bit down there. They'd been digging tunnels for eighty years, so there was quite a complex of tunnels down there.

God got me through it [the tunnels]. Back then, I had a good sixth sense. You had to be real observant. You had to watch for booby traps, any traces of somebody in there. The

Lord was with me. That's what I have to attribute it to now. Over the years, I used to fight and argue with Him and wonder why He put me through those things, but evidently He had a reason, and I resigned myself to the fact that, yeah, He was with me.

TOP: A U.S. infantryman is lowered into a tunnel by members of his 1st Cavalry Division reconnaissance platoon during Operation OREGON, April 24, 1967.

BELOW: U.S. infantrymen lob 81-mm mortar rounds at a suspected VC position during Operation WAHIAWA, a 25th Infantry Division effort to clear the Filhol Rubber Plantation in the Cu Chi area, May 16, 1966.

It took me thirty years, but I found another friend of mine, Paul Frisbee, from Vietnam. He didn't run tunnels. When I visited him and we were talking, I told him, "I had a hard time when I came back from Vietnam. I was a mean son of a bitch, you know, and I just didn't want nobody around me." He looked at me and laughed. I said, "What are you laughing about?" He says, "What do you mean, when you got home?"

They actually didn't refer to us as "Tunnel Rats," like those in the Big Red One. They had an engineering unit that that's all they did, run tunnels, and they had an organization called the Tunnel Rats. They had a unit that, when they found tunnels in their area of operation, which was right across the river from us, that unit or team would come out and run the tunnels.

Whereas, our unit was kind of like, when someone found a tunnel, they would say, "Okay, who's going to run it?" In this case, it was usually Gary and I who ran the tunnels, and once you did that, it's kind of like you did

it forever thereafter, until either you went home or something happened to you. You're more than likely going to be the one to run the tunnel. But it was strictly on a voluntary basis. If you freaked, you never had to go back in a tunnel again.

You could do that real easy. I mean, you could get down in the tunnel and the walls would start closing in on you. You'd hear noises, and you might start shooting, and you could get cranked up real easy and lose it completely and probably go insane if you weren't careful.

We found a lot of tunnels, especially when we got into an NVA base camp or VC base camp and we started checking the bunkers out. When you get down inside them, the bunkers would have tunnels leading off of them. Sometimes, if you were fortunate enough, you could find the entrance to a tunnel. Two of them we found through just pure luck because two NVA, or two VC in one particular tunnel, came out of the tunnel while we were there. They were killed, and we found the tunnel where they came out.

That happened on two different occasions in the year I was there. But most of the tunnels were very well camouflaged, and I think they had specific rules concerning how to dig the tunnels, how to make the trap doors so they would fit, and once they closed that trap door, you couldn't even tell that it was there. We would be in areas where you'd walk along and you'd look down and you'd see little piles of dirt all over the ground. Well, they would be digging tunnels somewhere in that area, but they would spread the dirt all out through the jungle so they wouldn't have a pile of dirt somewhere that was suspicious.

A lot of trap doors were small. Most of the entrances were at angles, and you'd go in and make a right angle or left angle or maybe a left turn. The GIs had a habit of just tossing a grenade into a tunnel and saying, "Well, that takes care of that," but it wouldn't do any damage because the first section of tunnel, if you examined it, you'd go in and would make a turn, and you'd just drop down and make another turn, or you'd go in and make a right or left turn [and this configuration blunted the blasts].

They would tie ropes on to us, about a one-eighth-inch rope, but you had to reel out a thousand-foot reel of rope, and you could run that all out and never find the end of the tunnel. The rope would hinder you; you couldn't move; you're dragging this rope behind you, and, I mean, it was probably good because you were going down trap doors and then different trap doors, and after a while you said to yourself, "Well, where am I? How do I get back out of here?" So the rope was a good trail to follow.

It happened a couple of times that you could hear movement up ahead. We didn't always run tunnels as a team. Sometimes, you just went down by yourself, and I went in a couple by myself. Once, I came into a room—this one had big rooms and another had some bamboo beds; they take bamboo and split it up and make beds and stuff—and there were two or three guys in there. They were wounded. I don't know whether it was a hospital or just a recovery area. But they weren't seriously wounded, I don't think. Anyway, they had their weapons up against a wall, and I kind of stumbled in there. When I came in there and shined the light, *boom*, it was like Keystone Cops. They were there and I was here, and they started reaching for their weapons, and I started shooting. When that happened, it's like flashes. Flash, this happens; flash, that happens; people are hollering and screaming. People are shooting, and when you're shooting a .45 in a tunnel, I think you immediately go deaf. Your heart is pounding. It's all reaction. You really don't think, you just start shooting, and you want to get out of there any way you can.

Running tunnels, you develop the ability to not think, but shoot. You don't want to hesitate. If you hesitate and think about it, you're the one that's probably going to die. So if there's movement or a noise, you shoot. That's what I did. I shot and got the hell out of there as fast as I could. Once I got out, I realized I was still alive, but I was just so pumped up from all of that, scared to death.

On the surface, they said: "What's down there; what's down there?" I said, "Well, nothing." What I did was take a charge back down, halfway down the tunnel, and collapsed the

I mean, you could get down in the tunnel and the walls would start closing in on you. You'd hear noises, and you might start shooting, and you could get cranked up real easy and lose it completely.

—C.W. Bowen

ABOVE: During Operation
SILVER SPRINGS, 1st Infantry
Division sergeant Charles
A. Duckett, of Indianapolis,
Indiana, enters the storage
cellar of a farmhouse to
search for a concealed tunnel entrance or evidence
that it has been used by
the Viet Cong, January 20,
1967. The operation was
conducted thirty miles
north of Saigon, close to
the Iron Triangle, an area
largely controlled by the
Viet Cong and riddled with
a seemingly endless warren
of small tunnels that
formed something like a
series of giant anthills.

tunnel, set the charge off. I'm sure the entire
tunnel wasn't collapsed or anything, because
once we got outside, it just went *boomp*, just
shook the ground.

—C.W. Bowen

*Because of his small size and daring,
Sergeant Art Tejeda had the right stuff
to become a Tunnel Rat, and like the
rest he volunteered for the challenge and the
extra money. One day in the tunnels, with a
new Tunnel Rat, John Riley, Tejeda ran into
a VC underground guerrilla.*

So, after a little conversation, he [John Riley]
said, "Well, it's the law of the land; it's my
tunnel." I said, "You're right. Okay, you go first.
I'll be right behind you." And we crawled

inside the tunnel, and we must have gone in
maybe forty feet, and I couldn't believe it; the
tunnel widened and it got bigger. To the right
were brand-new RPG-2s [rocket-propelled
grenades] with night scopes. They were still
wrapped in paper, hadn't even been fired.
We found boxes of RPG rounds with booster
caps. Riley said, "See, I told you."

I told John, "Shut up," because when he got
excited, he was very loud. Like I've said, you
don't talk inside a tunnel, you whisper,
maybe. So we kept crawling, and he says,
"There's more." So we kept crawling another
ten, twenty feet, and we came across brand-
new AK-47s—again, wrapped up, never been
fired—and ammunition, crates and crates of
brand-new ammunition, not dirty, not
muddy: it was all brand new. Again, John said,

> **I tried to squeeze by John . . . and [as] he was backing up trying to let me go by him, flashlights pointed down the tunnel . . . there were three VCs looking straight at us. They opened up, and the next thing I saw was this green, yellow, and red-colored flash and a loud bang.**
>
> **—Art Tejeda**

BELOW: Specialist 4 Moses Green, of Jamaica, New York, a medic of the 173d Airborne Brigade, pours water over an exhausted Tunnel Rat, Staff Sergeant Melvin C. Gaines, of Los Angeles, California. Sergeant Gaines has emerged from a search of several hours in the sweltering heat and foul air of a Viet Cong tunnel complex in the Iron Triangle northwest of Saigon, 1967.

"See, I told you; I told you." I answered, "Be quiet. Don't talk." Whispering, I said again, "Be quiet."

So we kept crawling, and then we hit a trap door, crawled down through it, found some more weapons, bigger caches, all brand new. There must have been enough weapons there to outfit maybe five hundred men. There was ammunition to supply maybe five hundred rounds per man. So it was a big cache of weapons. At this time, again, for the third time, John said, "See, I told you; I told you." He got excited again, and I told him, "Keep your voice down. In fact, let me take the point." I said, "Well, let me just get by you over here."

So we went farther, maybe another ten feet, and I looked up—because as you're crawling through these tunnels, you have to understand, you have to look to the sides, on the floor, overhead, because you don't know what Charlie [the VC] can put there. Then, I saw a trap door above me, which was a trap door that I had seen before on another trip through the caves in the area I was exploring. This led me to conclude that I had cleared one part of this cave before. I told John somebody was down there. Then, I looked to the right side of John, and there was a canteen with a pistol belt nearby.

So I knew for sure that it was the same tunnel and that the two connected. Then, I said, "Well, we cleared one end, so what's on the other end," which led to the left. I tried to squeeze by John, and my left hand went to the left, and as we were turning, and he was backing up trying to let me go by him, flashlights pointed down the tunnel, and there were three VCs looking straight at us. They opened up, and the next thing I saw was this

green, yellow, and red-colored flash and a loud bang.

The next thing I knew I was on my back; the blast had flipped me around. I got my .45 and pointed it down the tunnel and emptied out the clip. I didn't hear any more sounds or anything. I tried to rouse John, but he wasn't moving. I put my hand on his chest, and his heart wasn't pounding or pumping. He was dead. The next thought came to me quickly. It said, "Get out; it's time to get out." So I reversed my course and started crawling out of that tunnel, which seemed to take me an eternity.

I knew I was hurt, but I didn't feel pain or anything. I thought it was heat mostly, perspiration, and I was very tired. I remember a long time ago they used to have a TV program called the *Twilight Zone*, where you saw this fog filtering in. It was like that. I could see my mother's face, so lifelike, and I saw her face just drifting, getting closer, ever so closer, and I tried to touch her face with my hand. I called out, "Mom," and she didn't say anything; she drifted out, and drifted farther and farther away. Then, I saw my fiancée's face. And it got closer and I talked to her. I told her, "I'm tired. I'm sleepy." I said I knew I was hurt, but I wasn't feeling any pain. I was just sleepy, ever so sleepy and tired. She told me, "Art, you're hurt. Get out of that tunnel." I said, "No, I'm tired." I had never heard her cuss, but she cussed at me that day, and she said, "Damn you, Art, get up and see the sun for one last time."

So I started crawling out. I crawled, and then I found that first level, dragged myself up, and collapsed. I saw her face again, and she said, "Get up, get up. See the sun one more time." I remember passing all the weapons and the ammo, and I was getting closer to the surface. I fell down a third time, and I was just so sleepy, so tired. I felt comfortable, and I wasn't hurting. I finally saw light, and I got myself out of that tunnel.

While I thought I was covered by perspiration below in the tunnel, I found when I got to the surface that I was covered completely in blood. One of the bullets had gone through John, and it got me in the face, my jaw. It's still back here. Blood was squirting out of the wound like a water hose, and I was walking around. They called for a medic, and I could hear them cry out, "Medic! Medic! T.J.'s hurt." So this medic came over, one of the doctors, and grabbed me. I turned around and knocked him into a bomb crater, cold-cocked him. I said, "Get away from me." I said, if I can remember right: "Give me a gun! Dig him out! Dig him out! Get me a gun!"

Another medic tried to grab me, and I knocked him down. Then, my captain came by, Captain Bridgeman, and he said, "T.J., you're hurt, you're hurt." I said, "Leave me alone," and he put his arm around my shoulders, and I collapsed. I must have blacked out from loss of blood—that's what it was from. They ripped open my pants leg because I said, "My leg hurts, my leg hurts." I could see the doctors ripping my pants leg open, and I had a hole in my thigh, a good eight inches long by two inches wide.

That was one of my scariest days in Vietnam. Before I knew it, they called me into a medevac [medical evacuation] station, and from then on it was just history. But it was like a sense of losing a good guy, a sense of being close to death, the glory of knowing that, hey, man, I uncovered a whole bunch of weapons, or my friend and I did, John and I, that wouldn't be used against us anyway because we had uncovered them. So that was something good.

—Art Tejeda

 Specialist Fourth Class Ken Cory volunteered to be a Tunnel Rat because of his small size.

You could be standing next to a tunnel entrance and be six inches away from it and never know it; they were that well hidden. But as far as getting prepared to get into the tunnels, the first thing that would be eliminated would be anything that I was carrying. When you went into a tunnel, you carried the minimum amount that you could carry. We would take off our combat shirts. Most of the time, I would carry a T-shirt in my pack.

I wouldn't wear one, but I would carry a T-shirt just because [the combat shirts] were baggy. Because they were baggy, they could catch on things. They had pockets and they could drag on things, and the VC were ingenious in putting booby traps in the tunnels, and so you did not want to wear or carry things that had a tendency to flop around or catch on to things. So we would strip down to the bare minimum, which would be our boots, our pants, and a shirt.

Then, depending on how we had decided to go in, whether it was me first or one of the Kit Carson scouts [former Viet Cong working as scouts for U.S. units], that would determine

TOP AND BOTTOM: Specialist 4 Roy Reeden, of Pitcher, Oklahoma, cautiously prepares (top) and sets off (bottom) a plastic-explosive charge at the mouth of a VC tunnel northeast of An Khe in Binh Dinh Province, June 9, 1967. Unfortunately, these tunnel systems often had multiple escape points, so that the effects of caving in an entrance were limited to only the period of time when U.S. troops physically occupied the area. This tunnel was discovered by troops of the 12th Regiment, 1st Cavalry Division (Airmobile), during Operation PERSHING.

what equipment we were taking with us. The person that went in first would typically go in with just a web belt, a pistol, and a knife or bayonet or a probe of some sort. The backup guy would come in with more, and with a web belt. We might carry a couple of hand grenades with us. In some cases, I would carry a rifle. I had a special type of M16, called an AR-15. It's a small commando rifle with a collapsible stock. It also had a silencer on the front of it. And if I were the rear man, I'd sometimes carry that because it gave you more firepower. But the Tunnel Rat that was second was always the armed one. The first guy could not work a tunnel holding a flashlight, and probing the ground, and being armed at the same time. You just didn't have enough hands to do it, so it was always the second individual in the group that would actually carry the exposed weapon.

The most dangerous part would be psyching up to get into the tunnel. That was the part that was really the most frightening because you didn't know what you were getting into. Sometimes I ran into tunnels, later on, that would have a false entrance. Right underneath the entrance, they'd put a mantrap, a large punji pit.

Typically, you'd have to drop through the tunnel to get to the bottom, and if you would go into one of those and drop down, instead of landing on solid ground, you'd land in a punji pit, a larger mantrap. That's what it was designed for. You never knew for sure if the enemy was just going to be standing there, waiting for you. He might be sitting in the tunnel, ten meters down, knowing that you were coming in. One of the things that we tried doing is, once you had the top open on a tunnel, you'd have a shaft of light that would go in, and it would light up a portion of the tunnel in the bottom.

—Ken Cory

 Sometimes the denizens of the tunnels—the animals and insects—proved to be the greatest challenge.

There was one spot that was just alive with spiders. I remember that the guy behind me in the tunnel wasn't particularly crazy about spiders. He was a brave guy; he had won medals for all kinds of stuff, but he didn't like spiders. He was trying to get me to come back and clear out the path for him. The guy in front of me had the flashlight, and he could see where he was putting his hands and knees and so forth, and he was just kind of maneuvering through there. We're just talking about "maneuvering." We're talking about a tunnel two and a half feet wide. As for me, with no flashlight, it was just a matter of the crunching sound telling me that we were in the spiders. They get on your clothes and things like that. But I don't think they were bad ones because none of us got sick. But nobody likes bugs crawling on them, especially spiders. And this sergeant behind me was adamant that I would go back there every once in a while and try to clear a path for him with my feet.

And he followed me. After we got a little bit further down, we were just trying to find an exit. That's all we were trying to do. Let's forget the weapons; we don't care about the glory anymore. We just want to get out of there. You start thinking, we could be lost in here for a long time, or we may never get out. It's kind of crazy, but I guess it could happen. Then, I heard this squeaking. I looked around the bend, and it got louder and louder. I thought there were rats or something in the tunnel.

We got around this corner, and the guy with the light shined it around, and it looked like a million bats. Well, I'm sure there were several hundred bats that just came right at us through this little five-square-foot tunnel. You saw them from about ten or fifteen yards away coming right at you. All you could do was just lay down flat. You could feel the wings hitting you on the back of the head and on the back. They weren't coming after us. They were just trying to get away.

—Gerry Schooler

BELOW: Paratroopers of the 503d Airborne Infantry Regiment, 173d Airborne Brigade, dive out of a C-130 onto the JUNCTION CITY battlefield, February 22, 1967. The soldiers landed at a drop zone three kilometers north of Katum in the only combat parachute jump during the war, and the first since the Korea War.

Operation JUNCTION CITY

Another major search-and-destroy operation of 1967 was Operation JUNCTION CITY, conducted by II Field Force. The object of the attack was the destruction of the Viet Cong's Central Office of South Vietnam (COSVN) as well as the destruction of any VC and NVA installations encountered. While it was only one of a number of such operations carried out in 1967 throughout South Vietnam, it was one of the largest and was executed in three phases.

On February 22, five American brigades arrayed themselves in a horseshoe-shaped formation in the western part of War Zone C, with the 25th Division along the Cambodian border forming the western segment of the horseshoe, and the 1st Infantry Division and 174th Brigade in the north and along Provincial Route 4 shaping the rest of the horseshoe. At the outset of the main attack, a brigade of the 25th Division and the 11th Armored Cavalry

Regiment charged through the open end of the horseshoe in the south to conduct operations, with the blocking forces (the sides of the horseshoe) containing the enemy and attacking him whenever and wherever possible.

In phase one, a multidivisional force composed of U.S. forces and an ARVN corps launched operations in War Zone C, in northern Tay Ninh Province. In phase two, American forces conducted coordinated airmobile ground operations in the eastern part of War Zone C, where they were to continue to destroy COSVN and NVA forces and installations. In both phases, the object was to draw the enemy into a fight by attacking his base areas. In phase three, JUNCTION CITY became a brigade-size operation near Tay Ninh, where the 25th Infantry Division would assume operational control.

During the operation, the enemy, for the most part, cannily refused to fight, abandoned his base areas to the allied soldiers, and eventually eluded the encircling forces in the wild tangle of jungle, which he knew far better than

LEFT: Moving through the jungles and bush of South Vietnam was exhausting work. Here, in Tay Ninh Province northwest of Saigon, troopers of the 11th Armored Cavalry Regiment ford a stream with an M113 armored personnel carrier during Operation JUNCTION CITY.

the Americans and their allies. The Viet Cong decided to hazard their supplies and bases rather than risk annihilation. While the VC lost some 1,776 men killed, and abandoned huge amounts of medical supplies, ammunition, and some 800 tons of rice, within a short time they again returned to the area. Some 366,000 artillery rounds and 3,325 tons of bombs had been rained down on the VC, but as one military analyst noted: it took several tons of ordnance to kill a single VC.

JUNCTION CITY, however, did affect the COSVN, which responded by moving its head-quarters, hospitals, supply depots, and training centers out of Vietnam and into Cambodia. During and immediately after the conclusion of JUNCTION CITY (on April 15), two Special Forces camps were constructed in the area of operations. They would become easy targets for the enemy, who attacked from their nearby camps in Cambodia, and very difficult to support. JUNCTION CITY had proved an expensive operation that demonstrated just how difficult it was to bring the enemy to bay in the jungles of Vietnam.

1ST SQUADRON, 1ST CAVALRY REGIMENT (ARMORED CAVALRY)

Detached from the 1st Armored Division and deployed to Vietnam as a separate armored cavalry squadron, the 1st Squadron, 1st Cavalry Regiment, arrived in-country in 1967 and was attached to the 196th Light Infantry Brigade. The regiment was composed of three cavalry troops and a single air cavalry troop. Troop D of the squadron was deployed to Vietnam in July 1968 and attached to the 101st Airborne Division until 1969, when it rejoined its squadron. One of the United States' most battle-honored units, the squadron added an additional thirteen battle streamers to its tally in Vietnam while serving in Chu Lai, Da Nang, Tam Ky, and Thach Khe. The 1st Squadron departed Vietnam on May 10, 1972, after accounting for more than six thousand confirmed enemy dead.

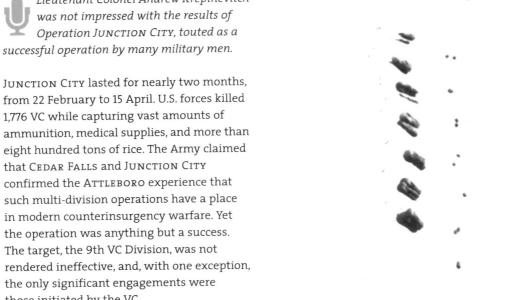

BELOW: A paratrooper watches as supplies are dropped from a C-130 Hercules for his unit of the 173d Airborne Brigade during Operation JUNCTION CITY, March 7, 1967. In this operation, U.S. Air Force planes guided by combat control teams dropped hundreds of tons of jeeps, trailers, trucks, and ammunition in support of ground troops in Tay Ninh Province.

Lieutenant Colonel Andrew Krepinevitch was not impressed with the results of Operation JUNCTION CITY, touted as a successful operation by many military men.

JUNCTION CITY lasted for nearly two months, from 22 February to 15 April. U.S. forces killed 1,776 VC while capturing vast amounts of ammunition, medical supplies, and more than eight hundred tons of rice. The Army claimed that CEDAR FALLS and JUNCTION CITY confirmed the ATTLEBORO experience that such multi-division operations have a place in modern counterinsurgency warfare. Yet the operation was anything but a success. The target, the 9th VC Division, was not rendered ineffective, and, with one exception, the only significant engagements were those initiated by the VC.

—Lieutenant Colonel Andrew F. Krepinevitch, U.S. Army, in *The U.S. Army in Vietnam*

LEFT: Enemy trucks on their way to supply centers in Laos and Cambodia move down the Ho Chi Minh Trail past trees defoliated by chemical agents and shredded by repeated U.S. air strikes. Along this well-defended route, SOG (Studies and Observation Group) soldiers air-dropped in small teams to disrupt the flow of enemy men and materiel. More than sixty thousand NVA troops were stationed along the trail to provide security for the shipments, so the encounters were quick and sometimes bloody.

Ho Chi Minh Trail

In order to move supplies, troops, and military equipment into South Vietnam in the face of an armada of B-52 bombers and U.S. Air Force fighter-bombers, the North Vietnamese took advantage of the sanctuary allowed them by the Americans in Cambodia and Laos. Soon after the Americans entered the war, tens of thousands of enemy soldiers trekked south-ward along the Ho Chi Minh Trail, an elaborate, multi-route road network that extended through northeastern Cambodia and southern Laos, opposite and parallel to Khe Sahn in the north and running as far south as Tay Ninh. Along these roads rolled trucks carrying hundreds of thousands of tons of ammunition,

weapons, and other supplies. So dense was the jungle canopy over the route that allied aerial reconnaissance pilots had to rely on infrared sensors, which picked up the heat of the truck engines, to conduct attacks.

Starting in 1964, the North Vietnamese began transforming the original primitive trails of the area into a more workable road network. The architect of this project was an engineer officer, Colonel Dong Si Nguyen. Supported by several engineer battalions and local labor, Dong built bridges and roads capable of carry-ing large trucks. In addition, he set up anti-aircraft defenses against inevitable U.S. air attacks. Hospitals, barracks, fuel depots, and supply warehouses were built in underground facilities, protecting them from possible U.S. bombardments. The Communists recruited all

4TH INFANTRY DIVISION

Arriving in Vietnam from Fort Lewis, Washington, in September 1966, the 4th Infantry Division deployed to the II Corps Tactical Zone, with the exception of its 3d Brigade and the division's armor battalion, which were attached to the 25th Infantry Division in III Corps. The 4th Infantry Division was engaged in combat as part of Operation ATTLEBORO, September 14–November 24, 1966, and Operation JUNCTION CITY, February–May 1967, two of the largest operations to date. Throughout 1968 and 1969, the division continued border operations, and in 1970 invaded Cambodia, destroying North Vietnamese sanctuaries. The 4th Division occupied the largest area of operations in Vietnam and fought in eleven major campaigns in which twelve of its soldiers received the Medal of Honor. By December 7, 1970, the division had departed Vietnam and was stationed at Fort Carson, Colorado.

sorts of specialists—drivers, mechanics, traffic managers, doctors, and nurses—to be stationed along this roadway. While only ten thousand North Vietnamese moved along the trail in 1964, by 1967 the trail teemed with as many as twenty thousand soldiers a month.

After General Creighton W. Abrams assumed command of MACV in mid-1968, U.S. Army intelligence officers learned about the magnitude of the activity along the Ho Chi Minh Trail through intercepted radio traffic emanating from enemy stations along the route. Abrams's experts soon broke the code. From this information, they obtained a good account of the numbers and disposition of infiltrating groups moving down the trail and their likely destinations. The trail acted as a staging area. Traffic was coordinated by the General Directorate of Rear Services in Hanoi and administered by more than twenty numbered way stations along the route (like Binh Tram 44, Base Area 600). Beside the trail were numerous supply warehouses and communications liaison groups, all with numbered designations. Under the command of the 559th

Transportation Group, more than forty thousand North Vietnamese helped operate the trail, including those stationed at anti-aircraft batteries, in medical and engineer units, and as supporting security forces.

During the Tet Offensive in 1968, U.S. intelligence discovered that more than two hundred thousand NVA troops were being infiltrated down the trail into South Vietnam. For some time, the Joint Chiefs of Staff and General Westmoreland had pleaded with President Johnson to allow them to carry the war into Laos and Cambodia to interdict the Ho Chi Minh Trail, always without success. Military leaders believed that the supply route was absolutely necessary to the ability of the North Vietnamese to carry on the war. As long as the trail was in operation, it perpetuated one of South Vietnam's greatest vulnerabilities: a long border almost completely open to its enemy. Finally, a CIA-inspired clandestine operation manned by the Studies and Observation Group (SOG), composed of Special Forces and other elite troops, was formed to attack the trail in small-scale but effective secret operations.

BELOW: Soldiers of the 25th Infantry Division's 4th Battalion, 23d Infantry Regiment, in action near the division's base camp at Cu Chi in 1968.

John Plaster discusses the importance of SOG operations along the Ho Chi Minh Trail.

The great majority of North Vietnamese troops and supplies reaching the battlefields of South Vietnam came down the Ho Chi Minh Trail. The road entered South Vietnam either through Laos or through Cambodia. The key to the entire war was what was happening in Laos.

If the North Vietnamese were going to stage an offensive, they had to mass troops and supplies in Laos. It was the critical lifeline to their entire war effort. They knew that, so they defended it heavily. At various times, there were as many as forty thousand to sixty thousand troops stationed there, just defending that trail system, versus perhaps sixty Special Forces troops at any given time that were running operations behind their lines.

If it were not for all those enemy troops devoted to that mission, we would have wreaked havoc, and we did, even then, whenever we found a vulnerable location. For example, I know J.D. Bath found a five-hundred-ton cache [of supplies].

Can you imagine the repercussions within the North Vietnamese command to lose as much rice as a whole division consumes in six months because security wasn't tight. Or we'd find truck parks, where they'd hide their trucks during the day to run them at night. We'd call in air strikes and destroy whole truck parks, thirty, forty, maybe fifty trucks. All of a sudden, there's this terrible gap in the Ho Chi Minh Trail where they can no longer move supplies until they move replacement trucks down. I assure you that the commander of that area is going to have hell to pay explaining why it was that his security was not strong enough to prevent the Yankees from finding a truck park and calling an air strike in on it.

SOG's primary mission was intelligence-gathering, to learn what the enemy had and where it was in Laos and Cambodia, the so-called sanctuaries of Cambodia. In the case of Laos, when we found a significant target, we called air strikes on it.

—Major John Plaster, U.S. Army Reserve, Retired, Special Forces recon leader, MACV-SOG

In Vietnam, Second Lieutenant Bill Townsley flew an O-2A, a military version of a Cessna Model 337, a tiny, unarmed aircraft with twin tail booms and tandem-mounted engines. Townsley was a forward air controller, and his job was to locate targets and bring in U.S. aircraft to attack them. Many of his targets were along the Ho Chi Minh Trail.

The next thing after being a fighter pilot was to be a forward air controller because you could be a battlefield commander. So we all listed the O-2A second in our list of desired positions because it was tactical. The mission in the beginning was at forty-five hundred feet, and we put in our strikes from that altitude.

We were told in the beginning, in our intelligence briefs, that it was a fairly dangerous place [over the Ho Chi Minh Trail]. When I first got to Saigon, they said, "Look at the guy to your right; look at the guy to your left: one of you is going to get an aircraft hit in your tour." You know, you looked at the guy at the right and the left and said, "Okay," and we all pointed to each other and said, "You be it." But I ended up with three hits when it was all over, so I took it for everybody.

On my seventh mission, on January 18, 1969, I was shot down. I was flying with my right-seater, combat training instructor pilot

ABOVE: A U.S. Air Force CH-3E "Jolly Green Giant" helicopter crewman prepares to drop a "Spike buoy" ADSID (air-delivered seismic-intrusion detector) along a suspected NVA infiltration route along the Ho Chi Minh Trail to monitor enemy troop and supply movements. The impact at ground level would bury the device up to the stabilization fins or even deeper, leaving only the antenna protruding aboveground. The principal NVA countermeasures—jamming and attempting to imitate the detector's transmission signals—were generally ineffective, and ADSIDs proved to be increasingly valuable tools in U.S. intelligence and interdiction efforts, particularly at Khe Sanh.

Major George Blair, when a 37-mm anti-aircraft gun hit us. I was a second lieutenant at the time. We had struck a target to the left, and I was pulling away, trying not to be constant [on a predictable course]. As I pulled away, George said, "Let's go back and take another look." I remember coming back level, and away we went. It struck—*whoomp!*—in the back end of the plane. To this day, George says, "Well, our right wing was shot off," and I say, "No, our boom was split in half."

The plane went into a flat spin, and it just tightened up. Of course, then you go into the slow-motion aspect of life that you get into when you're in that survival mode, I guess. We had about forty-five hundred feet to get out of the aircraft.

I called, "Mayday! Mayday!" George was trying to recover the aircraft; I was trying to recover the aircraft. It was just going straight down. So we tried to get out of the aircraft. As George got out, I think he hit his head on the strut, and it knocked him out. I dove out, pulled my ripcord, looked up to see the chute, and heard the plane crash. I looked down, saw the flames, and then I saw George's chute open, just about that fast.

The bad guys were shooting at me, so I started swinging in the chute as much as I could for whatever good it did. I'm not dead, so they didn't hit me. I hit the ground and landed about fifteen feet to the right side of the crashed airplane. My chute was caught in a tree, so I had to leave it. I just took off through the woods.

I got about fifty yards from the plane, jumped across a little stream, and got under a bush as best I could. I had a white helmet on, so I dug a hole for it real quick. I had a gold Cross pen in my pocket, so I took that out and threw that in the helmet. I had a book, my T.E. Lawrence, *Seven Pillars of Wisdom*, and I tossed that in the hole, too; then I just sat there and waited.

I could hear the bad guys come to the plane. Again, I was only about fifty yards away. Then they started shooting up the woods. I was a soldier, and some of us make it and some of us don't, and I was going to try till I died. So [I thought] we'll see what happens. We were

told in our intelligence briefing that the Pathet Lao [Laotian Communists] and the NVA along the trail did not take prisoners and that we should always save a bullet for ourselves if we wanted to take that option. That wasn't my option.

I had dug up an anthill, so I was covered in ants, but I wasn't going to move. I had to keep them out of my eyes and my nose; I didn't care about my ears, but I had to keep them out of my nose. You know, you do strange things, like cover your nose up and breathe in like that, you know, and snuff them out of your nose again, that kind of thing. Then, I decided, they taught me to eat ants. So I started eating some of them. After about an hour, two hours, they finally went away. Things had quieted down, and I could hear airplanes overhead. My whole mode was to get on the radio as soon as I could because I knew the aircraft were ours.

Well, as I got on the radio I could hear George talking [he had been rescued]. He thought I was dead. I wanted to prove to him that I wasn't. You're saying, "No, no, I'm not dead," but I couldn't talk very loud, you know. I think the radio was a PRC-46. I learned very quickly that I could talk through the tube on the radio; they hadn't taught us that, but if I talked through the tube, then I could keep my voice from going all over the countryside.

With the bad guys only fifty yards away, I could hear them talking normal talk, so I figured they could hear me if I got up to a normal conversational volume. My chief concern was to make no noise while I was on the ground.

The helicopter got close, and it started getting shot up. It took off and I'm there and everything gets real quiet. I knew that the Sandy, the A-1, is a search and rescue for me. The Sandy said, "Let's go off channel [on a different frequency] a minute." He went off channel, and I knew that they were going to have to leave me because it was getting dark. They came back on and told me that they were going to have to leave, that I'd have to dig in, and they wondered if I had my equipment. I told them I had the works, not to worry. They took off, and it was very silent,

LEFT: Riflemen of the 1st Infantry Division leap from a UH-1D Huey from the division's 1st Platoon ("Champagne Flight"), Company A, 1st Aviation Battalion, during an assault north of Saigon. The door gunner watches to make sure everyone is out before signaling the pilot to lift off, and the soldier in the foreground, fearing that the rope coil hanging from his shoulder will fly into the tall grass, presses it tightly to his chest as he hits the ground. A Company's 2d Platoon was called the Commancheros; the 3d Platoon was known as the Longhorns.

BELOW: Sometimes, the skies of Vietnam swarmed with helicopters carrying troops and supplies to the front. Here, a cloud of Hueys descends toward a landing zone.

Death from Above

ABOVE: A Huey fires a pair of 2.75-inch rockets from its two M3 24-rocket pods. Rockets could be fired in pairs or in full salvos of forty-eight. Stabilizing tailfins expanded into position after the rockets exited their launch tubes.

BELOW, LEFT: One of the most commonly used weapons-system combinations on a Huey was the minigun (a) and 7-rocket pod (b). The great quantities of ejected shell casings produced by door- and externally mounted machine guns flew to the rear during combat operations, often causing severe damage to tail rotors.

BELOW, RIGHT: The XM159 19-rocket pod (a) in combination with an XM18 7.62-mm minigun pod (b) on a Cobra's wing stub, and another minigun (c) in the chin turret.

ABOVE: A 1st Cavalry Division gunner picks out a target for his safety-strapped M79 grenade launcher.

ABOVE: Twin M60 7.62-mm machine guns on an external mount.

ABOVE: A .50-caliber tail gun, shown here, was frequently affixed to Chinooks, which were also issued lighter machine guns—first the .30-caliber, and later the M60—for their forward doors. The bag at left catches ejected shell casings. Ultimately, the most deadly weapon was the door gunner himself.

ABOVE: Shell casings fly as a gunner returns fire over Vietnam's Central Highlands.

and I just waited. I could hear all the commotion around the airplane that had crashed. Plus, I could hear an encampment of troops a little bit farther away, a lot of talking and yelling.

So I just waited. They were jabbering, none of which I understood, but I had always sworn that there were about three or four of them, and as they were walking by, two of them were trying to calm a third guy. I swear the third guy was saying something to the effect, "No, there's still one guy out here; there's still one guy out here." They headed about fifteen yards away from where I was and on to their encampment, and nobody looked for me. I was left alone and thought, "Well, this is good. I might make it." I just waited until darkness fell, then I started setting out all my equipment. I had a problem with that because it was all wrapped up in this kind of wax paper that made too much noise.

As the Sandy left, he said that my signal for getting up in the morning would be an F-100 Misty going with afterburner over my head. I said, "Great, understood, see you in the morning." As night fell, they [the NVA]

weren't looking for me because they thought I'd been picked up. I could hear their encampment, like a factory off to my east about two hundred or three hundred yards. The soldiers had walked in that direction earlier, so I knew that that's where their encampment was. Then, later on that night, trucks came in and shut down about three hundred yards to my northwest.

So, with my survival compass with the luminous dot on the pointer and the one on the dial, I was able to klick off exactly what heading [the enemy] were, and then I just remembered the numbers: one hundred meters, one hundred degrees, two hundred meters, and so forth.

In the morning, the Sandies came, apparently trying to wake me up or to get me on the radio. But I was not going to get on the radio because it only had so much life in it, and I didn't know how long I was going to get stuck there with everything that was going on around me.

Finally, when the F-100 came overhead and went afterburner, it was time for me to come up, and they asked me if I'd been sleeping,

and, yes, I had been sleeping during the night. But I told them I was fine now, and everything's ready to go, but we got a problem, you know, we got the various targets that we have to hit in order to get me out of there. So we did, and I went from being an air FAC one day to a ground FAC the next. We hit all those targets; they just hit the whole area, spent about three or four hours doing that in the morning.

They almost hit me with white phosphorus smoke, what we called a Willy P [or Willy Peter]. It landed about fifteen yards from me, exploded, and the phosphorus ball just dissipated right over my head. I got on the radio quickly and said: "Knock it off! Knock it off!"

They stopped for a moment, and I got out my mirror and started flashing with it. Well, I didn't want to get up and expose myself from my bush, so I just held it up. The sun was rising in the east, so the only place I could see the Sandies was off to the west, so I just was doing an angle shot, where I could get the mirror to flash upon a nearby leaf. Every time I saw a Sandy near that leaf, I'd move the mirror back and forth, keeping it focused on him. That's how I got myself out. I still have that mirror to this day.

They finally brought in the chopper, a "Jolly Green Giant." Before they brought it in, they said, "We're going to put down some salad," which meant tear gas. They were going to spread tear gas over the whole area and come in after me. I said fine, and actually I'd been trained extensively in that previously, in the Marines.

They brought in the chopper about two hundred yards or so from me. I could see the penetrator coming down, and just as it got there, the chopper started taking off. The penetrator kept coming down, but the helicopter started going very fast and basically left me behind. I'd been sitting up, and suddenly I was standing, and he was leaving me. But the penetrator was on the ground, being dragged through the jungle.

So I started chasing the penetrator. I got my radio and my pistol and started chasing it, and I caught up with it about fifty yards up the hill, grabbed it, pulled the seat down, and

said get me up. You know? Thumbs up. That thing was wound up tighter than a drum, and I just remember sitting there, seated with my pistol, just going around and around in a circle. They got me indoors and made sure they had me on board.

Everybody was crying because the blade wash had brought the tear gas into the helicopter. That kind of surprised them, so that's why they had taken off so abruptly. They got me on board, and I experienced an adrenaline rush, the result of being picked up. I went into the shiver mode. They laid me out, covered me up, gave me a cigarette, and I was happier.

I'd flown out of Da Nang, but they took me back to Nakhon Phathom in Thailand. That's where we landed, and I asked for a steak sandwich and a glass of milk. There was a crowd of two hundred or three hundred people waiting for me. It was a big deal for a second lieutenant, so that was nice.

—Colonel (then Second Lieutenant)
Bill Townsley, U.S. Air Force
forward air controller, Retired

ABOVE: Viet Cong in the Mekong Delta area south of Saigon, 1966. The guerrilla at right carries an American M1 carbine, a favorite weapon of both pro-government and insurgent Vietnamese because of its light weight, reliability, and detachable 15-round box magazine.

ABOVE: Platoon sergeant Oden Smith, of Colorado Springs, Colorado, scans the wood line to his front while Private Jerry Christensen, of Mattoon, Illinois, maintains contact with D Company, 3d Battalion, 7th Infantry, March 19, 1968. The soldiers are taking part in a 199th Light Infantry Brigade sweep in the Bien Hoa area called Operation Box SPRINGS.

BACKGROUND: Smoke was often "popped" to indicate to airborne helicopters the location of troops needing to be evacuated. In this case, a UH-1D "Dustoff" helicopter has answered the call for help and is preparing to land and evacuate the wounded, October 10, 1967. Sergeant Nick Schneider, 199th Light Infantry Brigade, is guiding in the medevac helicopter. Previous to the arrival of the air ambulance, messages on a radio net would have designated the area where the wounded were being held and described the number of men to be extracted and their condition.

From the time he entered the U.S. Army, John Plaster aspired to be in the Special Forces, to be a Green Beret. He achieved that goal, and when he arrived in Vietnam, his friends suggested to him, without being specific, that the best assignment for him was Command Control North (CCN) in the Studies and Observation Group (SOG), an organization with very dangerous secret assignments. Plaster joined up.

My first mission was with Recon Team New Mexico. We flew up to our launch site, my team leader and I and a guy by the name of Stevens, and we were to insert into Laos. While we were waiting to insert, our two other team members, two other Americans, arrived. They had just returned from attending SOG's Recon Team Leader course. Their names were Billard and Simmons. We were literally minutes from launching when Stevens came over to me and informed me that he had just checked with the pilot, and the aircraft would be overgrossed [over-weighted] if all of us went.

He had to leave one man behind, and because I was the least experienced, it was me. I was the new guy, and had never been on the ground before. So all I could do was wave to them as they left me there. That was to have been my first mission. They were all killed that night. So, the naivete in me was gone now....

[Some time later.] In March 1970, there had been a series of convoys running on Highway 110 [the Ho Chi Minh Trail] in southern Laos. They went up to the border of South Vietnam, then they disappeared. Supplies were being stockpiled for some major action, intelligence officers believed, so the commander of MACV, General Creighton Abrams, asked the chief of SOG, Stephen E. Cavanaugh, to see if he could find out where all these trucks were going and what the enemy were preparing to do. Cavanaugh analyzed the situation and decided the most logical way to find out was to go after someone who was accessible and knowledgeable, not some senior North Vietnamese officer but someone who knew where the trucks were going, what they were

carrying, and what the priority was. Therefore, the key person to snatch would be the lead driver of a truck convoy, because he had to know where the supplies were being picked up and sent.

The driver probably saw the manifests of what was being loaded because he'd be accountable, and he was the guide for his entire convoy. So he had to know where they were going. Of course, if this intelligence could be developed, the result would be a series of B-52 strikes on those locations.

Unfortunately, the first team inserted to capture a driver had a shootout with the North Vietnamese along the highway. In the process, the lead truck driver was killed. Fortunately, none of our team was wounded, and they got out. They successfully ambushed the convoy but did not bring back the driver. So a second attempt was mounted [Operation ASHTRAY], which I commanded—two recon teams, mine and Fred Krupa's Recon Team New Hampshire.

We trained exclusively for this operation for two weeks. We focused and drilled on how do you stop a truck at night? How do you signal at night? What kind of explosives do you

JOHN PLASTER

BELOW: SOG recon team members Sergeant John Plaster (left) and Sergeant Glen Uemura keep low in a Laotian bamboo grove during an air strike on the NVA anti-aircraft gun that's preventing helicopters from extracting their team, circa 1969–1970. Plaster found that at least ten SOG and fourteen other Special Forces teams were wiped out during cross-border operations; not one of the eighty SOG team members missing in action ever turned up on North Vietnam's list of POWs.

ABOVE: The Viet Cong were very resourceful, and outfitted themselves with everything from sandals made out of U.S. Army vehicle tires to rucksacks made out of U.S. supply sacks. Here, a VC guerrilla wears an improvised backpack emblazoned with the words "Donated by the people of the United States...not to be sold...."

use? How do you hog-tie a prisoner in five seconds to get him out of there? What would you do if he were chained to the steering wheel, as our intelligence suggested some drivers were, so that they could not abandon their trucks in the middle of an air strike?

We analyzed all these kinds of problems, things that had to be planned for. We developed a plan and drilled it day and night. Finally, for our final dress rehearsal, which was live fire and at night, we pulled it off in like ten seconds, from the time I detonated claymores until we grabbed our volunteer driver. It was a canned exercise; it wasn't for real. But we were ready now to play ball.

We landed about two kilometers south of Highway 110. It took us two days to get to the road. I still remember that first night, as we lay on a hillside about two kilometers from the highway. We could hear trucks rolling down it at night. It was exciting and

a little scary. We knew they were there, and the next night, we would be down on that highway. We reached the trail by about noon the next day. We backed off and just kept the road under surveillance during the day. We wanted to get an idea of what kind of foot security they had walking up and down the road. Meanwhile, I selected the ambush site, and Fred Krupa, the captain of the other recon team, and I discussed the ambush position at length.

By the book, it was a terrible position because it was on the downhill side of the road, which is contrary to the book. The position was in a thin bamboo grove, which is a very noisy place and not good cover, either. But it was such an unlikely place that I thought it would be the perfect ambush position. The North Vietnamese were famous in this area for running whole platoons, forty or fifty men, in sweeps along the road, looking for ambushes.

I believed they would not sweep such an unlikely place. They'd come by, shrug their shoulders, and pass by. That's the way it turned out. That evening, we waited until you could barely see your hand in front of your face. I deployed security teams to our right and left, one American with two Montagnards [Vietnamese mountain people from the central and northern parts of the country] on each flank. Our assault team was situated in the center. I kept the medic and the radio operator about a hundred meters behind us. When I had our guys set, I went out on the highway. It was a creepy feeling to be out there on Highway 110.

I put three claymore mines in a semicircle; these would fire shaped charges. Because it was going to be a fairly dark moon, there'd be just enough light for the ambush and sufficient light to see each other as we fled through the jungle. But it would be dark enough that the enemy wouldn't be able to see us clearly to follow and fire at us. In the moonlight, I was just barely able to make out a tree across the road. That was to be my sign. The plan was that I would set off the claymores, command-detonate them so that all three would fire simultaneously. I would align that tree with the front tire of the truck and collapse it with explosives. In the meantime, we lay on the downhill side of the road.

We thought that we'd only be there a few minutes because we had already had trucks rolling by even before dark, but we waited two hours for a truck to pass. Finally, here came this line of trucks. I could hear them from a long way off because it was a very still night. It was almost a buzz to start with that kept getting louder and louder. Finally, the first truck rounded the corner about two hundred meters away, at a curve in the road.

The convoy was just a few trucks, per our plan. As the first truck approached, everyone got down low, as we had planned. I waited for the tire to line up with the tree, then I ducked down and fired the claymores. They created a tremendous roar. But I had erred in the excitement of the moment, and instead of closing my right eye, which was my dominant eye for shooting, I left both eyes open. So now I experienced this terrible flash from the claymores. I was still executing, but my vision was kind of washed out for a couple seconds. I hollered, "Assault!" and we all got up on the highway. John Yancy, my assistant team leader, jerked open the door and grabbed the driver. I ran around the truck to take out the assistant driver, but there wasn't one.

Richard Woody ran around to the rear, in case there were any troops in the back. Instead, there were supplies inside the truck. Fred Krupa, my fellow team leader, covered the hood of the truck, in case there was a threat of someone coming over the back. We're almost creeping as we do all this, jerking the doors open, thrusting our weapons in, but there was no resistance. So it was only the driver. He'd never encountered an American in his life, but he knew to say, "No kill! No kill!" We had one of the very first pairs of these experimental plastic restraints that police use today in America. As quick as he had him secured, Fred Krupa led the driver back to the rallying point.

Then I hollered, "Withdraw!" But to make sure that the signal would be heard, Richard Woody blew a whistle, like in our rehearsals. He blew twice on the whistle, and when he

ABOVE: SOG Recon Team (RT) Louisiana, at Quang Tri, just a few of the two thousand American and eight thousand handpicked indigenous troops engaged in disrupting NVA, VC, Pathet Lao, and Khmer Rouge units inside their own territory. The Americans along the back row are (left to right) Specialist Ken Van Arsdel, Sergeant David A. Maurer, and Sergeant David Badger.

blew the second time, a North Vietnamese soldier hiding in the jungle along the road shot him twice.

Meanwhile, our teams were detonating claymores and throwing tear gas to delay any pursuers. I grabbed Woody and returned fire. Woody had taken an AK-47 bullet through his arm, and it was broken. That's terrible, terrible, horrible pain, but he wasn't griping at all, a great soldier, a strong man. I took his weapon away from him, wrapped him up, and led him back into the jungle.

Just then, an enemy truck came around the curve in the road. The trucks had kept an interval out of fear of bombing. I was sure that just the sound of that explosion would bring North Vietnamese troops running. Our intelligence had estimated that there was a North Vietnamese battalion base camp within about a thousand meters of our position. That was five hundred North Vietnamese troops. So we couldn't stay there very long at all. But we had to buy a little time, so I stayed back there alone and played patty-cake with the North Vietnamese for a few minutes.

Fortunately, we had developed time-delay munitions. We took ordinary hand grenades and modified them with nonelectric blasting caps and a time fuse. The quickest one was

TOP: SOG RT Michigan hurries through a bomb-damaged bamboo grove in Laos, 1968.

BOTTOM: Sergeant Bob Bechtoldt and a Khmer member of RT Auger move cautiously through a stream in the Golf-80 target area of Cambodia's notorious "Fish Hook" region.

set for thirty seconds and the longest one was set for like eleven minutes. So as we were pulling back, designated men within the team were throwing these, creating a virtual mine-field of all these things that would be cooking off in the next up to forty-five minutes.

The North Vietnamese by now were at the truck, and I was falling back as I engaged in a little shootout with them. We'd also thrown a satchel charge in the truck, and a thermite grenade sat right on the hood of the truck. The satchel charge detonated first, and it was like two and a half or three pounds of C4 explosive. When it exploded, all firing ceased around the truck. It was a major explosion. That just did the initial reaction force in right there. But then they started firing wildly into the jungle. Fortunately, the truck caught fire, and the thermite grenade eventually deto-nated. Now we had a beacon for our incoming fighters, and when a night FAC later arrived, he was able to use that fire to define targets. Our men bombed up and down that road all night long, and it kept the enemy pinned down. The enemy was so preoccupied with trying to avoid the bombing that they never caught up with us in the jungle.

—John Plaster

Impact of the Air War

By 1967, President Johnson had unleashed a much more damaging air attack on North Vietnam, and it became an increasing problem for the Communists. The rate of sorties rose from some twenty-four hundred a month in 1965 to eight to nine thousand a month by late 1966. In addition, more targets were being chosen in the generally off-limits Hanoi area, which threatened the security of North Vietnam's leaders as well as their military infrastructure. Thousands of trucks, railroad cars, and ships were destroyed, as well as bridges, roads, oil facilities, and heavy industries. Unintended collateral bombing damaged schools, hospitals, homes, and offices, forcing the North Vietnamese to employ more than half a million workers to repair the damage and to man air defenses. The state of North Vietnam's agricultural production was also affected, and food and medical supplies dwindled, malnutrition increased, and the general morale of the people plummeted.

In March 1967, the American air attacks targeted the Thai Nguyen iron and steel works and pounded the area around Hanoi incessantly. The North Vietnamese began to fear that the Americans' expanding attacks would include

ABOVE: As an F-100 Super Sabre pulls out of its bombing run, the concussion wave from its own ordnance visibly radiates from the detonation point, February 22, 1967. This is one of the 210 U.S. air strikes that pummeled the Iron Triangle immediately before swarms of helicopters air-landed the 173d Airborne Brigade during Operation JUNCTION CITY.

the dikes along the Red River, which would cause hundreds of square miles of North Vietnamese farmland to be flooded and the city of Hanoi to be submerged under eleven feet of water. Their fears were not misguided, for U.S. military planners were studying an "iron bomb" that could be used for just such a purpose.

In virtually all cases during this period, the U.S. target officers, the persons who chose the specific sites for bombardments, were President Lyndon Baines Johnson and Secretary of Defense Robert McNamara—not trained military planners in Vietnam or the Pacific. While the main weakness of the U.S. air attacks was that they lacked surprise, mass, consistency, and constancy, the escalating aerial bombardment nonetheless unnerved the North Vietnamese leaders more than they wished to admit, and caused them to wonder if the Americans might be preparing to invade the North.

From June 1965 onward, B-52 strategic bombers were part of the U.S. arsenal for ROLLING THUNDER, but in the initial stages of

the war, they were used primarily to counter guerrilla activities in South Vietnam. A single B-52 could carry fifty-one 750-pound bombs—twenty-seven in the bomb bay and twelve under each wing. The planes were devastating weapons when used to cover a large area of operation, and they had excellent navigation and bombing systems aboard that allowed them to operate night and day in all weather and to drop their tonnage with extraordinary accuracy. Security breaches, however, became a serious problem. These lapses were often the result of idle chatter by Americans over their communication channels; but more often the leaks came from the necessity for the Strategic Air Command (SAC) to announce its plans to air traffic authorities in the same way as civilian carriers. In addition, the North Vietnamese had a potent spy network in South Vietnam.

In mid-1967, when Secretary of Defense McNamara attempted to rein in the scope of ROLLING THUNDER, the "hawkish" Subcommittee of the Senate Arms Service Committee, led by Senator John C. Stennis (D-Mississippi), called McNamara and Admiral

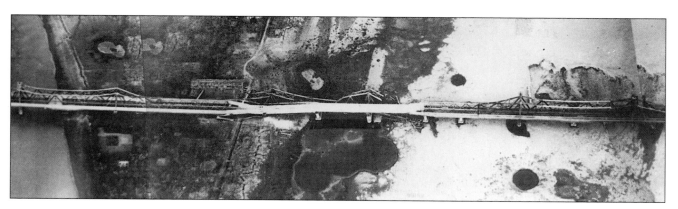

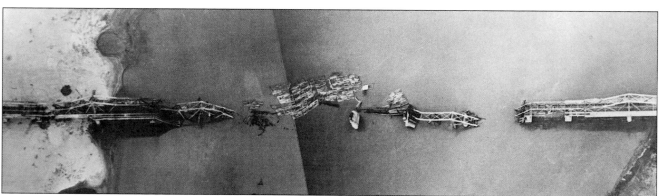

LEFT: During a September 1963 inspection of the military and political situation in South Vietnam (seated, left to right), Chairman of the Joint Chiefs of Staff, General Maxwell D. Taylor; Secretary of Defense Robert S. McNamara; and MACV commander General Paul D. Harkins are briefed by ARVN and U.S. Army advisors. McNamara treated the war as if it were simply another business management problem. This attitude, combined with the Joint Chiefs' refusal to believe that the United States could lose the war militarily, set the stage for a long, drawn-out conflict in which enemies of the United States brought maximum pressure on America's will to win, or even to support the South Vietnamese in their own fight.

Ulysses Grant Sharp Jr., Commander in Chief, Pacific, to testify on the matter. The committee concluded that military voices on such matters, which had long been disregarded, should be heeded. So the bombing of North Vietnam continued, off and on, until the end of the war.

 Pilot Jerry Hoblit believed that the Vietnam War effort was poorly focused.

My generation of military people was very much concerned about what happened to the generation of professional military people in Germany in the 1930s. We didn't want that to happen to us. Way before the war in Vietnam intensified, I had recognized that that was a hot spot I might end up fighting in, and I studied it. The first thing I learned was that the Communists, after the Geneva Accords, killed seventeen thousand schoolteachers one year in Vietnam—only because they were potential leaders in their communities. So they were taken out and shot.

Our history today seems to forget that in [the twentieth] century the Communists have killed 100 million people. Most of those people were in countries that they controlled. That's the evil that we've put behind us. I'm very glad that I participated in that. I'm not

happy with the specific war and the poor way in which we managed that, but I'm not against the overall purpose of it.

—Jerry Hoblit

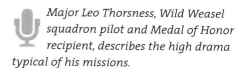 *Major Leo Thorsness, Wild Weasel squadron pilot and Medal of Honor recipient, describes the high drama typical of his missions.*

We were always first in. We'd air-refuel and then lead the gaggle in. Our job was to stay in there until the last flight was out, to suppress the SAMs. So whereas the strike pilots coming in had a fixed target—they would go here and there, drop their bombs, and they'd be time over target, TOT, maybe two minutes— we'd be trolling around in there for maybe twenty minutes. In the summertime or the dry season, we had to wait till the dust cleared because McNamara said if you destroyed a target, you couldn't put another flight of bombs on there. So it took longer for the dust to clear in the dry season.

There were times when we couldn't even use our afterburner to cover that last flight because there'd be about five minutes between them. So it was just a statistical analysis that if someone was over the target

Wild Weasels: The SAM Killers

On November 21, 1966, the U.S. Air Force began fielding a "Wild Weasel" SAM-killing mission. Radar-detection devices and weapons were installed on North American F-100F Super Sabres based at Eglin Air Force Base in Florida. At the outset, the aircraft inventory consisted of only four planes, soon augmented to six planes, with more planes of other varieties added later. The F-100Fs were quickly reassigned to Korat Royal Air Force Base in Thailand, where they soon tested their SAM-killing potential. From the start, the attacks were effective, but not without great losses in men and aircraft. More effective U.S. weapons systems and aircraft had to be developed to lessen the costs of the operation. The Russians, it was learned, had been supplying North Vietnam with modern radar-guided missiles with effective command-and-control systems that resulted in extremely lethal ground fire.

The North Vietnamese weapon of choice was the SA-2 GUIDELINE surface-to-air missile, popularly called the SAM. So successful were the SAMs that Air Force pilots were forced to devise a variety of evasive measures to prevent being shot down and killed. SAMs were most dangerous at high altitudes, but when U.S. planes dropped to medium altitudes to avoid them, they were vulnerable to flak from the potent NVA anti-aircraft batteries. Near ground level, planes were exposed to low-tech small-arms fire that created its own menace. But SAMs were the most feared weapons, so an intensive effort was undertaken to learn how to evade them and to develop weapons systems capable of opposing them.

The AGM-45 Shrike missile was one of the answers. The Shrike, with its own detection and homing system, when properly positioned for attack by a pilot, could lock in on a SAM site and kill it. The advantage of the Shrike was that it could be used in operations against SAMs while at a standoff range of a couple of miles.

Wild Weasel pilots were "sticks," outstanding pilots. The second man on board—an electronic warfare officer,

BELOW: A deadly trio of F-100s during early air operations against North Vietnam.

JACK DONOVAN

or EWO—was referred to as a bear. He served also as the aircraft's navigator. One of the first EWOs, Captain Jack Donovan, after being briefed concerning the Wild Weasel mission, responded caustically, "You've got to be shitting me." At that stage in the program, his response was sensible, for the missions initially had all the characteristics of a suicide run. Donovan's remark was made into an acronym, YGBSM, and became the favorite slogan for the Weasels.

The first sorties were extremely perilous, but they continued until better systems and tactics could be developed. But the missions, throughout the entire war, were extremely hazardous because the Weasels were used in the vanguard of strike aircraft on bombing runs, their object being to lure the NVA radar sites to fix and fire on them, after which they avoided the SAMs and destroyed

ABOVE: EWO Mike Gilroy (standing, fourth from left), pilots, and other electronic warfare officers of the 354th Tactical Fighter Squadron—the first Wild Weasels—at Takhli Royal Thai Air Base, Thailand, July 1966. Gilroy later wrote that, forty-five days after they began operations against North Vietnamese targets, "We had one airplane left. Of our sixteen people, four had been killed, two were POWs, three had been wounded (two seriously enough to cause their return to the States for extended medical treatment), and two, I'm sorry to say, quit." Standing, left to right: Tom Pyle (POW); Bob Marts; Nes Maier; Mike Gilroy; Bobby Martin; Ed Larson (shot down August 7, 1966, rescued, WIA); Gene Pemberton (shot down July 23, 1966, KIA); and Buddy Reinbold (WIA). Kneeling, left to right: Bill Sparks, Curt Hartsell; Ed Rock; Joe Brand (shot down July 23, 1966, KIA); Ben Newsome (shot down July 23, 1966, KIA); Glenn Davis, and EWO Charles "Carlo" Lombardo. Not pictured: Bob Sandvick (POW) and Don Singer (shot down August 17, 1966, KIA).

their launching site, clearing the way for other aircraft to enter North Vietnamese airspace in greater safety. The pilots and EWOs were members of numbered Wild Weasel squadrons. One of their planes was emblazoned with

the provocative title "Jail Bait," an example of their warrior élan.

The F-100F was replaced early on by the EF (Electronic Fighter)-105F Thunderchief, called the Thud, a faster, longer-range aircraft armed for the first time with the Shrike missile and AGM-78 standard anti-radiation missiles. The F-105F was armored and could take a lot more punishment than the earlier F-100Fs. In 1969, the Air Force included the F-4C Phantom II in its inventory of Wild Weasel aircraft over North Vietnam. Many of the early Weasel pilots, after their tours of duty, were returned to Nellis Air Force Base, Nevada, where they conducted classes for new pilots at the "Willie Weasel College." By the time the Wild Weasels, warriors par excellence, perfected their tactics over North Vietnam, they remained in effect for many years to come.

OPPOSITE: A B-52 Stratofortress releases its load of "iron bombs" on Communist targets. Originally intended for nuclear warfare, B-52s ear-marked for missions over Vietnam and its environs were reequipped to carry up to eighty-four 500-pound bombs or forty-two 750-pound bombs internally, plus twenty-four more bombs externally on wing racks. Commonly operating in three-aircraft cells, they could completely saturate a one-by-two-kilometer target box or thoroughly disrupt operations in a one-by-five-kilometer area. The number of B-52s employed against Communist targets from bases on Guam and in Thailand ebbed and flowed throughout the war but ultimately exceeded two hundred aircraft—nearly a third of the strategic fleet—during the eleven-day Christmas Bombing of 1972, which forced the North Vietnamese to the negotiating table. During that campaign, at least 1,242 surface-to-air missiles were fired against the Stratofortresses and other U.S. aircraft. Fifteen aircraft were brought down, prin-cipally the longer-range B-52Gs, which carried an electronic countermeasures suite inferior to the B-52D's. The B-52G bomber was affectionately known among both troops and air-crews as BUFFs, for "big ugly fat fuckers," or the more public relations–friendly "big ugly fat fellows."

area for two minutes versus twenty minutes, the odds of being shot down were about ten times greater. And that was our mission.

The concept, obviously, was that this was the first war in which there were surface-to-air missiles. So, we being the United States, our military industrial complex came up with a concept of let's develop a missile that will home in on the radar. The missiles they fired at us were radar controlled. Let's see if we can find a missile that'll destroy that radar. Let's put a system together. We'll put an electronic warfare officer in the backseat of a fighter and have a pilot do the maneuvering, and have the warfare officer refine all this techni-cal data, and see if we can't find an aiming system where we can destroy those surface-to-air missiles, either on the ground or figure out how to evade the SAMs after they are launched at these first-in groups, the Wild Weasels. Then, we'll destroy the radar after that, and the launch fields.

Just like in World War II or the Korean War, there were bridges. There was POL [petroleum storage depots]. There were supply lines, railroad lines, those types of hard targets. Those were the targets for the strike force, the flights of four airplanes coming in with their big bombs. Our job was to go in just ahead of them and to hold down those surface-to-air missile sites or destroy them, and to allow those people in the bombers to do their jobs of interdiction and destroying the enemy's fuel supplies, rail lines, and those things.

—Leo Thorsness

Leo Thorsness fulfilled his vows to the Air Force and his nation for a variety of reasons.

I didn't question my mission. I was ordered to go in and do it. And I didn't question it for several reasons. One is that I'd been trained to do it. I was a professional fighter pilot. I was at the top of my career, my flying was good, and I was recognized for that. They picked those kind of people to be Weasels. I suppose I had a certain amount of pride in that, also, when we went to Vietnam; really, the antiwar

thing hadn't really started yet when I went over there in 1966. I think another thing is, I'd have been embarrassed not to do my mission. Everybody was doing their job to the best of their ability, with rare exceptions. If I had all of a sudden said, "I don't believe in this cause; I guess I won't go," I think pride would have prevented me from saying that. Maybe that's foolish pride; maybe it was youthful pride. But most young people don't seem to ques-tion their government. I grew up in a patriotic home, and I was red, white, and blue when I went over there.

I would add, surprising maybe to most people, that when I got home I was maybe more red, white, and blue than before. That was simply because I'd had a chance to look at Communism from within the very bowels of the system for six years [from inside a prison camp, the Hanoi Hilton, one of the worst].

You know, there are a lot of things wrong with our country, but it's all relative. When you compare it with that dictatorial, no freedom, autocratic system [Communism]: I was so proud to be an American. And we came home to a country that was much less red, white, and blue than when I left. We came home to a country that had lost confidence in our institutions, our family, our religion, our government, our military, our school system, even. It was a difficult adjustment. We came home so proud to be Americans to a country that was—what's the opposite of proud—so much less proud than when we went.

—Leo Thorsness

Jerry Hoblit, a pilot in a Wild Weasel squadron, operated over wartime North Vietnam, where 63 percent of the pilots and their electronic warfare officers did not survive their 100-mission tours of duty. Hoblit describes the necessity of their risky operations.

The Weasels were organized in Southeast Asia at one of our bases as a separate squadron, and they were integrated at another base within the existing fighter squadrons. They were special because they represented a watershed in the history of aerial warfare.

One of the biggest lessons of the twentieth century in war is that you can't conduct a battle unless you control the airspace above that battle. Classically, the way this has been done is with fighter aircraft, first by getting air superiority over the battlefield area, and then maintaining it.

Well, the aircraft versus the surface-to-air missile was a duel. It was Dodge City at high noon. It was similar to other military duels: tank versus tank, fighter aircraft versus fighter aircraft, or even submarine versus submarine, in some respects. But in one very important respect it was different. That is, that the adversarial systems were operated in very different environments and used very different technologies and weapons to deal with one another.

Therefore, when you're a fighter pilot engaging another fighter pilot, for instance, you can project from your system to his system, and the differences, usually small, will dictate and control your tactics. In the case of the surface-to-air missile versus the aircraft, they were very different. So we had a very complex set of technologies interfacing with tactics that we had to deal with. What was similar to the other duels, however, was that the final result was almost always fatal to one of the two adversaries. Our mission was not a suicide one; it was a very high-risk mission and one that was typical of other things in aviation. It wasn't good if you weren't prepared, and it wasn't good if you didn't pay attention. But if you paid attention and you were prepared, then it was probably no more dangerous than many other missions performed by members of all services.

The greatest legacy is, when our ability to maintain air superiority was fundamentally threatened, the Wild Weasel arrived on the scene and restored our ability to control the air over any battlefield, anyplace.

—Jerry Hoblit

ABOVE: An AGM Shrike anti-radiation missile launched from an F-105 streaks toward a North Vietnamese SAM site's radar transmitter during a December 1966 U.S. air strike.

 Bill R. Sparks explains the purpose of the Wild Weasels from his perspective.

What the Weasels did, when we did it right, was keep the SAMs off the good guys' [strike pilots and bombers'] backs so they could get in and get out. Now, a lot of things happen to a strike pilot. We're all there strictly to help the strike pilot out. Okay, everybody there wasn't lugging pig iron, but we were trying to help the strike pilots out. Those guys were getting shot at; they had to roll and go down a slide with all the flak coming up at them—not a good way to make a living, a horrible way to make a living, actually. Then, they had to survive a pull off, getting out of town,

getting rejoined, and making a getaway. So anything you could do to keep them from being distracted on the way in was worth it. Maybe "distraction" is a silly term. But to keep the distraction level as low as possible was what the Weasels would do.

So if they had to go dance with missiles— you could dodge a missile. You can do it. I had a RAND Ph.D. tell me that it was impossible. I didn't know whether to laugh at him or become angry, because, you know, I had spent seven months dodging missiles, and this guy tells me it's impossible. Well, bunk. You can dodge them.

We called it dancing with them. So if you keep the guys with the heavy loads on them from dancing with the missiles, then (a) he doesn't have to jettison his bombs, and (b) he gets to the target on time. It makes his job a lot easier. The MiG cap [the Weasels' Air Force protectors] did the same thing, kept MiGs off our backs. So basically the mission was real simple: whatever you could do to make the strike pilot's job easier is what you were supposed to do.

—Lieutenant Colonel Bill R. Sparks, U.S. Air Force, Wild Weasel pilot

 Mike Gilroy, electronic warfare officer, portrays the chaos of the Wild Weasel program at its inception.

Well, we started out pretty badly in Vietnam. We arrived there on July 4, 1966. We had eight aircrews and six airplanes; forty-five days later, we had no airplanes, and of our sixteen people we had four who had been killed and two were prisoners of war. Three of our pilots had been wounded, two of which had wounds that were serious enough that they had to go back to the States and couldn't fly anymore, and one fellow had quit.

You're going at 500 knots, and this missile is going at Mach 2.5, and how do you dodge it? They told us, "Well, you light the burner and get some airspeed up, and when it gets right up about there, pull real hard."

You answered, "What do you mean, 'right about there'? Is that about a hundred yards away or three hundred yards away?" And

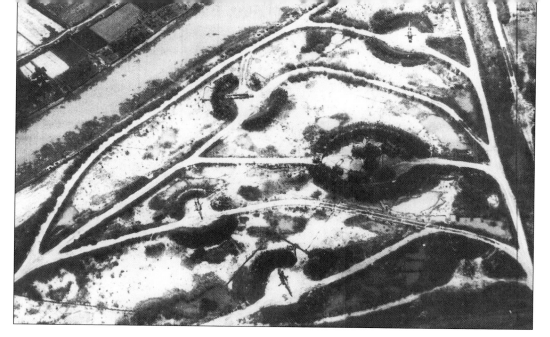

LEFT: An aerial reconnaissance photo of a SAM battery beside a canal in the Red River Delta area of North Vietnam. Visible are six SA-2 GUIDELINE missile launch sites partially protected by berms. The large berm at center right encloses electronic support equipment and a Fan Song fire control radar system—the target of the Wild Weasels' deadly intentions. If destroyed, the battery will be forced to fall back on the SA-2's ineffective optically directed guidance system.

they said, "Well, you'll know. You'll know." So it was pretty rudimentary training, and we sort of learned as we went along. No developed tactics existed on how to do that, so we made a lot of mistakes in the beginning. If you survived, you learned, and you brought your lessons back, and you passed them on to someone else.

But the danger was not something that you dwelled upon. There was a lot of peer pressure there, maybe not spoken but implied. When you finished your mission and you went to the bar at night, you sat there and had a drink with your buddies. You wanted to be as brave as they were during that day.

The worst thing that could happen to you was if someone called you a candy ass because you didn't press on when you should have.

—Mike Gilroy

 Fear was not something that had much relevance for Wild Weasels, as EWO Tom Wilson explains.

No, no, you didn't have time for fear. In the airplane, when you were going into the target, you felt no fear because you couldn't. You didn't have time for that sort of thing. You had to get up, sort of like for a football game, get yourself mentally prepared; therefore, when you're in a combat situation—and people might get killed and everything—you don't stop and ponder the situation. You can't. You don't have the luxury. When you land, you still don't have the luxury.

—Tom B. Wilson

 Major Leo Thorsness believed his EWO, Harry Johnson, was a lifesaver for him.

I'd never flown with a crew member before. I was a fighter pilot used to a single-place airplane. All of a sudden, I got this crew that I have to coordinate with. But Harry turned out to be a frustrated would-be fighter pilot, and he was a great EWO. I taught him how to fly. There was a stick in the backseat of a 105, so we'd go up to the [refueling] tankers. I'd carry pictures of the suspected SAM sights with me. I'd plug in, we'd get our fuel, then we'd wait for all the strike people [incoming bombers]. I was studying those pictures right up till the last minute, and then I'd fly.

But Harry, in only one flight out of ninety-two missions did he question my judgment. We were out on the [Red River] Delta, by ourselves, and we were trying to get a SAM site. And he said, "Leo, we're hanging out kind of far." Because he was so hesitant to criticize my portion of the duties, my job, I paid a lot of attention to him. But somehow we ended up being very well matched. We were both aggressive, and we both realized that, at some point, we were better off to back out and come back tomorrow rather than go to the point where you're just about certain to back out.

But in the heat of things, Harry had three eyes. Twice he saved my butt, our butt, because he saw MiGs coming in that I wasn't aware of. And yet he's looking at the scope, he's listening to all that stuff, he's tuning his knobs, and I don't know how. Maybe all navigators are cross-eyed, but Harry could be looking at two spots at the same time, and he could listen to about three different radio signals and stay on top of it all. So without Harry, I would have been shot down; we would have been shot down long before we were.

—Leo Thorsness

 There was a critical necessity for electronic war officers, as noted by pilot Jerry Hoblit.

Well, the air battle always has been very intense, very complex, and very difficult to sort out. This didn't change particularly for the "bear," the EWO in the Wild Weasel business, but it was amplified quite a bit. The fighter pilot's basic problem is that he has too much coming at him. Too much information is coming into his cabin. What he needs, what his lifeblood is, is processed information. He has to have the wheat separated from the chaff, and he has to have it done real time, split-second time.

That's what Bear Wilson did for me. He kept track of what the enemy was doing from an electronic standpoint, from the missile standpoint, from the surface-to-air missile standpoint. I was keeping track of what the other things were doing, the MiGs, the strike force behind me, and the management of my flight. But he kept me advised of the primary threat, the threat that not only was a threat to us, but the threat that we intended to deal with and make less of a negative threat. It took a very special person to look at all the things that he [the EWO] looked at and to communicate that to the guy in the front without further loading the guy in the front with information.

He had to sort it out, understand what the enemy was doing, anticipate what the enemy was going to do, and communicate that to me in a very minimal fashion. Sometimes, he would do that with only an inflection of voice, even a grunt, while we were pulling Gs, and it could tell me lots of things. Very few people could do what Bear Wilson did. Only two or three did it well. Bear Wilson was unquestionably the best of any of them.

—Jerry Hoblit

 Jerry Hoblit was aware of the reputation pilots have for daring and partying, and he made no extenuating excuses for it.

All Weasels were fighter pilots, and all fighter pilots in those days—well, not all, of course, but nearly all—were pretty heavy drinkers and pretty heavy party folks. It was part of the culture. It had always been part of the culture since World War I. I think it probably still is part of the culture. I don't think we did it to relieve stress, particularly. We didn't think about stress in those days. We thought about a job to do, and we did it. We thought it sure would be nice to relax, though, after some intensity.

—Jerry Hoblit

BELOW: U.S. Air Force pilot Jerry Hoblit (right) and his "back-seater," Electronic Warfare Officer Tom Wilson.

Contrary to popular belief, flying an airplane is not very hard. It's very easy. Using an airplane is hard. And there's a heck of a lot of difference between the two. When you fly a fighter, you put it on like a shirt, and then you forget about it. It does what you want it to do; you think about it, and your plane is there. I mean, you do not constantly fly. Flying is easy, real easy. But using the plane properly—that's where training comes in. The most successful crews shared something in common. Both the front- and back-seater were pretty aggressive. The back-seater [the EWO] was very good on all successful crews.

The back-seater had to really be knowledgeable and know what he was doing. So you can sort of divide it up into two different pieces, if you will. Your EWO, your "bear," was totally knowledgeable, or at least you wanted to believe that he was totally knowledgeable. After all, you wouldn't hire a ham-fisted surgeon, would you, and this guy's far more responsible for your life than any surgeon would be. So your bear was knowledgeable and had to be, and you trusted him implicitly to know the systems, and to listen to these funny little squeaks and squawks and watch these funny little curvy lines, and from that tell you what was going on. And he's looking at a two-inch CRT [cathode ray tube] to do this. Listening to all sorts of things, right?

Now, in my particular case, Carl Lombardo had joined the U.S. Army two weeks before I started in the first grade in 1941. He had been an electronic war officer since the second class of Old Crows in 1942. He knew more about electronic warfare than almost anybody else in the Air Force—he'd forgotten more than most anybody else would ever know. He was an opinionated, obnoxious, hard-nosed human being, and I never met a man that I liked better or trusted more, and I loved him dearly and still do. But Carlo knew what was

going on, and he didn't take anything from me at all. I mean, as far as he was concerned, if he wanted to be a pilot, he would have been one a long time ago, and he didn't need some teenage jerk in the front seat telling him what to do. He was always there, he always was right, and I believed in him. Now all I had to do then was to take his inputs and make sense out of them, with what I was seeing, and my experience level of what was there, and what we were supposed to do, and what everyone else was supposed to do, and be in the right place at the right time. Put us between the [NVA] threat and the [U.S.] force, so that we could be in place to put it down however this had to be done— any threat to the force.

So the concept was simple; the tactics were complex, and the actuality was very interesting. You didn't have one threat; you had a lot of threats. Okay? There were twenty, roughly twenty to twenty-two SAM sites in North Vietnam. At any one time, we'd kill them; they'd bring in some more; we'd kill them, and they'd bring in some more. They'd wear out, and they'd bring in some more. Normally, for starters, when you say North Vietnam, that doesn't mean all of it. The area of interest was really the area around Hanoi, and for anybody who has been to Las Vegas,

ABOVE: The two-seat F-105F, or "Thud," formed the backbone of the U.S. Air Force SAM suppression missions during Operation ROLLING THUNDER. The electronic warfare officer in the "backseat" tracked North Vietnamese radar systems, while the pilot acted as gunslinger.

ABOVE: A Bullpup missile is launched at an enemy target from a U.S. Air Force F-100 (center), January 1, 1966.

it's about the size of Las Vegas valley. It's not all that big. It's a lot smaller than the Los Angeles basin. In that area, they would have the vast majority of their sophisticated defenses. I have seen eighteen SAM sites up at one time in an area the size of Las Vegas valley. And that's interesting. And I don't know how many gun layers [artillery] because we couldn't count them. I don't know, maybe thirty, forty maybe, at one time were up [monitoring us].

Now, if you throw into that all the radars that are looking at you so that they can direct MiGs your way, and talk to the guns, and talk to the SAM sites to tell them what you're doing, and direct them, you got a heck of a lot of electronic activity going on. So it's easy to get sidetracked. You start up here, and a guy comes up [detected enemy radar]; you start heading north, and a guy [enemy radar] comes up northeast of you; so you point your nose at him. And he drags you out a while; he grabs your attention; he locks on your nose; and he pulls you along; he pulls you up; and

about that time you're, "Oh, I'm going to get this guy," he's done. He shuts down [his radar], and a guy comes up over here at your left, and you, "Oh, I'll get him," and you charge over in that direction, and he drags you along a little bit farther with your attention. About that time, [radars] 1 and 6 come on, and you are "Dr Peppered." You've got one at 10 [o'clock], one at 2 [o'clock], and one at 4 [o'clock], and they all three shoot [at you] at the same time. About that time, you wish you'd taken up driving a garbage truck instead of being a fighter pilot, and you try to get out of there the best way you can.

You cannot dodge missiles from three directions at the same time. You can't even dodge them from two directions at one time. So you had to play a game. It was a head game, okay? They were trying to play games with your heads; we were trying to play games with their heads. And it was the most interesting game you ever played in your life. And all this time, there are all sorts of people talking. You'd have twenty-some-odd folks in the [attack] force at one time. Normally, you'd have sixteen fighters carrying bombs. Sixteen bomb droppers. You'd have four Weasels. And you'd have at least one MiG cap—four F-4s— with air-to-air ordnance to keep the MiGs off you, right? Sometimes, we would double-MiG cap it. You'd put one MiG cap up front and one behind, if they really got obstreperous.

They kept trying to get you and liked to bother the Weasels. They used to bother the Weasels because if they kept us busy, we couldn't do our jobs. So we put four F-4s up with the Weasels to keep them [the enemy] off the Weasels so that they could do their jobs, because normally the Weasels would go in a little bit ahead of everybody else.

So you get this big glob, you know, a lot of people are talking; you got guard channels where a lot of people are talking; you've got all sorts of things happening; you've got airplanes that are looking from different radars; other places that are relaying other information up to this big mouth; "Red Crown," "Big Eye," and a bunch of other people who were talking to you. All of this is going on and distracts you. Plus, occasionally, they'd shoot missiles at you, and you've got flak going off all around you, which was distracting. So the whole thing was an exercise in discipline. How can I keep my cool; how can I watch what's going on; how can I listen to Carlo Lombardo with gusts of thirty thousand words a minute in the backseat and keep aware of whatever else was going on and not get totally discombobulated and lose my mind. It was an interesting way to make a living. By the way, I keep using the term *interesting*. There is an Arabic curse I learned that says, "May you be born in interesting times." And those were interesting times.
—Bill R. Sparks

In his low-key, modest manner, Leo Thorsness describes the actions for which he received the Medal of Honor as a major in air combat over North Vietnam.

I received the Medal of Honor because of what most medals are awarded for, trying to rescue someone. I received the Medal of Honor because I was trying to rescue my downed wingman and direct the rescue operation. Most Medals of Honor are given not because you killed a bunch of people, but because you saved your buddy or something. In my case, my wingman had been shot down, and there were two of them in the airplane, and a MiG started attacking the two men as they floated down from their airplane. So I attacked that MiG and ended up shooting it down. About that time, some MiGs were on our tail. So we escaped out of there at low-level supersonic speed "on the deck" [very close to the ground], through valleys, and came back around one more time, and were trying to make radio contact with my wingman, with their little handheld radio.

BILL R. SPARKS

As I started to make that contact, we were out of fuel, so we went some distance and found a tanker, and while we were on the tanker, I'm saying that I need some help, we're going back in, I need a flight with me. Well, there's always mix-ups, so it turns out there was nobody available to go with me. That's how things happen sometimes. So Harry and I, we had a little bit of ammo left, and that's about all. We went back in ourselves, and it was just about the time we got over to where my wingmen were, and we found ourselves surrounded by five MiGs. They were circling up there, and I just happened to fly in the middle of them, and hosed away at them, and pieces started coming off

ABOVE: Electronic Warfare Officer Mike Gilroy (right) is presented with "100 Mission–North Vietnam" and "Yankee Air Pirate" patches at the conclusion of his 100-mission tour of duty, April 12, 1966. Gilroy, in turn, presented his crew chief with a case of beer. With Gilroy are (from left) Lieutenant Colonel Phil Gast, commander of the 354th Tactical Fighter Squadron, and Colonel Bob Scott, commander of the 355th Tactical Fighter Squadron.

of them. But by that time, we had more of them on us, and one more time I went back through the valleys and finally got away from them. Finally, another flight came in and took over the rescue operation. I was close to a tanker, and all of a sudden over the radio—you never used first names over the radio—I heard this voice that said, "Leo." I answered, "Tomahawk 3 here, yes," or whatever. He said, "I've got six hundred pounds, I don't know where I am, and I'm about to eject."

So I called my tanker and put him on the same channel, and I said, "Tanker, you come farther north and home in on this guy, and Harry and I'll try to make it to Thailand on the fuel we've got." And this guy, I know his name, he hooked up with a zero indication remaining. Coasting downhill, he hooked up to the tanker, and they saved that one. Then, we climbed to thirty-five thousand feet, and a 105 will glide two miles per thousand, so we were seventy miles out, indicating about zero, and I pulled it back to idle, and started gliding, and we ran out of fuel just after we touched down in Thailand. It was just a mission that lasted a long time, a couple of refuelings in there, and we probably should not have survived it, but you don't think, you know, will I be rewarded for this. Some people say you should have been criticized for it, because the odds of being shot down were great.

It was just my job. He was my wingman; there was no question that my job was to come in and direct that operation. If things fell apart, and I was the only one there, then I was the only one there. But there were a couple Sandy airplanes coming up, rescue airplanes coming up there while we were there. As I was coming back in after refueling, Sandy 2 called, saying, "Sandy 1 is going in. Sandy 1 is going in." The MiGs are upon these little propeller airplanes. He kind of said, "What should I do?" I said, "Keep turning your airplane as hard as you can turn it. They can't stay with you. And keep talking, and I'll home in on you." He kept talking, and I just used my automatic direction finder, homed in on him, and went right

through those MiGs, and they did what I hoped they would. They followed me, and he got away.

But going through the mind is you have a job to do, and that's all there is to it. There's no question of should I or shouldn't I when somebody's hurting. He's your wingman.

I was proud [about receiving the medal], and I was humble. I'd read Medal of Honor citations before I went to the White House, so I knew what kind of men I was going to join in this society. But I found out with the tap code in prison that I had been submitted for the Medal of Honor. I was shot down eleven days after this mission I flew, for which I later got the Medal of Honor. Eleven days later, I was shot down. But someone came into the squadron about that time, and he was tasked to write this Medal of Honor citation. Then he was shot down. So with a tap code, about maybe a year, year and a half after I was there, I found out that I'd been submitted for the Medal of Honor.

I came home after six years of being there [the Hanoi Hilton]. Nothing was in my records about that. It was blank for that day. I looked at my back-seater's records, and he'd received the Air Force Cross, which is the next-highest medal. He kind of gave me a hard time about that, but he said there's something going on here. So, at any rate, I was contacted by the Air Force and told that I'd been submitted for the Medal of Honor, but that it was going back through channels. And I said, "Why is that?" They didn't really answer that, but the reason for it was that we had seven people who were prisoners of war who collaborated. That's a difficult thing to say because we had seven Americans who collaborated, and they, the Air Force, even though the medal wasn't for prison time, they didn't want to be embarrassed by awarding someone if he were one of them. It went back through the system, and it took another nine months or so. So I think I'm the only Medal of Honor recipient that has been approved by two administrations, two presidents. My wife, who is Swedish, thinks it's because I'm Norwegian and all that.

—Leo Thorsness

Fixed-Wing Aircraft

BACKGROUND: The devastatingly effective AC-47 gunships were created by adding a trio of 7.62-mm miniguns to decades-old C-47 cargo planes. Called Spooky (its call sign) or Puff by ground troops, an AC-47 could pour nonstop fire on a target as it orbited around it in a banked turn until the job was done. Daylight missions frequently involved protecting vulnerable truck convoys, while, at night, a Puff was always in the air—with more on call on the ground—to help beat back sudden enemy attacks on isolated firebases.

INSET, BELOW: A "murderers' row" of miniguns along the port side of an AC-47 at Bien Hoa, November 1965.

ABOVE: While AC-47 Puffs were used principally for local defense, the much larger AC-130 Spectre gunships, adapted from C-130 Hercules transports, were offensive weapons. Equipped with four miniguns, four 20-mm Vulcan cannons, and advanced night-observation equipment, AC-130s began search-and-destroy missions along the Ho Chi Minh Trail in October 1968. The Spectres quickly established a reputation as the most efficient "truck killers" along the trail, and later models incorporated such improvements as infrared imaging systems, searchlights, and two 40-mm Bofers cannons on some aircraft. The last Spectre variant sent to Vietnam was the AC-130H, armed with two miniguns, two Vulcans, a Bofers, and a long-range 105-mm cannon for use against heavily defended targets.

ABOVE, LEFT: An early production model of the OV-10 Bronco, an extremely versatile reconnaissance and attack aircraft designed specifically for counterinsurgency operations. The Bronco could be easily reconfigured to carry seemingly endless combinations of weaponry, including 5-inch Zuni rockets, mini and Gatling guns, plus general purpose and cluster bombs. The OV-10 could take far more punishment than a helicopter but lacked maneuverability and required a long runway to get airborne.

ABOVE, RIGHT: An OV-1A Mohawk observation plane belonging to the 1st Cavalry Division takes on some badly needed gas, circa September 1965. Because spotted targets often disappeared before they could be intercepted by attack aircraft, Mohawk pilots and ground crews soon began to arm their planes with a varied assortment of bombs, rockets, and minigun pods to catch fleeing enemy units before they vanished. The OV-1B Mohawk carried a side-looking airborne radar, for mapping the ground on each side of its flight path, in an extremely long, thin pod under the fuselage.

LEFT: An AD-1 Navy Skyraider "Spad" awaits its turn to take off from the USS *Oriskany* as a Crusader catapults off the angled flight deck. Propeller-driven Skyraiders didn't require the use of a steam catapult to get airborne in spite of carrying bomb loads of up to eight thousand pounds. Known for their extreme accuracy during attack runs, the AD-1 types were also acquired by the U.S. and Vietnamese air forces, in which they served until the fall of Saigon. Navy Skyraiders were withdrawn from operations over North Vietnam, but not before downing two MiG-17 jets with their wing-mounted 20-mm cannons.

ABOVE: The A-37 Dragonfly was a light, close-support aircraft designed for a counterinsurgency role. Highly prized for its ability to be "turned around" between missions in as little as ninety minutes, it carried a wide range of munitions on reconnaissance and night-interdiction missions over Vietnam and Laos. Numerous A-37s were incorporated into the North Vietnamese Air Force after the fall of Saigon.

RIGHT: Barely clearing the treetops, a U.S. Air Force Skyraider lofts a 100-pound bomb on Viet Cong guerrillas spotted by a Vietnamese forward air controller, April 1965.

LEFT: AC-1 (later C-7) Caribous taking on fuel at Korat, Thailand. With a C-47-size wingspan of just ninety-six feet—four feet fewer than the Provider's—the Caribou could deliver thirty-two soldiers, two jeeps, or two M274 Mules to even smaller and more crudely constructed strips. The popular aircraft was originally flown by Army pilots but was grudgingly turned over to the Air Force in late 1966, after a long, fractious struggle between the services. Caribous were also flown by the Australian contingent in Vietnam.

BELOW: A C-123 Provider lands on a narrow airstrip in Tay Ninh Province during Operation ATTLEBORO, November 1966. The Provider began as a 67-troop glider (XCG-18), then became a powered assault transport (XCG- 20) before going into full-scale production as a troop carrier well suited to operations on small airfields and even hastily prepared strips. C-123s were configured to dispense chemical defoliants such as Agent Orange.

RIGHT: Getting the "go" signal from the catapult officer, an F-8E Crusader pilot prepares to launch from the deck of the USS *Bon Homme Richard* en route to a target in North Vietnam, March 1967. Armed with four 20-mm cannons and an equal number of Sidewinder air-to-air missiles, this all-weather fighter was also equipped to carry up to five thousand pounds of bombs. The air war in Indochina opened with strikes by Crusaders on North Vietnamese PT boats, and it was the mainstay of the U.S. fleet's fighter operations until it was largely supplanted by the F-4B Phantom II.

CENTER: A bomb-laden U.S. Air Force F-4C Phantom flies in support of ground operations in South Vietnam, circa spring 1967. The Phantom was capable of flying at twice the speed of sound and quickly established itself as the premier air-to-air interceptor when armed with up to eight Sidewinder or Sparrow missiles, yet it could also carry sixteen thousand pounds of bombs for close air support of ground troops. The aircraft was so clearly superior that even the U.S. Air Force, in an unprecedented move, adopted the Navy jet as its standard fighter.

BOTTOM: A U.S. Navy A-7A Corsair II prepares to launch from a carrier off the coast of Vietnam. Based on the design of the Crusader, the Corsair was armed with half the number of 20-mm cannons but carried a prodigious bomb load of fifteen thousand pounds—more than twice that of a World War II–era B-17 bomber. The later A-7E in Vietnam service mounted a Vulcan multi-barrel cannon in place of the two 20-mms.

LEFT: F-105D Thunderchiefs, also known as Thuds or Lead Sleds, are refueled by a KC-135 Stratotanker while en route to North Vietnam from their base in Thailand, November 1966. Not known for its agility, the F-105 was nevertheless very fast and a solid performer capable of delivering fourteen thousand pounds of bombs on target as it bore the brunt of Air Force bombing missions into heavily defended areas of North Vietnam. The Thunderchief's air-to-air armament consisted of a Vulcan multibarrel cannon, and, although it could be armed with Sidewinder or Sparrow missiles, it generally depended on its great speed to get itself out of harm's way. Later in the war, two-seat F-105F "Wild Weasels"—with an electronic warfare officer in the "backseat"—performed superbly in the air-defense suppression role by targeting and destroying Communist radar systems and SAM sites.

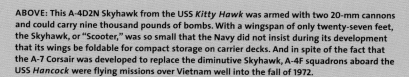

ABOVE: This A-4D2N Skyhawk from the USS *Kitty Hawk* was armed with two 20-mm cannons and could carry nine thousand pounds of bombs. With a wingspan of only twenty-seven feet, the Skyhawk, or "Scooter," was so small that the Navy did not insist during its development that its wings be foldable for compact storage on carrier decks. And in spite of the fact that the A-7 Corsair was developed to replace the diminutive Skyhawk, A-4F squadrons aboard the USS *Hancock* were flying missions over Vietnam well into the fall of 1972.

ABOVE: An A6-A Intruder taxies to a deck catapult that will launch it from the USS *Forrestal*, circa 1968. The Intruder was an all-weather ground-attack aircraft capable of dropping a remarkable seventeen thousand pounds of ordnance on target in the dead of night and during Vietnam's notorious monsoon season. The special electronics managed by a navigator/bombardier accounted for much of the aircraft's weight, and a version of the Intruder, the EA-6A, with lessened strike capability but greatly increased electronic countermeasure facilities, made its appearance late in the war. It was the predecessor to the postwar EA-6B Prowler and is most easily distinguished by the radome atop its tailfin.

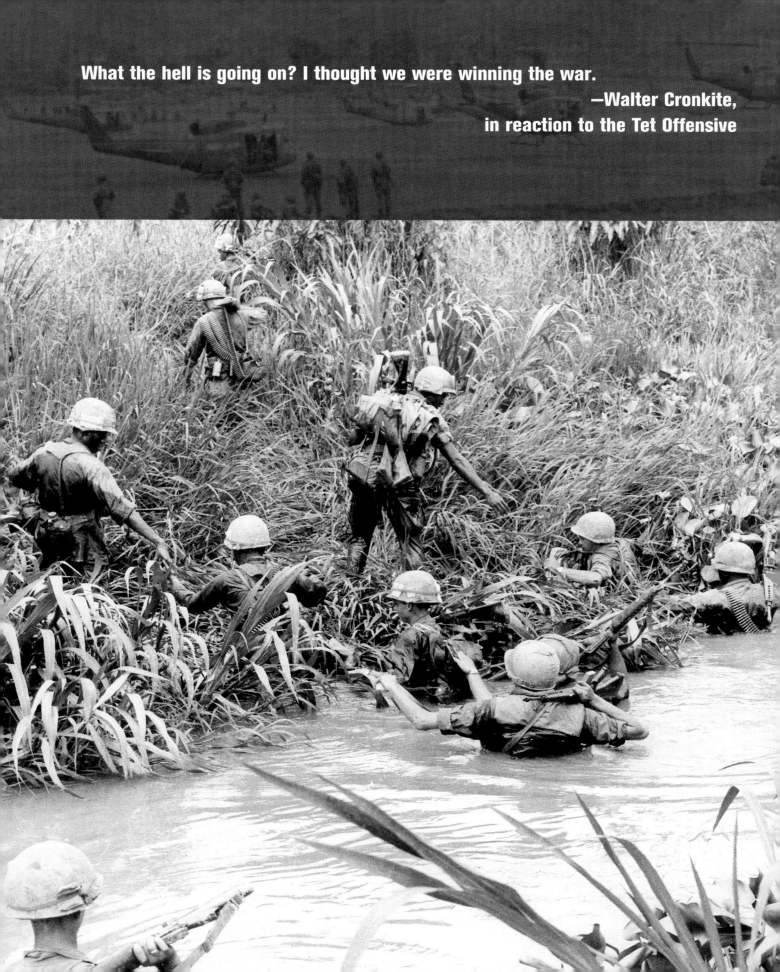

What the hell is going on? I thought we were winning the war.

—Walter Cronkite,
in reaction to the Tet Offensive

Chapter Three

LIMITATIONS ON A SUPERPOWER

While General Westmoreland was conducting large-scale search-and-destroy operations in the hinterlands of Vietnam, the Communists were active at the village level throughout South Vietnam, employing their well-practiced arts of manipulation and coercion to gain ever-greater control over the South Vietnamese people. They made their homes in the small villages of South Vietnam, allowing Viet Cong agents to gain intimate knowledge about the power structures within the hamlets and the vulnerabilities of those in charge. As a result, once the Communists declared open warfare on their own people, no one was safe. Village leaders were assassinated and friends of the United States were murdered and their homes burned. Every road, every trail became a potential ambush point or site of a booby trap meant for U.S. troops or their Vietnamese friends. The allied pacification program was foundering, a trend that increasingly concerned President Johnson and his advisors.

Pacification

Washington recognized that winning military battles was only a part of winning the war; the pacification of South Vietnam was critical to the

success of the overall war effort. Pacification, as the term was used in Vietnam, referred to the establishment of local governments at the province level that were loyal to the South Vietnamese government. The successful implementation of pacification required the destruction of the Viet Cong's illicit shadow government; the involvement of the people in the actions of the local government; the protection of the people and local leaders from Communist intimidation and reprisals; and the free flow of commerce along waterways and roads. Pacification also included nation building, the winning of the "hearts and minds" of the populace to the interests of the national government. It would entail constructing hospitals, fostering agricultural programs, and providing security in the local areas so that democratic processes might flourish. Other issues of importance were land reform, inflation control, the curbing of corruption, and increased rice production.

The Johnson administration decided to combine the war effort and the pacification effort into one office in South Vietnam, the Office of the Assistant Chief of Staff for Civil Operations and Revolutionary (later Rural) Development Support—or CORDS. Robert William "Blowtorch" Komer, a dynamic and innovative administrator, was given charge of the office on May 29, 1967. Komer was successful

PAGES 140–141: In riverine operations, infantrymen were always prepared to do plenty of wading—but hopefully not much swimming, because of their heavy rifles and other equipment.

ABOVE: In the White House, President Johnson and Special Assistant Robert W. Komer (seated) mull over the lengthening war in 1967. Komer later went to Vietnam to centralize and reinvigorate the moribund, fragmented counterinsurgency effort through his Civil Operations and Revolutionary Development Support (CORDS) program.

RIGHT: A 3d Marine Division machine gunner at Con Thien cleans the feed system of his M60, September 1967. Con Thien, and the other firebases to the east of Khe Sanh, were close enough to the DMZ to be regularly bombarded by NVA heavy artillery, making resupply problematic and forcing the periodic rationing of water. Showers and shaving became things of the past, and the men were allowed, when necessary, to sport beards.

beyond anyone's expectations. He organized an enviable relationship among MACV (the U.S. military), the South Vietnamese government, and the civilian agencies. Because of his dynamic personality and shrewdness, he invariably had General Westmoreland's support, and when Westmoreland was replaced in mid-1968, Komer gained General Creighton Abrams's support.

The success of the pacification rested upon the ability of the local militias to secure their areas. These paramilitary soldiers, Regional Forces (RFs) in the provinces and Popular Forces (PFs) at the village level, were called the Ruff-Puffs. They were initially poorly armed and trained. Under Komer and his successors at CORDS, they grew in strength from 300,000 in 1967 to 532,000 by 1971. Their arms improved from obsolete World War II rifles to M16s. Eventually, some 353 Mobile Advisory Teams trained them. Officered generally by castoffs from the regular South Vietnamese Army, they suffered more casualties than the ARVN. Even though they operated under severe handicaps, Regional and Popular forces continued to hamper VC operations and damage the Communist infrastructure. In late 1967, while the Ruff-Puffs attempted to contain the VC and National Liberation Front (NLF) in the populated parts of South Vietnam, the U.S. Army and U.S. Marines continued to pound away at NVA main force units at Con Thien, Song Be in Phuoc Long Province, Loc Ninh, and Tak To, killing more than 4,586 of the enemy. In the last engagement, four regiments of the NVA were virtually annihilated.

William C. Westmoreland

General William C. Westmoreland was born in 1914 in Spartanburg, South Carolina, a member of a distinguished family. A graduate and "First Captain" at the U.S. Military Academy in his youth, he fought in World War II and the Korean War, in which he commanded troops in North Africa, Sicily, Normandy, and Germany. By 1952, he had become a brigadier general and subsequently served as superintendent of the U.S. Military Academy, commander of the XVIII Airborne Corps, and filled high positions at the Pentagon.

In January 1964, Westmoreland became deputy commander of MACV under General Paul D. Harkins, and by June replaced Harkins as commander, MACV. Westmoreland was responsible for initiating and supervising the attrition strategy practiced in Vietnam that led to the expansion of U.S. forces in that country to 525,000 men by June 1968. Ultimately, this strategy was abandoned. During Westmoreland's watch in Vietnam, he operated within the strategic limitations placed on the U.S. military in Vietnam, which included the allowance of North Vietnamese sanctuaries in Cambodia, Laos, and North Vietnam. Arguably, these limitations led to an American defeat. Many of the faults laid at Westmoreland's doorstep can be attributed to the policies of Presidents Johnson and Nixon.

Military Assistance Command, Vietnam (MACV)

Westmoreland was removed from command of MACV in June 1968 and replaced by General Creighton W. Abrams. At that time, Westmoreland was made Chief of Staff of the U.S. Army, considered a face-saving appointment by some. Thereafter, the general was considered a political liability and had little influence on Presidents Johnson or Nixon.

LEFT: Soldiers erupt in a spirited roar of approval after a speech by General William Westmoreland, commander, MACV, commending them on their operations against the Viet Cong in Hau Nghia Province, twenty-five miles northwest of Saigon. Westmoreland (center) was at his best in these personal encounters with the troops, in this case the U.S. Army's 27th Infantry Regiment, 25th Infantry Division, the "Wolfhounds."

The Brown Water War

Along the rivers and streams of the Mekong Delta region in South Vietnam, a brown-water war existed from 1948 to 1972 that was vast in scale and deadly. The brown-water, or "riverine," war consisted of some of the same components as land war, except that rivers, streams, and creeks substituted for roads and highways, and tanks, personnel carriers, and artillery had corresponding brown-water equipment. In the Mekong Delta, where ingress and egress was extremely difficult along roads, waterways were the natural highways of commerce. They also became lines of communication along which supplies, weapons, and soldiers traveled and fought in the Delta area.

Brown-water tactics were similar to ground-force tactics, and involved close cooperation and coordination between ground and naval forces. One of the main focuses of such operations in South Vietnam was the Mekong River and its tributaries: the My Tho, Ham Luong, Go Chien, and Hou Giang (Bassac) rivers. Dense vegetation and trees, ideal for ambushes, bordered the waterways, where some 40 percent of the population of Vietnam resided. By mid-1966, one-third of these people were under VC control.

As early as 1964–65, North Vietnam had begun supplying the Viet Cong in the Mekong Delta with weapons and supplies, using junks, sampans, and other boats to transport war materiel along rivers and in international waters. On March 16, 1965, the U.S. Seventh Fleet organized Task Force (TF) 71 in an operation called MARKET TIME. The operation's purpose was to interdict the influx of enemy goods

arriving in South Vietnam through an air-sea effort. In the South China Sea, TF 71 minesweepers searched boats and seized contraband. Along inland waterways, U.S. Navy high-speed "Swift boats" and U.S. Coast Guard boats intercepted the enemy. These efforts were conducted in cooperation with the South Vietnamese Sea Force and Coastal Force. By 1966, VC supplies coming into the Mekong Delta by water were severely curtailed, and by 1968, half a million junks and sampans had been searched. While this aggravated legitimate sea traffic, the locals soon appreciated the improvement in security that resulted from the searches.

U.S. Navy ships also provided fire support to inland operations, and by 1969, the Seventh Fleet had fired more than ninety thousand projectiles at enemy targets ashore. A large number of amphibious landings were also conducted. In 1967, U.S. Marines conducted fifty-three landings in the I Corps area alone. The Marines quickly learned to lower their casualties by avoiding beach assaults. Instead, they often air-dropped behind the VC using helicopter squadrons to land six hundred men at a time, creating chaos and casualties among the enemy.

In Operation GAME WARDEN, the Navy used PBRs (river patrol boats), which moved at speeds of up to twenty-five knots and mounted three .50-caliber machine guns and a 40-mm grenade launcher. When they met heavy opposition, helicopter gunships and artillery supported the PBRs. LSTs (landing ship, troops) were used as floating bases for the PBRs and were sufficiently armed for self-protection. But the PBRs, while useful, failed to carry out their intended mission of supply interdiction and VC suppression. By 1965, there were more than 70,000 VC in the Mekong Delta. A year later, allied strength in the Delta reached 150,000; this was still not sufficient strength when applied against dedicated guerrillas familiar with the area.

In 1966, a new concept was developed:

(MDMAF), soon called the Mobile Riverine Force (MRF). It consisted of two reinforced infantry battalions (a reduced brigade) and the boats of River Flotilla One: River Assault Squadrons Nine and Eleven and River Support Squadron Seven. The force used fifty-two ATCs (armored troop carriers); ten monitors (riverine "battleships"); four CCBs (command-and-control boats); thirty-two ASPBs (assault support patrol boats); and two LCMs (landing craft, mechanized) for refueling. The U.S. Army components in the joint force were elements of the 2d Brigade, 9th Infantry Division. An aggregate of five thousand men was involved in the operations.

The MRF had two bases, a fixed one at My Tho and a Mobile Riverine Base (MRB). The latter moved periodically to new target areas, carrying with it three barracks ships, a repair ship, a tug, an LST, and a net-laying ship. Artillery barges and helicopter landing barges (platforms) were MRF operational innovations. This unique force could move one hundred to two hundred kilometers in twenty-four hours and, after anchoring, launch day or night operations in thirty minutes. Before the MRF dissolved in the summer of 1969, it had performed a number of highly successful operations.

OPPOSITE: A PBR (river patrol boat) crewman takes aim at a suspected Viet Cong ambush site along a flooded canal, October 1966. PBRs were armed with twin .50-caliber machine guns forward and a single .50-caliber aft, while the less plentiful and slightly larger PCFs (fast patrol craft, "Swift boats") mounted twin .50-caliber machine guns above a small deck house and another .50-caliber gun carried aft, with an 81-mm mortar on a common pedestal mount. Capable of twenty-four and twenty-eight knots, respectively, they sailed rings around the steel 75-ton monitors, and RPG rounds were known to pass completely through these lightly armored, fiberglass- or aluminum-hulled craft without exploding. Unlike the ARVN, which contained numerous motivated and well-led units, the South Vietnamese Navy was at the bottom of the funding and personnel chains. Consequently, their riverine forces were less aggressively handled than that of their American counterparts, but still provided a valuable guard and reaction force along the inland waterways.

LEFT: One of the many motor gunboats used to supplement, and ultimately replace, the various French-built river patrol craft is delivered to the South Vietnamese Navy, May 1967.

ABOVE: A South Vietnamese "baby monitor" plows through the receding waves of an ocean-going ship in the major shipping channel to Saigon, circa spring 1966.

TOP LEFT: Navy ATCs could ferry forty or more troops into battle and were armed with one 20-mm cannon and two .50-caliber machine guns in individual turrets on a raised superstructure. Their distinctive sectional canvas roofing provided the troops some protection from the equatorial sun and rain. The ATCs plied the Delta at speeds of up to eight knots.

BOTTOM LEFT: Like the ATCs, the monitor gunboats were modified LCMs. But while the aft portion of a monitor carried the same weaponry as its cousin, a pedestal-mounted 81-mm mortar was sited amidships, and an armored turret behind the monitor's "spoon bow" contained a quick-firing 40-mm gun and a .50-caliber machine gun. Craft armed with a pair of flamethrower turrets in place of the 81-mm mortar were called Zippo Monitors, and the comparatively quiet ASPBs (assault support patrol boats) were purpose-built monitors not derived from LCMs. All riverine craft of these types were fitted with an outer screen of bar armor that allowed maximum visibility and ventilation while minimizing the effectiveness of armor-piercing RPGs.

LEFT, INSET: A freshly painted LSIL (landing ship, infantry, large) left over from French colonial days patrols the main shipping channel between Saigon Harbor and the South China Sea. Originally an American-built LCI (landing craft, infantry), this could be one of several such vessels turned over to the French by the British in 1946. It is armed with a 76-mm gun, a 40-mm Bofors, two 20-mm Oerlikons, plus multiple machine guns and heavy mortars.

BELOW: A row of ATCs and an LCM lie moored to barracks ship USS *Benewah* in the Mekong Delta region south of Saigon, September 1967.

RIGHT: The "mothership" USS *Harnett County* lies anchored in the brown water of the Mekong Delta, one of four LSTs pulled out of mothballs and converted to patrol craft tenders (AGPs) supporting riverine and 9th Infantry Division operations in the Delta. Two other LSTs were converted to barracks ships capable of housing more than eleven hundred servicemen; containing evaporators that could produce up to forty thousand gallons of fresh water daily; a sixteen-bed hospital with X-ray, dental, and bacteriological facilities; in addition to a laundry, library, and tailor shop. All living and many working spaces were air-conditioned. The extra booms attached to the *Harnett's* port side allow its PBR squadron to moor alongside, and a Huey sits at the edge of the ship's broad landing pad that, in an emergency, could handle the operation of two helicopters simultaneously when additional deck space was cleared.

BELOW: A UH-1H Huey of the 9th Aviation Battalion prepares to set down on the sixteen-square-foot landing pad of an ATC(H) (armored troop carrier with helipad) during Operation CORONADO I, July 26, 1967.

BELOW: ATCs transporting soldiers of the 2d Brigade, 9th Infantry Division, carefully thread their way through a canal near Dong Tam, September 1967. Submerged mines and ambushes were a constant threat in such restricted waterways.

INSET: The recovered hulk of an LCVP (landing craft, vehicle and personnel) destroyed by a mine during operations in the Mekong Delta.

RIGHT: U.S. soldiers take a break in front of a bunker. The homemade sign above the entrance proclaims, "Home is where you dig it."

BELOW: U.S. Marines keep their weapons and an extra radio battery pack dry as they ford a stream. Both Marines have attached native grasses to their helmets to break up their outlines.

The Tet Offensive

In late January 1968, General Vo Nguyen Giap, the victorious commander over the French at Dien Bien Phu in 1954, began the Tet Offensive. To prepare his army for this effort, Giap had for some time been secretly massing Viet Cong soldiers, supplies, and armaments across the length of Vietnam. The attack would be widespread and conceived in such a way as to create panic and confusion among the U.S. and South Vietnamese armed forces, to foment a popular uprising among the unaligned South Vietnamese, and perhaps stir pandemonium within the U.S. news media. Even if the offensive failed to achieve all its tactical goals, sudden violent assaults, conducted countrywide, might still create a major North Vietnamese psychological victory by undermining the American public's willingness to continue the war.

By mid-January, it was clear that the volume of traffic on the Ho Chi Minh Trail was reaching astounding levels: seven NVA regiments from three divisions had taken up positions on both sides of the Laotian–South Vietnamese border. NVA commandos were also infiltrating South Vietnamese cities hidden aboard wagons of farm produce, where they carried their weapons and supplies. While the U.S. news media, prompted by the Johnson administration, was heralding one U.S. victory in the war after another and seemed oblivious to serious threats to the allied war effort, General Westmoreland, by the end of January, had canceled all active military operations and was preparing for a major enemy offensive. He expected the attack around the time of Tet, Vietnam's festive lunar New Year holiday. But no one, not the South Vietnamese nor the Americans, expected the attack precisely during Tet. American intelligence also had no idea exactly where the attacks would occur.

At 0300 hours on January 30, NVA forces attacked six cities and towns in the center of South Vietnam. All of the attacks were driven back. U.S. intelligence immediately recognized these aborted attacks as miscalculations. Giap, it was confirmed later, had originally ordered the attacks to occur on January 30. At the last

minute, he had moved the attack time to January 31. His unresponsive communication network, however, had failed to inform all of his units of the change. This tipped his hand, costing his offensive the key element of surprise. After the initial attacks, U.S. units were put on maximum alert and warned of the likely continuation of attacks.

The South Vietnamese began their Tet festivities and fireworks despite the fighting. The Americans dug in, expecting a battle. The next day, January 31, a large force consisting of some eighty thousand NVA and VC soldiers and cadres launched a countrywide offensive on more than forty cities and towns in South Vietnam. In one of the largest attacks thus far in the war, the Communists attacked Saigon, Quang Tri, Hue, Da Nang, Nha Trang, Qui Nhon, Kontum City, Ban Me Thuot, My Tho, Can Tho, and Ben Tre. Most of the attacks were quickly repelled, but significant fighting continued for

BELOW: A rocket attack on Da Nang Air Base announces the start of the Tet Offensive in Vietnam's northern provinces, January 30, 1968.

up to a month afterward at Hue, Khe Sanh, and elsewhere. One of the failed but high-visibility attacks was that by a VC hit squad on the U.S. Embassy in Saigon. A radio station, the presidential palace, and the headquarters of the general staff and navy were also assaulted.

During the various attacks, the VC suffered disastrous casualties among their regular soldiers and especially their political cadre—perhaps as many as forty thousand dead. The Communists had expected a widespread uprising by the South Vietnamese people against their government, but this failed to materialize. However, because of the way Tet was reported in the press and on television in the United States, it had an immense impact on U.S. governmental leaders and the American people and resulted in a major North Vietnamese psychological victory that affected the war's outcome.

Before the Tet Offensive, U.S. soldiers, like Tunnel Rat Gerry Schooler, began discovering caches of equipment hidden in underground caves.

So they [the Viet Cong] had to pretty much either carry what they needed or stockpile it and come back to it. That's one of the things they used the tunnels for: they'd stockpile stuff everywhere. It was very common to find a small tunnel entrance, explore it, and find a cache with maybe thirty or forty weapons; I'm talking about brand-new AK-47s, usually bathed in grease and wrapped in plastic.

They would just put them in a little cutaway inside of the tunnel and leave them there for future reference, along with muni-

tions. One of the things that we didn't realize in November and December of 1967 was that the Tet Offensive was going to use these weapons at the end of January 1968. So we started finding a lot more of those areas, like the Ho Bo Woods in the Iron Triangle, which were staging areas for the Viet Cong.

People wondered why we didn't find big caches, ones that had thousands of weapons in them. I think the VC thought they needed to spread their weapons and supplies out, so that one or a number of lucky finds didn't immobilize their whole project.

—Gerry Schooler

U.S. Marine scout sniper Charles "Chuck" Mawhinney recalls enemy activity during Tet. Sometimes, as he and his spotter proceeded stealthily through the nocturnal world of the sniper, they were called upon to kill their enemies at long range, aided by a telescopic sight and a see-in-the-dark "Starlight" scope. With these tools of his trade, Mawhinney visited instant, unexpected death upon the Viet Cong and the NVA.

If anything ever went right for me as a sniper, it did in this one instance, the night when I set up along a river. We were probably three hundred to five hundred meters in from the riverbank. It was getting late that evening. It was February 14, 1968. I remember that day because it was Valentine's Day. That evening, right before dusk—it was during the 1968 Tet Offensive—our observation aircraft flew over and said there was a large, large number of NVA regulars across the river moving towards our position.

1ST INFANTRY DIVISION

The 1st Infantry Division, the "Big Red One," arrived in Vietnam from Fort Riley, Kansas, on October 2, 1965, and served through 1967 in the III Corps Tactical Zone, where it fought the 9th Viet Cong Division. From September 14 to November 24, 1966, it engaged in combat in the largest operation to date in Vietnam: Operation ATTLEBORO, in Tay Ninh Province. From February through May 1967, the division and other units fought the Communists in Operation JUNCTION CITY. During Tet, the division bolstered Saigon's sagging defenses, and, by March 1968, the division was situated near Lai Khe, where it conducted pacification operations. The Big Red One, in July 1969, participated with ARVN soldiers in a war effort described as Dong Tien (Progress Together), and, by April 1970, the division had returned to Fort Riley, Kansas.

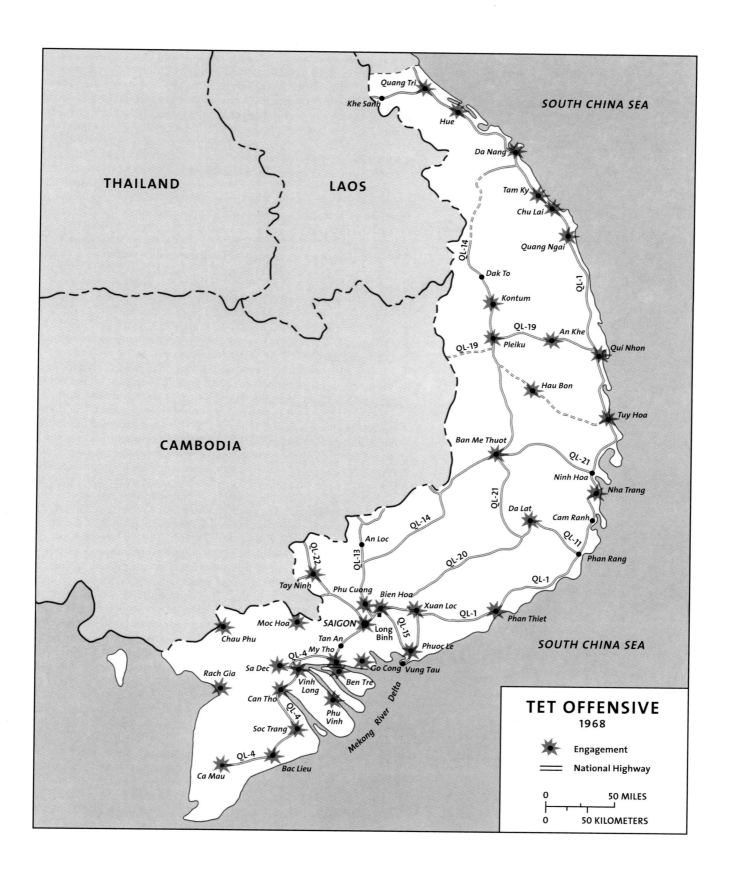

SOUTH CHINA SEA

THAILAND

LAOS

Quang Tri

Khe Sanh

Hue

Da Nang

Tam Ky

Chu Lai

QL-14

Quang Ngai

QL-1

Dak To

Kontum

QL-19

An Khe

QL-19

Pleiku

Qui Nhon

Hau Bon

Tuy Hoa

CAMBODIA

Ban Me Thuot

QL-21

Ninh Hoa

QL-21

Da Lat

Nha Trang

Cam Ranh

QL-11

An Loc

QL-14

QL-13

Phan Rang

QL-22

QL-20

QL-1

Tay Ninh

Phu Cuong

Bien Hoa

Xuan Loc

QL-1

Moc Hoa

SAIGON

Long Binh

QL-15

Phan Thiet

Chau Phu

Tan An

Phuoc Le

SOUTH CHINA SEA

My Tho

Go Cong

Vung Tau

QL-4

Rach Gia

Sa Dec

Ben Tre

Vinh Long

Mekong River Delta

Can Tho

QL-4

Phu Vinh

Soc Trang

QL-4

Ca Mau

Bac Lieu

TET OFFENSIVE

1968

⬟ Engagement

══ National Highway

0   50 MILES

0   50 KILOMETERS

ABOVE, LEFT: Raquel Welch is joined by GIs pulled (willingly, one presumes) from the throng attending the Bob Hope show at Da Nang, December 18, 1967. Her husband, Marine F-4 pilot Patrick Curtis, later described himself as "just another clown in green" as he sat ten rows back from the stage. Curtis, however, had played the infant Beau Wilkes in *Gone With the Wind* and grew up four doors down from Bob Hope. Much to the pilot's horror, Hope pointed out Curtis and introduced him as Welch's husband. The resultant booing from eighty-five thousand envious U.S. servicemen was deafening. Curtis was later shot down on his 284th mission and spent many months in a Navy hospital.

ABOVE, RIGHT: John Wayne, seen here during the filming of *The Green Berets*, made several trips to Vietnam. The "NVA general" in this scene was played by a U.S. Army major named William K.S. Olds, of Honolulu, Hawaii.

RIGHT: Evangelist Dr. Billy Graham crosses paths with Bob Hope at Qui Nhon Airfield during one of Graham's trips to "minister to our troops by my prayers and spiritual help."

So that evening, I sat down with the company commander and asked him if we could take our Starlight scope and go down to the river and observe the area where the NVA were operating. He gave us permission, so we left the lines and went down there. It was one of the pitch-perfect places where the river had receded a place, like you've seen how a river cuts out, eddies into the bank. It gave us some cover, and we dropped down there with the Starlight scope that night. The river was probably a hundred and ten yards wide, but very shallow in that area because the river had widened out. We sat down there that evening with the Starlight scope for a couple hours. We started noticing the enemy moving a little bit on the other side of the river.

To my surprise, an NVA scout walked across the river and came out probably within twenty or thirty yards of me. He walked clear across the river and never had to swim. At one time, the water was about up to his neck, but he didn't have to swim. He walked out on the bank on the side next to us, and he was close enough that night that I could hear the water dripping off of him; that's how close he was. I had the M14 on him, the Starlight on him. I had a 20-round clip in it, and I had the rifle on semiautomatic.

He walked up onto the bank, looked around, and then he started towards the high grass, the elephant grass. Probably there was ten feet of shore until you got into the elephant grass. That's where my company was, in this elephant grass, back in there five hundred or six hundred meters. The NVA scout started towards the elephant grass, and I started to go ahead and just pass him [kill him] because I couldn't let him get between the company and me. But right before I fired, he stopped at the edge of the elephant grass. He stood there for a moment, walked back down by the bank, and then he decided to cross the river again and go back.

So we let him cross the river, and I told my partner, "You know, this might get real interesting." Well, it did. Later that evening, here they came. They were probably ten feet apart. An entire line of NVA started across the river, on the same route the scout had taken earlier. They had all their gear on, their packs on, and were holding their rifles up. They started to cross the river. As soon as the first one started up the bank on our side, I went to work. I got sixteen rounds off that night as fast as I could fire the weapon.

ABOVE: A U.S. Army tank firing from behind dirt revetments pounds enemy positions near Highway 19E during the Tet Offensive. A jet aircraft streaks toward the same target. Air-ground actions took a terrible toll on the Viet Cong during Tet, depleting their ranks and causing their morale to plummet. At the same time, news media in the United States trumpeted the story that Tet was a massive Communist military victory.

He walked out on the bank on the side next to us, and he was close enough that night that I could hear the water dripping off of him. . . . I had the M14 on him, the Starlight on him. I had a 20-round clip in it, and I had the rifle on semiautomatic.

—Charles "Chuck" Mawhinney

25TH INFANTRY DIVISION

The 25th Infantry Division was sent to Vietnam in 1963, and, by December 1965, its 3d Brigade was posted in the highlands near Pleiku. When the rest of the 25th Infantry arrived in Vietnam, in early 1966, the division was deployed against the enemy in the III Corps Tactical Zone along the Cambodian border and in the Saigon area. In January 1967, the 25th was engaged in operations in the Iron Triangle, northwest of Saigon. It later participated in Operation JUNCTION CITY, February 22–May 14, 1967. During the Tet Offensive in 1968, the division fought in the Saigon vicinity. Later, it conducted operations in the Cu Chi area, and, in spring 1970, the division advanced into Cambodia searching for NVA sanctuaries. By December 1970, most of the 25th Infantry Division had withdrawn from Vietnam.

Every one of them was a head shot, dead center. Next, the soldiers started drawing small-arms fire from the other side of the bank because the NVA there didn't know what was going on; all they could hear was shooting. I could see these bodies floating down the river. They started drawing more small-arms fire, and we retreated and went back to our company. The enemy never did cross the river that night.

—Charles "Chuck" Mawhinney

 *General Bruce Palmer Jr. worked with General Westmoreland in several roles, including the position of Westmoreland's U.S. Army deputy and as commander of II Field Force, Vietnam. Palmer knew Westmoreland intimately.*

[Westmoreland] rose to high rank through outstanding performance in World War II and the Korean War.... [He was a] shrewdly calculating, prudent commander who chose the ... conservative course. Faultlessly attired,

Westmoreland constantly worried about his public image and assiduously courted the press.... [He] liked to stand on the hood of a jeep and gather a relatively large group of soldiers, preferably paratroopers, around him.... Correctly formal, with his emotions under tight control, Westmoreland was predictable in manner.... [Ultimately, Westmoreland became] a national scapegoat, blamed for everything that went wrong in Vietnam.

—General Bruce Palmer Jr.,
U.S. Army, Retired, in *The 25-Year War: America's Military Role in Vietnam*

The Siege of Khe Sanh

One of the most violent battles during the Tet Offensive occurred at Khe Sanh, in the I Corps region of South Vietnam, not far from the DMZ and North Vietnam. As early as November 1967, U.S. intelligence detected NVA divisions moving southward toward the DMZ. Two of

RIGHT: A U.S. Marine surrounded by sandbags talks on his landline to other Marines on the base during the siege of Khe Sanh. The NVA had to abort the siege after the military situation in Hue and elsewhere demanded greater support. Rumors circulated, not completely unfounded, that if the Communists made an all-out attempt to take Khe Sanh, a nuclear response was possible.

these divisions, the 304th and the 325C NVA, appeared to be headed toward Khe Sanh. Two other NVA divisions, the 320th and a regiment of the 324th, were moving in the same direction. They eventually set up within supporting distance (twelve miles) of the 324th and 325C divisions outside of Khe Sanh, giving General Giap a total of some thirty thousand to forty thousand available men. U.S. and ARVN forces in Khe Sanh consisted of only six thousand Marines and ARVN rangers commanded by U.S. Marine Colonel David E. Lownds.

On January 2, 1968, the two opposing forces made first contact when a six-man enemy patrol led by an NVA regimental commander was detected while on a reconnaissance mission outside of Khe Sanh. Marines killed all but one of the patrol members. On January 20, the Marines captured an NVA deserter who told them that an attack on Hills 881N and 861 was scheduled for that night. At 0530 the next morning, small-arms fire, rockets, artillery, and mortars pounded the Marine base. During the attack, their ammunition depot blew up.

Meanwhile, Khe Sanh Village, some two or three miles away, was overrun, and heavy fighting broke out on Hill 861 until Marines cleared it of the enemy. On the same day, General Westmoreland ordered Operation Niagara implemented. This action brought B-52 aircraft into the struggle, as well as already available tactical air units, artillery, and mortars. The 1st Battalion, 9th Marines, reported to Lownds on January 22 and manned the southwest perimeter of the base. On January 27, the ARVN 37th Ranger Battalion arrived and was placed on the eastern edge of the base defenses.

A Special Forces camp at Lang Vei, five miles southwest of Khe Sanh, was virtually destroyed by PT-76 tanks on February 7, and, on the next day, the 1st Battalion, 9th Marines, was overrun by an NVA battalion. The Marines counterattacked and drove the enemy from their positions, killing 150 of them. Giap's plan was to assault Khe Sanh with the 304th Division attacking along an axis from Lang Vei to Khe Sanh Village. Then, at the appropriate time, the final assault would penetrate Khe Sanh from

BELOW: U.S. Marine machine gunners lie atop trench cover as they search for enemy movement. Stopping an 82-mm mortar round was the minimum requirement for overhead cover. It was determined that one layer of runway matting overlaid by two or three layers of sandbags and loose dirt would fit the bill. Inside, bunkers had six-by-six-inch timbers in each corner and in the center for support. The NVA in Laos, however, fired artillery rounds of up to 130-mm and 152-mm that could easily penetrate any bunker on the base, and even a dud could be driven four feet into the hard, red earth.

Marines of a signals or headquarters unit near the Demilitarized Zone hug the earth as incoming rounds explode nearby during 1968. Fire bases established as much as two years earlier by the 3d Marine division along Route 9 (which generally paralleled the DMZ separating North and South Vietnam) extended from Khe Sanh in the west through The Rockpile, Ca Lu, Camp Carrol, Cam Lo, Guo Linh, and Cua Viet in the east. Often the scenes of fierce fighting, these bases were well within the range of heavy artillery situated in North Vietnam and Laos.

the south and west and capture it. Suddenly, Giap changed his plan. Some military commentators say a crisis developed at Hue that caused him to withdraw five of his battalions for battle there. Whatever the reason, artillery and mortar fire continued to rain down relentlessly on Khe Sanh, with more than thirteen hundred rounds dropping on the base on February 23. Lownds expected a ground attack at any moment.

On February 29, acoustic and seismic sensors detected enemy troop movements east of Khe Sanh. The Marines responded by showering artillery rounds on the area. In addition, radar-equipped fighters strafed and dropped bombs on the area. An NVA assault on the ARVN 37th Rangers' position was destroyed by these attacks before it reached the wire entanglements surrounding the base. Another NVA attack at 2330 hours was decimated, and a following assault at 0315 hours was crushed as well. This last assault seemed to finish the NVA, for on March 11 they began withdrawing. On April 1, Lownds's Marines and the ARVN rangers were relieved by the U.S. 1st Cavalry Division (Airmobile).

Much speculation has been made concerning why Giap withdrew from Khe Sanh without making a Dien Binh Phu–like attempt to capture it. Some analysts say the horrendous air and artillery fire U.S. forces rained down on his troops made capturing the base too costly. Others, however, have noted that the Communists may have been aware of talks between General Westmoreland and President Johnson concerning the use of an atomic weapon against Giap's troops if they massed to take the base.

3D MARINE DIVISION

In June 1965, the 3d Marine Division arrived in Vietnam and assumed the mission of protecting the air base at Da Nang. The Marines subsequently began attacking Viet Cong–infested villages in the area. By 1967, the division was fighting conventional operations near the Special Forces camp at Khe Sanh and in the eastern DMZ, where it created strongpoints, sensors, and obstacles impeding North Vietnamese incursions into the South. During the Tet Offensive in 1968, NVA attacks against northern population centers were repulsed by the Marines, except at Hue, where the Leathernecks fought bitter house-to-house engagements before ejecting the NVA. Meanwhile, at Khe Sanh, the Communists besieged the Marines for seventy-seven days before the 1st Cavalry Division broke the encirclement. By 1969, the 3d Marine Division had retired to Okinawa.

RIGHT: A U.S. Marine stands watch on an observation tower as a chaplain holds Mass on Hill 950, July 31, 1967. The hill, north of the U.S. Marine base at Khe Sanh, was one of the key defenses for that base in Quang Tri Province. A fierce firefight occurred on the hill in 1967, fought by members of the 1st Battalion, 26th Marines, against Communist forces.

The U.S. Marines were stationed at Khe Sanh to give muscle to U.S. defenses along the DMZ. The Marines, elite troops, are given more rigorous training than ordinary soldiers and, for that reason, have a high reputation for stern discipline while under heavy fire. They were ideal for the role of meeting main force NVA units. Marine morale is inculcated in them from the start of their training. Thus, Charles "Chuck" Mawhinney, a Marine scout sniper in Vietnam, felt fully prepared for combat.

I was pretty much conditioned for what was going to be in boot camp. I pretty much had an idea what was going to happen. I had friends that had gone in before me that explained what was happening. It was all I expected it to be. It was a good conditioning program; it was good training. They were also working hard on the Vietnam conflict that was going on. So there was a lot of that added in to our basic training. They explained some of the training, some of the techniques, the reason for the physical conditioning, the reason that we were doing some of the exercises we were doing. When we got to Vietnam, we'd be conditioned and be able to maintain and hold our own. After boot camp, after basic training, they gave the people that qualified as "expert" with the rifle an opportunity to go to the Scout Sniper School that the Marines had just started.

I probably went through the fourth or fifth school. We had about a 50 percent washout rate in Scout Sniper School. But the school was condensed down to about three and a half weeks at that time. So it was a very tedious school. We ran from daylight till dark and then into the night. Sometimes, days would go by with only an hour or two of sleep for us.

—Charles "Chuck" Mawhinney

Another Marine, Bernard Jones, enlisted in the Corps on March 18, 1965, when he was seventeen years old. He describes his harsh training more graphically. The outcome of the training was the molding of intrepid fighters.

It was quite a jolt to the system—in your face. The first night I was there, I asked myself, "What the hell did I do to deserve this?" But everyone gets the same treatment. You did what you were told, and if you didn't, you paid for it. I remember we were on the parade deck one day and were at ease. We weren't supposed to move, but a mosquito bit me, and I slapped it. The sergeant came over to me and told me to meet him in his office when the parade was over. Another guy had done the same thing, and we went over to the office together. The sergeant told us to face each other. He told me to punch the guy that was with me in the stomach as hard as I could. We had to punch each other. It didn't hurt too much, but we were a little sore the next day. But if you slapped a mosquito in the jungle, you could get killed.

I was on the firing line one day, and I forgot to put the safety on my rifle when I was supposed to. The sergeant came over and realized what I had done. He pulled the bolt back and had me put my thumb in [the receiver]. He let the bolt slam a couple of times. Blood was running out of my thumb, and now I have an M14 thumb; I never forgot to put my safety on again.

—Bernard Jones

BELOW: An ABC television news crew covers the arrival of a U.S. Marine convoy at the "Rock Pile," near Khe Sanh. The seven-hundred-foot-high Rock Pile was used as an artillery site when the siege of Khe Sanh was lifted during Operation PEGASUS, in April 1968, by the 1st Cavalry Division (Airmobile) with the help of five Marine battalions, mostly from the 26th Marines.

RIGHT: Sergeant James Fenling, of Brooklyn, New York, catches a few winks during 173d Airborne Brigade operations near Bong Son, November 4, 1968.

BELOW: During the Tet Offensive, April 3, 1968, U.S. Marines riding atop an M48 tank cover their ears as their gunner fires 90-mm rounds at the enemy.

> **For me, the war in Vietnam broke me, almost killed me, but medics helped me get strong at the broken places.**
>
> **—Senator Max Cleland**

MAX CLELAND

Lieutenant (and later U.S. Senator) Max Cleland, 1st Cavalry Division (Airmobile), arrived in Khe Sanh in early 1968 to relieve the siege. Armed to the teeth in his flak vest and steel pot, and with his M16 in his left hand and grenades on his web gear, he was ready to fight. Tragically, one of his grenades became detached from his gear, fell to the ground, and exploded, blowing off an arm and both his legs. Only quick action by Navy medics who were present saved his life.

My flak jacket, my flak vest, helped save me. My steel pot was blown off, and my left hand was saved because it was behind me. It was holding my M16. My right arm was blown off instantly; my right leg was blown off instantly, and my left leg was so mangled it was amputated within the hour. So there I am, lying on the ground, my windpipe shattered. I can't speak, I can't talk, and I'm lying on the ground bleeding and dying. Well, unbeknownst to me, a team of four Navy medical corpsmen attached to the Marine Corps were right there on that hill. I mean, Providence, the good Lord, was looking after me. There were four medics, not just one but four, right there on that hill, and they rushed to me.

I can remember when they started cutting off my uniform. I thought, you know, the military uniform is sacrosanct. I thought, here I am, missing almost two legs and my right arm, and I'm thinking, "God, don't cut off my uniform."

But the team knew what they were doing. So they started cutting off my uniform to make a tourniquet to stop the bleeding. They called in an immediate Dustoff, or helicopter, a Huey. That was, in effect, my lifeline, but while I was lying there, they took care of me and made sure I got on the medevac helicop-

ter that got me to the division aid station. There, other medics took over. I had an IV put in while I was in the chopper on the way to the bunker, and one shot of morphine. They started asking my name, rank, and service number, and I'm thinking, "You've got to be kidding me, man." I guess it was, you know, we've got to tag this body properly. So I looked up at one medic and said, "Do you think I'm going to make it?" He said, "You just might." I figured, under the circumstances, it was a word of encouragement.

So I was put on a helicopter again and flown to a Quonset hut on the South China Sea. All of this was done within an hour, and a team of five surgeons saved my life. But it was the medics that got to me first, and it was the medics in the helicopter that got the IV in, and it was the medics in the bunker in the division aid station that I think ultimately saved my life.

[Cleland added, quoting author Ernest Hemingway]: "The world breaks us all. But afterward, many are strong in the broken places." For me, the war in Vietnam broke me, almost killed me, but medics helped me get strong at the broken places.

> —Senator (then Lieutenant) Max Cleland,
> 1st Cavalry Division (Airmobile)

The I Corps region in the northern part of South Vietnam had been a hotbed of enemy activity even two years before the Tet Offensive. In the late fall of 1965, First Lieutenant "Barney" Barnum, a forward observer for the Marines, got his baptism of fire in the I Corps region as part of Operation HARVEST MOON. When his rifle company commander was shot during an ambush of their column, the young lieutenant assumed command.

HARVEY C. BARNUM JR.

This was a major ambush. The first thing I noticed when I looked up from underneath my helmet and found myself on the deck were all these young Marines looking at me, almost saying, "Okay, lieutenant, what the hell are we going to do now?" And the first thing I did with my radio operator and scout sergeant was to contact the artillery, and we went into motion.

I couldn't bring the rounds right where I wanted them on a couple of positions because they were a little erratic, especially at the maximum range. I had enemy on three sides of me, so I fired on two sides. I was given some helicopter gunships that I utilized on the right side. The enemy to my right was where I launched a counterattack. I had my hands full.

This was the first time in the Vietnam War, and this was in 1965, that an enemy regiment with shoulder patches, uniforms, and the whole bit had come in contact with us. When the ambush was triggered, they were smart, they picked out that company commander of mine, with a map in his hand and a radio operator behind him with that big-whip antenna.

The first round that triggered the ambush hit and mortally wounded my commander and killed his radio operator. Maybe a half hour into the battle, after I went out and brought him back, he died in my arms. I took over the rifle company. It all goes back to every Marine is a rifleman first. Every Marine officer is a lieutenant of Marines.

Yeah, we got out alive. They figured my company overcame ten-to-one odds. We did it as a team. There were no superstars that day.

I'll tell you, they did anything I asked them to do when I asked. If somebody got shot doing it, then someone else was there ready to do it. It just shows that teamwork overcomes. I'll tell you, you get Marines, when they see their buddies shot up, they're fired up. It's a pretty strong motivator.

So the artillery, at that point, was my third priority. My first priority was the infantry, running the infantry company. Then, when I had the helicopter gunships come on, I had them right there, and they could fire at exactly what I wanted them to, and they were of great benefit.

You know, when you're in combat, you're directing, you're leading, and you're not thinking about yourself. You're thinking about doing your job. All these young Marines are looking at you, and they're ready to do something, but they're scared, and you've got to point them in the right direction, get them moving, and then you don't need a bullwhip on them, you just need to guide them and be out there in front of them. You know, it's not "Go do this!" It's "Follow me!" [It was a case of] supporting the young Marines and the great corpsmen I had with me, leading by example, standing up and doing things, and using common sense. If something didn't work, I tried something else. You know, we didn't stop; we never stopped. I had to make some tough decisions, and when I ran one counterattack to our right flank with a platoon, I had some people shot up.

But I knew if I didn't do that, they were going to get us. Later on into the battle, we were running low on ammunition. We were

All these young Marines are looking at you, and they're ready to do something, but they're scared, and you've got to point them in the right direction, get them moving. . . . You know, it's not "Go do this!" It's "Follow me!"

—Harvey C. "Barney" Barnum Jr.

cut off five hundred meters from the rest of the unit, and the battalion commander says, "You've got to come out. We can't come get you. If you don't come out, you're going to be in there by yourself tonight." I knew that if we were there by ourselves that night, it was all over, so I made some decisions.

The first thing I did was to have the engineers blow some trees down so I could bring in helicopters to take out the dead and the wounded. Then, I had everyone drop their packs in a pile, and we blew them up. Every piece of unusable equipment, we blew it up to make ourselves light for the breakout.

So I got everyone together, and I said, "Okay, we're going to go in squad rushes, and we'll set up a base of fire. After one squad goes, and they get across, the next one [goes] high-diddle-diddle. If someone is shot, you pick him up. We're not leaving anybody on the battlefield." That's what happened.

Someone got shot, two guys picked him up, and we just did it. I never ran so goddamned fast in my life, but I was the last one out.

Then, when I got out, the first thing the battalion commander said to me when I got over there was do you have everybody. We made a count and I had everybody. The dead and the wounded that didn't get out on the helicopter, we brought with us. Needless to say, there were a couple of supply officers, when it was all over, who were a little upset that I blew up some of their equipment. But we blew it up so that the bad guys couldn't capture it and use it. The same was true of our personal packs. A lot of guys afterwards were complaining that they had pictures of their wives in their wallets and stuff. Then someone said, "But we're alive."

—Colonel Harvey C. "Barney" Barnum Jr.,
U.S. Marine Corps, Retired,
Medal of Honor recipient

BELOW: To provide greater accuracy and to reduce his exposure to the enemy, a 9th Marines rifleman of the 3d Marine Division returns fire from the kneeling position during Operation PRAIRIE II, north of Cam Lo, March 2, 1967.

BELOW: In this dramatic image, U.S. Marines pick their way carefully through the wreckage of war as they use the cramped passageways between houses for protection from snipers, Hue, February 17, 1968.

Hue

The city of Hue, population one hundred thousand, was one of the principal targets of the Tet Offensive. Two-thirds of Hue lay inside the walls of the Citadel, the old imperial capital on the north bank of the Huong River; the other third was on the south bank. The city lay sixty-two miles south of the DMZ and six miles from the South China Sea. A long bridge connected its two sections. The Citadel, as its name implies, was originally a fortress encircled on all sides by a moat, or channel. The moat, moreover, was bordered by massive stone walls, forming a formidable defensive structure.

On January 31, 1968, at 0340 hours, NVA and VC forces attacked with seven to ten battalions supported by rockets and mortars. Concealed by fog, the Communists easily infiltrated the city with the help of collaborators and seized most of Hue, including the Citadel. Brigadier General Ngo Quang Truong, the commanding general of the South's 1st Vietnamese Army Infantry Division, managed to hold off the enemy in his part of the Citadel with only his headquarters staff until the Hoc Boa, or Black Panther Company, the division's reaction force, reached him. Ultimately, Truong

was able to hold only the headquarters area in the Citadel, the rest being occupied by the 6th NVA Regiment and the 12th NVA Sapper Battalion. Meanwhile, the 4th NVA Regiment mounted an attack against the MACV compound in southern Hue, which fended off the strike until relieved by elements of the 1st Marine Division. After an enemy assault on the compound by mortars and rockets, the 804th NVA Battalion attacked from the southeast but was driven back by the Americans.

By the next morning, a red-and-blue banner affixed with a gold star, the flag of the Viet Cong, flew from atop the Citadel. But the MACV and the ARVN division headquarters were still operating. Moreover, South Vietnamese Regional and Popular Force units, though surrounded, were still viable, and the 1st Signal Brigade's important multichannel rapid-relay complex was operating and providing communications links to Khe Sanh and Hue. All entrances to Hue, however, were blocked to allied reinforcements. They would have to break into the city.

With this mission in mind, the 1st Marine Division ordered the 1st Marine Regiment to Hue, and General Truong committed his 3d Regiment, 1st Airborne Task Force, and 3d Troop, 7th Cavalry, to the rescue of the besieged units. When these forces reached Hue from the north, the 806th NVA Battalion met them in a blocking position on Highway 1. South of Hue, the 804th NVA Battalion, with Company B, Sapper Battalion, and K4B Battalion, blocked the way, with the 810th defending in the southwest. U.S. forces barged through this blockade and proceeded toward the Citadel, encountering intense fire along the way. During the next few days, these forces received added support from the Command Group, 1st Marines; two other Marine command groups; three Marine companies; a Marine regimental command group; and a Marine tank platoon.

During the period of February 13 to 23, the battle for Hue raged on, reminiscent of the street fighting in World War II. In a close struggle, U.S. and South Vietnamese marines and the ARVN 1st Division assaulted the enemy across the breadth of the Citadel. Supporting the allied battle to drive the enemy from their entrenched positions were naval and ground artillery. A violent surprise attack against the enemy on February 23 to 24 by the ARVN 2d Battalion, 3d Regiment, forced the enemy to retreat, and at 0500 hours on February 24, the South Vietnamese red-and-yellow flag replaced the Viet Cong flag atop the Citadel. Following an artillery attack the next day, the enemy's last position was overrun. The battle for the recapture of Hue was over.

The devastating toll of the battle became apparent days later: some 8,000 NVA and VC soldiers were killed, and some 116,000 citizens in Hue were made homeless. But that was only a part of the loss. During the Communist occupation, 5,800 civilians in the city, as well as a few Catholic priests, had been systematically and tragically murdered and thrown in mass graves, some while still alive, as a result of their loyalty to the South Vietnamese government.

BELOW: A wounded U.S. Marine is dragged to safety during bloody fighting at the outer wall of the Citadel, on February 16, 1968. After failing in their siege of Khe Sanh, the Communists made an all-out attempt to take and hold Hue. Ultimately, the Tet Offensive was a failure and ended in the decimation of the Viet Cong.

LEFT: An aerial view of the old imperial capital city of Hue.

Medical Evacuation

RIGHT: Medics and infantrymen of the 25th Infantry Division hurriedly assist soldiers wounded by mortar or artillery fire. The job of the field medics assigned to each infantry company was to keep grievously injured soldiers alive until they could be transferred to better-equipped personnel in a "Dustoff," the nickname for medical evacuation (medevac) helicopters. The ten weeks of training that Vietnam-era medics received was far more extensive than that of earlier wars—and it showed. Fast airborne transit to field hospitals would have been of only moderate value if the patients had not been stabilized first; a tall order when one considers that Vietnam saw a higher percentage of "dirty" wounds than did World War II or Korea, as well as an increased shredding of flesh from the new high-velocity rounds. Fully 97.5 percent of the men who reached field hospitals in Vietnam survived their wounds.

BELOW: Soldiers "pop smoke" to guide in a medevac helicopter picking up wounded troopers during 1st Cavalry Division operations in the A Shau Valley, April 30, 1968.

LEFT: Running in a crouch to avoid the deadly whirl of helicopter blades, U.S. soldiers rush a wounded comrade to a waiting Huey. Despite the fact that the number of Dustoff aerial ambulances reached a peak of 116 in 1968, the extremely large number of helos readily available during operations—and the knowledge that speed was of the essence if lives were to be saved—frequently meant that the first flight out after the arrival of wounded would be a "life flight." Unfortunately, the sheer effectiveness of medical evacuation was known to have impeded some operations because even experienced commanders displayed a tendency to hold up an advance while the wounded were choppered out, thus giving enemy forces time to either get away to fight again, regroup and inflict more casualties during a counterattack, or simply direct mortar fire at a congested landing zone. As early as 1965, Lieutenant Colonel Harold G. "Hal" Moore, of the 1st Cavalry Division (Airmobile), warned that "troops must not get so concerned with casualties that they forget the enemy and their mission."

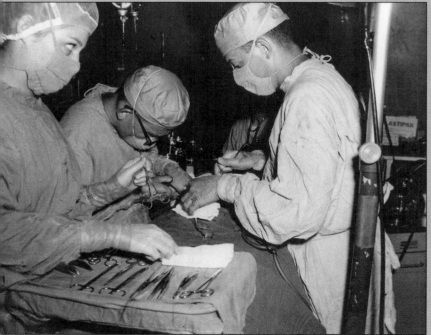

LEFT: Seriously wounded U.S. soldiers and Marines in Vietnam received a level of surgical care unheard of little more than a decade earlier. Here, Army doctors at a field hospital perform surgery using the most modern equipment in one of two air-conditioned and sanitized operating rooms, where up to four operations could be handled at a time. There were six MASH (Mobile Army Surgical Hospital) units; eight field hospitals, principally with the combat divisions; ten evacuation hospitals; two surgical hospitals; hospital ships *Repose* and *Sanctuary*, serving the Marines; a convalescent center; a POW hospital; and innumerable other facilities. The relatively static nature of the fighting and the ease of movement benefited medical operations and patient survivability, but some facilities, such as the 3d Surgical Hospital at Dong Tam, came under frequent artillery and rocket attacks. Excluding personnel injured in accidents or suffering from disease, medical facilities in Vietnam hospitalized 153,329 combat casualties and treated an additional 150,375 lightly wounded, who returned to duty.

LEFT: Convalescents relax in the recreation area of the 3d Field Hospital, near Saigon, May 1966. Most of these men will return to duty at the end of their hospital stays. The nurses chatting with the patients are Lieutenants Susan Eastman (center) and Helen M. Hafner (right), of New York.

BOTTOM LEFT: In the South China Sea off the coast of Vietnam, a nurse tenderly ministers to a patient just out of surgery in the intensive care ward aboard the hospital ship USS *Repose*, October 1967. Approximately seventy-five hundred women worked in the armed forces in Vietnam. The majority worked as nurses or in related medical fields, while others performed in a variety of roles, such as trainers, clerks, or military intelligence photo interpreters. The number of nurses peaked at nine hundred in January 1969. Some five thousand of these women were in the Army, nearly two thousand in the Air Force, five hundred in the Navy, and twenty-seven in the Marine Corps. Eight nurses died in Vietnam, including one mortally wounded during a rocket attack on Chu Lai in June 1969.

BOTTOM RIGHT: From 1963 to 1973, the Military Airlift Command evacuated 406,022 patients, including 168,832 battle casualties, to stateside hospitals from Vietnam. Here, at Walter Reed General Hospital, Captain Jeanne Phillips tends to the shoulder cast of an injured soldier with the help of an enlisted specialist. The patient's long hair and sideburns in this 1970 photo were not an uncommon sight in stateside hospitals, where relaxed grooming standards were often allowed in the late-war period.

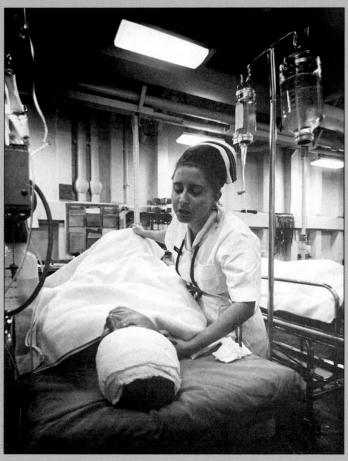

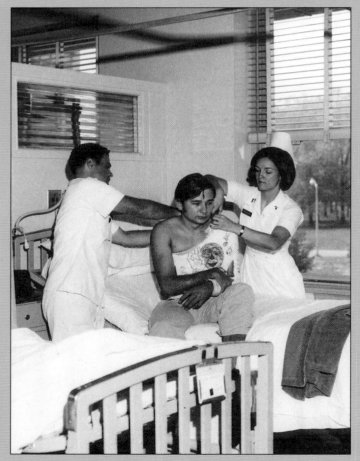

The Aftermath of Tet

The surprise of the Tet Offensive had a traumatic effect on American public opinion. President Johnson, Ambassador Ellsworth Bunker, and General Westmoreland had earlier expressed confidence over the situation in Vietnam, and Westmoreland had even used the term "light at the end of the tunnel" to express his optimism about the war. Meanwhile, the U.S. news media had reported one success after another in 1967, expressing few reservations about the conduct of the war. So the violence and scale of the Tet Offensive surprised most people. Even usually astute newsman Walter Cronkite said, "What the hell is going on? I thought we were winning the war." After this, Cronkite made no secret of his opposition to the war.

But as early as December 18, 1967, the chairman of the Joint Chiefs of Staff, General Earle Wheeler, had warned of the possibility of a desperate effort by the Communists, akin to the Battle of the Bulge. But his warning went unheeded by the press and the American people. On December 23, President Johnson said he feared "kamikaze" tactics in the near future as the Communists grew more desperate. But Johnson revealed none of this trepidation in his State of the Union speech. Even Hanson Baldwin of the *New York Times* warned in a series of articles before the Tet Offensive that the Communists were acting in ways calculated to affect American public opinion. When the Tet Offensive got into full swing, it became obvious that the Communists had completely misjudged the situation in South Vietnam, where the people had no intention of rising in revolt. The press, nonetheless, featured the offensive as a U.S. military disaster.

Since Tet, however, many historians have chosen to view the offensive as a major North Vietnamese military failure. But because Tet was reported persistently in the U.S. news media at the time as a U.S. military failure, the North Vietnamese reaped a great psychological victory. The events as reported in the press and on TV demoralized America's political leadership and, most importantly, President Johnson.

In February 1968, Clark Clifford became secretary of defense and directed a far-reaching study of the American strategy in Vietnam. Clifford met with the JCS and asked them a number of pointed questions: "How many men would it take to defeat the North Vietnamese?" None of them could say. "What is the plan for victory?" He was told, "There is no plan." When asked why not, the chiefs replied, "Because American forces operate under three major restrictions: the president has forbidden them to invade the North ... he has forbidden the mining of Haiphong harbor ... [and] he has forbidden pursuing the enemy into Laos and Cambodia." When Clifford asked the JCS how the United States could win with these prohibitions in place, the JCS suggested that the only way was by continuing the present attrition strategy. Based on this interaction, Clifford determined that the present strategy was hopeless and that the United States must diminish its involvement in Vietnam and exit the conflict.

In the interim, Clifford and his advisors decided to go back to the old enclave concept (a strategy rejected earlier in the war), and they began planning a new strategy referred to as

BELOW: Under heavy enemy fire and carrying an M60 machine gun, a Vietnamese paratrooper rushes to a firing position at a cemetery not far from the Airborne Advisory Headquarters at Tan Son Nhut Air Base during the Tet Offensive of 1968.

The War at Sea

RIGHT: CH-46 Sea Knight helicopters supporting the battalion-size Special Landing Force (SLF) "Alfa" line the deck of the amphibious assault ship USS *Okinawa*. The *Okinawa* and its sister *Iwo Jima*–class ships had flight deck "spots" for seven Sea Knights or four of the larger CH-53 Sea Stallions, and could accommodate up to nineteen helicopters. On call to conduct operations on very short notice and to provide immediate support to threatened units, the U.S. Seventh Fleet maintained two assault ships off the coast throughout much of the war. The *Okinawa* landed its force to assist Marines ashore on numerous occasions in 1967 and 1969, and in 1975, the ship took part in Operation FREQUENT WIND, the evacuation of U.S. personnel and Vietnamese during the fall of Saigon. It was not uncommon for wounded U.S. Marines and ARVN troops to receive emergency treatment at the extensive hospital facilities aboard the amphibious assault ships.

BELOW: A crewman prepares to fuel F-8 Crusaders parked along the starboard bow of the USS *Bon Homme Richard*'s flight deck on March 3, 1967, during the carrier's third combat deployment to Vietnam. Some 2,090 men called the aircraft carrier home as it conducted operations from "Yankee Station" in the Gulf of Tonkin on six occasions between January 1964 and November 1970.

ABOVE: At maximum elevation, the battleship *New Jersey* fires one of its high-explosive 16-inch shells at a target far inland, perhaps as distant as thirty miles. Some 800 pounds lighter in weight than the 2,700-pound armor-piercing shell it never had an opportunity to use against an enemy ship, a single high-explosive shell could obliterate an area roughly the size of a football field. The fact that one of its twin 5-inch turrets is also elevated suggests that the *New Jersey* was handling a second fire mission closer to the coast as well. Very heavy aircraft losses in the area of North Vietnam above the DMZ—more than fifty were lost while attacking the vital Than Hoa bridge—drove the reactivation of the battleship, but a bombing halt over the North to "escalate" the war was ordered just days before its recommissioning. With many of the *New Jersey*'s best targets removed from consideration, the ship was limited to a single extremely effective deployment, which, much to the chagrin of the Marines fighting in the I Corps area adjacent to North Vietnam and Laos, came after the Tet Offensive of 1968 but before the Easter Offensive of 1972.

LEFT: The heavy cruiser *Newport News* fires at a target near the North Vietnamese shore, December 1967. Armed with nine 8-inch and twelve 5-inch guns, the *Newport News* was sent on interdiction, fire support, and shore bombardment missions as far north as Hanoi's port of Haiphong, where in May 1972 it struck inland military facilities while the guided-missile cruisers *Oklahoma City* and *Providence* suppressed counterbattery fire. Weeks earlier, the Easter Offensive of 1972 had brought as many as six hundred NVA tanks into the South, with many within easy reach of naval guns. The U.S. Seventh Fleet's surface action group, centered around the *Newport News*, was quickly built up to at least twenty ships, providing round-the-clock gunfire support to ARVN forces in Quang Tri and Thua Thien provinces until the Communists were beaten back with very heavy losses. A tragic loading accident in the #2 turret (foreground) occurred later that year: the center gun exploded, killing twenty men. The remains of the weapon were removed and its gun port plated over for the rest of the ship's remaining three years of service before decommissioning.

RIGHT: U.S. Coast Guard cutter *Point League*, with two wounded aboard, stands off from a burning trawler it forced aground in the southern Mekong Delta after a running battle in June 1966. The Coast Guard provided twenty-six cutters in support of MARKET TIME, an operation designed to prevent arms and supplies from reaching the Viet Cong through South Vietnam's long shore-line. The steady movement of war supplies among the fifty thousand vessels, large and small, that sailed daily along the coast was particularly important to the Communists, because it was far more efficient to transport materiel by water than by land, and the load carried by a single 120-foot trawler was often enough to support the activities of a guerrilla battalion for a month. Assisted by fast patrol craft ("Swift boats") plus reconnais-sance aircraft, like the P-2 Neptune and SP-5 Marlin, the small WPB "Point"–class cutters quickly choked off the Communists' seaborne pipeline. Although numerous efforts were made to test the system by moving the supply runs to steadily smaller craft and "Chinese" junks, the coastal waters remained closed to anything more than piecemeal smuggling until the final offensive against Saigon in 1975.

BELOW: Aware that a particular stretch of rail line along the North Vietnamese coast was a tempting target for American warships, the NVA positioned two dozen Soviet-made 152-mm howitzers to intercept unwary attackers. Although World War II–era cruisers had good armor protection, the modern guided-missile destroyer USS *Lynde McCormick*'s half-inch steel skin offered no protec-tion against shells nearly as large as those fired from a cruiser's main battery. Here, geysers of water erupt around the *McCormick* as Communist gunners attempt to bracket the destroyer. The *McCormick* successfully zigzagged out of range, suffering only slight damage from shrapnel and no injuries to its crew, while the cruiser *Newport News* supplied suppressive fire and aircraft from the USS *Ranger* destroyed several of the would-be bushwhackers. During the war, sixteen Navy ships were struck by North Vietnamese shore batteries, but none were sunk.

LEFT AND BELOW: Workhorses of the air war over North Vietnam, the 60,000-ton *Constellation* (left) and the 32,000-ton *Oriskany* (below) amassed eight Vietnam deployments apiece. The displacement at full load of the *Oriskany* and other veterans of World War II averaged 40,000–45,000 tons, or approximately 35,000 tons fewer than the much bigger *Constellation* and its postwar sister ships, which topped out at up to 80,000 tons when going into combat. Despite this, however, the eighty-plane air wings on the more modern ships were only marginally larger because their smaller sisters generally fought with smaller aircraft. For example, while the *Constellation*'s two fighter squadrons were made up of F-4 Phantoms weighing 28,000 pounds and exceeding 58 feet in length, the *Oriskany*'s squadrons contained the very capable F-8 Crusader, which was more than 10,000 pounds lighter and 4 feet shorter. Likewise, the *Constellation*'s two attack squadrons were made up of A-7 Corsairs, while the *Oriskany*'s flew the diminutive A-4 Skyhawk until finally switching to Corsairs late in the war. The carriers *Coral Sea*, *Hancock*, and *Ranger* also had eight deployments apiece, the *Enterprise* seven, with the *Coral Sea* and *Midway* (four deployments) being of a late–World War II design that split the difference in tonnage between the oldest and newest carriers.

JERRY D. MORELOCK

Vietnamization. In the new strategy, the ARVN was to be strengthened to take over the war on its own. Clifford and his clique advocated: (1) the United States and Free World Forces pull back to guard population centers, (2) the air war against North Vietnam be suspended, (3) the burden of fighting the North Vietnamese be transferred as soon as possible to the South Vietnamese, and (4) while the United States phased its forces out of Vietnam, renewed negotiations would ensure a settlement and final U.S. withdrawal from the war.

Vietnamization

Through Vietnamization, as it was proposed, the armed forces of South Vietnam would become better equipped and educated and transformed into a viable opponent of North Vietnam before American forces evacuated the country. The problem in effecting this transformation was that years of conflict between the allied forces and the NVA had toughened the Communists but left many of the South Vietnamese forces largely untested. U.S. leaders understood that the Republic of Vietnam Armed Forces (RVNAF) was poorly prepared for the life-and-death struggle that South Vietnam would ultimately face against the Communists.

In light of this situation, in April 1968, Clark Clifford approved a two-phase program to upgrade and improve the RVNAF. Phase one of the upgrade would include supplying the South Vietnamese with more tanks, guns, and helicopters and providing their forces with greater mobility and firepower. Phase two, approved in December 1968, would entail a more drastic transformation: it called for creating, through training and incremental improvements, a self-sufficient RVNAF capable of waging a successful war against North Vietnam. When Richard M. Nixon was elected president, the Vietnamization strategy—considered by many a gamble—continued to be implemented. In Nixon's view, the United States had to transform the training of the RVNAF, encourage South Vietnam to enlarge its armed forces, and supply these forces with the latest weapons of war. At the same time, it would continue pacification and military operations against the NVA to maintain pressure on the enemy to negotiate. That was a tall order.

Nixon's Vietnamization of the conflict did not end the U.S. war of attrition against the NVA begun by General Westmoreland. Starting in mid-1968, General Creighton Abrams, now the MACV commander, began operations in the backcountry of South Vietnam that were reminiscent of Westmoreland's. The only difference was that the size of attacking units was smaller, and night operations—backed by prompt, massive firepower support—became more prevalent. "Body counts," the hallmark of attrition warfare, were still the focus, only this time the ratios were often more lopsided in the allies' favor than they had been in the past. This caused some critics of the war to wonder how this increase in U.S. killing power was possible. Critics were skeptical about the body counts: were all of these counted dead combatants, or were some of them civilians? Because the number of counted bodies always far exceeded that of captured weapons, the matter was the subject of serious debate.

While military operations continued under General Abrams, Henry Kissinger, President Nixon's new national security advisor, began negotiating a diplomatic settlement with the North Vietnamese based on (1) mutual troop withdrawals from South Vietnam by the North Vietnamese and the United States, (2) a negotiated settlement between the South Vietnamese government and the Viet Cong, and (3) an international conference between the warring parties that would establish safeguards for the agreements decided upon through negotiations. Kissinger was faced with a difficult mission, especially when confronted by the devious and guileful negotiators sent by North Vietnam's politburo.

Jerry D. Morelock believes that Vietnamization failed because the United States did not enforce the peace agreements it made with Hanoi and neglected to give adequate military support to the ARVN, and because the South Vietnamese were not yet up to the task of fending off the Communists.

The "insurgency" situation was so secure throughout most of South Vietnam by 1971–72 that I routinely drove alone to and from my duty location in the Citadel of Hue from my quarters in Phu Bai—about a thirty-kilometer round trip—armed with nothing more deadly than a .45-caliber pistol.

—Colonel Jerry D. Morelock, Ph.D., U.S. Army, Retired

My one-year tour in Vietnam, November 1971 to November 1972, coincided with the final phases of "Vietnamization" and the end of the American troop drawdown. This concept—gradually turning over responsibility for the conduct of the war to the South Vietnamese—was devised by the Nixon administration as a means of extricating the United States from the conflict without immediately submitting to a victory by Hanoi. It was the centerpiece of Nixon's "Peace with Honor" initiative.

The main reason Vietnamization ultimately failed and the Communists took over the South in April 1975 was that critical U.S. support—airpower, supplies, and equipment,

LEFT: Under the U.S. policy of "Vietnamization," ARVN troops were extensively reequipped with the most modern weaponry, and efforts were made to bring their training and competence up to the same standards that pertained in their airborne and marine units. Despite the upgrades, however, many of the basic social and political issues that undermined the effectiveness of the ARVN remained. Nevertheless, the newly fanged ARVN units performed well during North Vietnam's 1970 and 1972 offensives, giving war planners grounds for optimism at the time.

RIGHT: Specialist Johnny Seals, from Milwaukee, Wisconsin, eyes enemy positions while Specialist Ron Burbon, of Oxnard, California, reloads his M79 grenade launcher during a 1968 firefight between elements of the 101st Airborne Division and NVA regulars.

BELOW: A skirmish line holds in place while awaiting orders to move cautiously forward. Units generally tried to skirt or maneuver around open areas like rice paddies or grassy fields, but there was often no alternative to an advance directly through them. Large areas required an infantry company to move with two platoons abreast and men spread out as much as fifteen feet apart. Following at an appropriate distance, perhaps one hundred yards, would be the weapons platoon line, with the third rifle platoon skirmish line further back acting as both rear guard and reserve. In difficult terrain, the distance between men and platoons might be reduced by half, with the platoons echeloned one behind the other or, more likely, in a squad formation such as two forward and one back. In this case, the M60 machine gun teams would hang close to the platoon commander in the center.

9TH INFANTRY DIVISION

In 1966, the 9th Infantry Division was deployed to the III Corps Tactical Zone in Vietnam. From January through May 1967, the 9th conducted operations in Dinh Tuong Province against enemy forces. When the Mobile Riverine Force was created in 1967, the division was attached to it and began operations independent of fixed support bases, carrying its fire support in tow. In these mobile operations, division troops lived aboard ships docked at mobile riverine anchorages. During tactical operations, the troops traveled aboard Navy armored troop carrier boats preceded by minesweeping craft and armored boats ("monitors"). The division operated continuously along Mekong Delta waterways, conducting blocking, pursuit, and reconnaissance operations in conjunction with Navy SEALs, South Vietnamese marines, and the ARVN 7th Division. In August 1969, the 9th Infantry Division was redeployed to Fort Lewis, Washington.

etc.—was denied the struggling South Vietnamese by the American Congress, which by then no longer backed a war that it had staunchly supported since 1964. Nixon's secretary of state, Henry Kissinger, who had brokered the 1973 peace agreement with Hanoi, later noted that the Nixon administration never dreamed that the United States would be prevented from enforcing the peace agreement. Earlier, in the 1950s, we had successfully enforced a similar peace agreement in South Korea, where even today American forces remain stationed as a deterrent to renewed aggression by the Communist thugs in North Korea.

In theory, Vietnamization should have worked because the conditions throughout South Vietnam were conducive to it. Although the NVA, in general, continued to use guerrilla tactics in combating U.S. and ARVN forces, the Communist insurgency in South Vietnam was essentially dead by the time I arrived in Vietnam in 1971. Since most of the Viet Cong had been killed during the Tet Offensive of 1968—"sacrificed," some say in doleful tones, on the altar of American public opinion—the war in 1971–72 was carried on by NVA regulars arriving from the North via the Ho Chi Minh trail complex that ran through the "neutral" countries of Laos and Cambodia. Even this formerly privileged sanctuary had been seriously disrupted by Nixon's incursion into the Cambodian-Vietnam border region in 1970. The "insurgency" situation was so secure throughout most of South Vietnam by 1971–72 that I routinely drove alone to and from my duty location in the Citadel of Hue from my quarters in Phu Bai—about a thirty-kilometer round trip—armed with nothing more deadly than a .45-caliber pistol that I kept tucked away in the pocket of my jungle fatigues. Moreover, I frequently walked all over Hue and often visited my Vietnamese counterparts in their homes in various residential areas in Hue, Phu Bai, and Da Nang. There was never a time that I felt threatened or feared an insurgent attack. By 1971, the South Vietnamese were fighting invaders from the North, not their own dissatisfied countrymen conducting an insurgency.

LEFT: During a monsoon shower, a 173d Airborne Brigade paratrooper, Specialist 4 Robert Riley, peers out from a crack in his poncho. Riley took a moment off for a cigarette during a lull in the fighting below Bong Son, South Vietnam.

The main problem with Vietnamization, in my observation, was the spotty quality of ARVN forces. Some units were excellent, some mediocre, and some absolutely awful. For example, the ARVN 1st Division operated in my area of operations, side by side with the ARVN 3d Division, yet the contrast between the two was like night and day. The 1st was a veteran outfit that had fought for years, while the 3d was a newly formed unit filled with rejects and castoffs from other units. When the storm of the 1972 Easter Offensive broke in the North, the results were completely predictable—the 1st held its own while the 3d collapsed in terror and fled south en masse.

One of my Vietnamese counterparts working alongside me in the ARVN I Corps headquarters in Hue had been with the ARVN 3d Division when the powerful NVA Easter Offensive struck his unit. He related one incident in which a 3d Division formation of over one hundred mechanized vehicles, including tanks, was suddenly confronted by the approach of a single NVA T-54 tank. This officer said he was disgusted, disappointed, and personally ashamed that all of the 3d Division vehicles fled in panic at the sight of the lone NVA tank. When he told me the

Armor

TOP RIGHT: Tankers of the 1st Australian Task Force break for tea atop the turret of the lead Mark 5 Centurion. In addition to the range of ammunition available to main battle tanks, the Centurion's 20-pounder gun also fired a highly effective canister round similar to the U.S. "beehive."

CENTER RIGHT: The air-portable M551 Sheridan "armored reconnaissance assault vehicle" was armed with a 152-mm gun/missile system, which made it, functionally, the world's most powerfully armed light tank. Named the Rebel and belonging to the Americal (23d) Division's 1st Cavalry Regiment, this Sheridan's commander has hung smoke grenades along the side of his .50-caliber gun shield to supplement the smoke dischargers mounted on the turret.

BELOW: An LVTE supports U.S. Marines during a firefight near Da Nang. LVTs (landing vehicles, tracked) were less versatile than the M113, but arrived in Vietnam already in specific configurations. The E (engineer) variant was armed with an effective—and fierce-looking—plow for clearing away mines; the LVTR was configured with a crane and boom for recovery and repair operations; and the LVTH was equipped with a turret-mounted 105-mm howitzer.

LEFT: A driver carefully edges his M48A3 Patton tank off an LCM (landing craft, medium) in May 1967. Armed with a 90-mm gun, the M48A3 easily outclassed Communist T-54/55 tanks during the three offensives in which the NVA employed armor. The Patton proved itself to be a reliable fighter under harsh weather and terrain conditions, but its crews found that the turret needed the additional protection of extra track, road wheels, and sandbags to help negate the effect of hits from the increasing numbers of rocket-propelled grenades available to Viet Cong and NVA forces.

BELOW: The M113 armored personnel carrier (APC) was originally envisioned as simply an aluminum box capable of ferrying soldiers from one battle site to another at speeds of up to forty-five miles per hour. However, crews in Vietnam immediately found that it could be adapted to almost any use imaginable. Belonging to the 47th Cavalry, 199th Infantry Brigade, this APC sports a 106-mm recoilless rifle. Its deployed splash shield, intended to deflect water from the driver and deck hatches during amphibious operations, provides a handy place to store bulky extra gear. The shield to the commander's machine-gun mount is not one of the standard mass-produced types but a field modification produced sometime prior to April 9, 1968, when this photo was taken.

RIGHT: South Vietnamese M24 Chaffee light tanks lob 75-mm rounds at a "Communist shelter" in January 1963. The ARVN inherited a great miscellany of made-in-the-USA French armored cars, tanks, and half-tracks, including almost every variant of the M4 Sherman medium and M3 Stuart light tanks fielded during World War II. With the advent of direct American aid, the South's tank force was standardized around the M24 (including some left by the French) by the early 1960s.

LEFT: A "Little Helper," an M578 light recovery vehicle based on the M551 Sheridan light tank, sets off at high speed to assist an 11th Armored Cavalry Regiment vehicle in the Central Highlands, March 1968.

BELOW: In 1966, a gradual replacement was begun of ARVN Chaffees with the 76-mm-gun M41 Walker "Bulldog," a light tank with superior cross-country capabilities. But while more and more Chaffees were downgraded for use as static pillboxes, the M24 light tank figured prominently in the defense of Saigon during the 1968 Tet Offensive and was still being used at the time of the American withdrawal.

RIGHT: A 4th Cavalry M113 lifts and retracts its thirty-foot marginal terrain bridge (affectionately referred to as a porta-bridge) before moving on to its next objective, August 1969.

BELOW: Specialized vehicles based on tank and APC chassis played a key role in U.S. offensive operations by allowing armor elements to move quickly through rough or water-laden terrain. Here, a 9th Infantry Division AVLB (armored vehicle–launched bridge), based on the M48 Patton tank, is almost completely obscured by its expandable scissors bridge while wading a shallow Mekong Delta stream, July 1968. The AVLB is headed to a more difficult fording site, where its sixty-three-foot span will allow vehicles of up to sixty tons to cross safely.

BRIAN M. THACKER

story, this young ARVN captain was visibly moved, almost to the point of tears in frustration and shame, at what his comrades had done. In a similar vein, my section sergeant and assistant advisor in Hue, an American sergeant first class, related his own experiences during the first days of the NVA Easter Offensive, when he had served as an advisor to the ARVN 33d Artillery Regiment, a 3d ARVN Division outfit. In the offensive's opening days, the unit he was with panicked and abandoned not only their eighteen artillery pieces, but threw away their personal small arms; indeed, nearly five hundred M16s were reported lost by the unit. But that's not the worst part of his story. In a subsequent phase of the NVA offensive, as the enemy regrouped and continued their assault, the sergeant reported that this same 33d Artillery Regiment, having been resupplied with weapons, lost another eighteen howitzers and another five hundred M16s! This wasn't war; it was farce played out in a combat zone.

For Vietnamization to have succeeded required patience, support, and long-term commitment by the United States. Key to this would have been the freedom of American forces to intervene with any military action necessary to enforce the 1973 peace agreement. In effect, South Vietnam needed exactly the kind of commitment that America had given to the South Korean government and its military forces from 1950 to the present day. Indeed, the Republic of Korea [ROK] Army of 1950–53, during the Korean War era, was hardly more impressive and capable than the ARVN forces of 1971–72. ROK forces only

evolved into a truly outstanding military establishment over decades of U.S. support and training. The fact that the ROK Tiger Division that served in Vietnam was one of the NVA's most feared and deadly opponents suggests that the ARVN could have eventually become a highly trained, extremely effective force of committed professionals if given the critical time necessary to accomplish this transformation. Moreover, the fact that some ARVN units—the 1st Division, for example— fought bravely and well seems another indication that it was certainly possible that Vietnamization would have eventually been successful. Yet a crippled U.S. president, made virtually powerless by the Watergate scandal, combined with a Congress no longer willing to pay the price of South Vietnam's freedom, deserted South Vietnam long before the roots of Vietnamization could take hold. It took over 58,000 dead Americans to buy ARVN and South Vietnam a fighting chance to survive. Their sacrifice was thrown away by 435 politicians.

—Colonel Jerry D. Morelock, Ph.D., U.S. Army, Retired

When First Lieutenant Brian M. Thacker was assigned to the headquarters of a South Vietnamese unit in 1969, he hoped to learn more about coordination. He had no idea what he was getting in to. As part of his new assignment, he was given new, sophisticated equipment, weighing eight hundred pounds and mounted on a huge platform atop a mountain surrounded by almost an entire NVA division. When the

101st Airborne Division (Airmobile)

AIRBORNE

The 101st Airborne's 1st Brigade was sent to Vietnam in July 1965, followed by the entire division on November 19, 1967. Initially deployed in the III Corps Tactical Zone, the unit soon began combat operations throughout the I and II Corps Tactical Zones around Quang Tri and Thua Thien provinces and at Hue. By August 1968, the division had been converted into a fully airmobile unit and had abandoned its parachute tactics. Thereafter, the division began wide-ranging operations from Saigon to Dak To, including in the northern area around Phong Dien in I Corps. Throughout 1970, the division engaged in pacification operations at Quang Tri and Thua Thien. Late in the war, the division's command structure and aviation assets were employed in LAM SON 719, a major ARVN operation. By December 1972, most of the division was redeployed to Fort Campbell, Kentucky.

North Vietnamese began overrunning
Thacker's position, his South Vietnamese
captain assigned him to bring down artillery
fire to cover his unit's retreat. Thacker's heroic
actions earned him the Medal of Honor.
Afterward, he had the deepest respect for his
Vietnamese commander.

Well, I'm a lieutenant with less than two
years' experience looking at a captain, a
Vietnamese captain with ten or fifteen years'
experience. He was school trained in America,
fluent in English, a command of the English
language equivalent to mine or better, who
was fighting for his life and his way of life.
I wasn't going to command him at all, and I
wasn't able to tell him much at all as an

advisor. I did have some target-acquisition
capability that he didn't, and I could call for
the artillery fire in English, and they knew
my voice was an American voice, not somebody who could speak good English. So it was
his firebase; there was never any question
about that. When he was done with his job, it
was, "We can go now, it's okay"; he put his
advisor in the middle and got somebody out
on the point that knew where they were
going and could read a map. I took the rear,
and we left the firebases as a reasonably
coherent unit.

—(then First Lieutenant) Brian M. Thacker,
U.S. Army forward observer,
1st Battalion, 92d Artillery,
Medal of Honor recipient

ABOVE: Paratroopers
from the 101st Airborne
Division cut loose with
their M-16 assault rifles
against a Communist
bunker on Hill 937, May
1969. Although more
accurately named Ap Bia
Mountain, Hill 937 quickly
acquired the suggestive
sobriquet "Hamburger
Hill," when casualties
during the ten-day fight
to take the summit cost
the U.S. more than three
hundred casualties.

It was Americans coming home in boxes that tended more than anything else to turn public opinion against the war.

—Professor Lawrence W. Lichty,
in a speech to U.S. Army Public Affairs officers, 1983

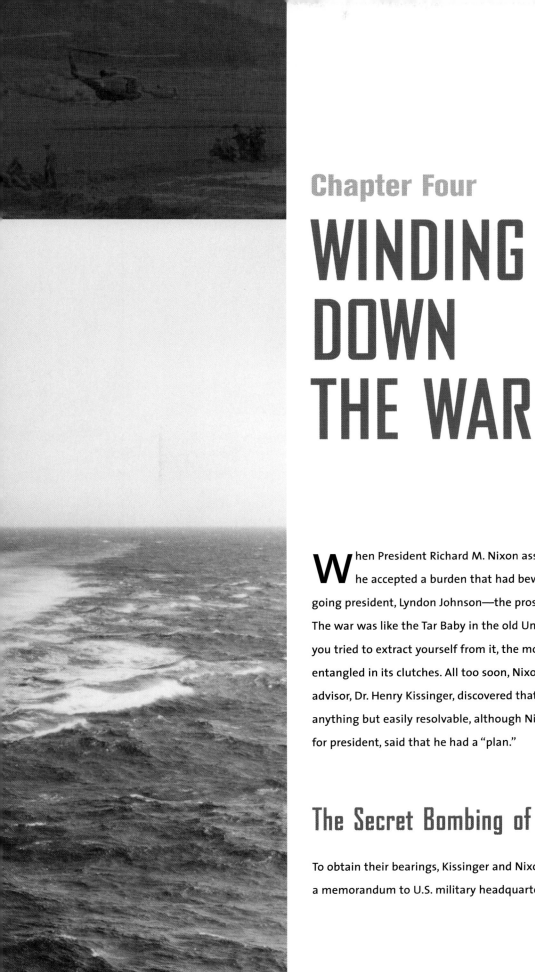

Chapter Four

WINDING DOWN THE WAR

When President Richard M. Nixon assumed office in January 1969, he accepted a burden that had bewildered the exhausted outgoing president, Lyndon Johnson—the prosecution of the Vietnam War. The war was like the Tar Baby in the old Uncle Remus stories: the more you tried to extract yourself from it, the more you seemed to become entangled in its clutches. All too soon, Nixon and his national security advisor, Dr. Henry Kissinger, discovered that the war was going to be anything but easily resolvable, although Nixon, when he campaigned for president, said that he had a "plan."

The Secret Bombing of Cambodia

To obtain their bearings, Kissinger and Nixon started out by circulating a memorandum to U.S. military headquarters and government agencies

PAGES 186–187: The battleship *New Jersey* on patrol
near the DMZ, summer
1968. The USS *New Jersey*
regularly hurled 16-inch
shells at this narrow neck of
South Vietnam abutting the
Communist North, reaching
targets more than halfway
to the Laotian border with
great accuracy. The damper
this put on hostile activity
was immediate and pro-
nounced. Before long, U.S.
Marine and MACV intelli-
gence were pleased—and
amused—to find that the
warship's mere appearance
near the coast was often
enough to prompt a quick
withdrawal inland by
enemy units. The decommissioning of the *New Jersey*,
and ninety-nine other Navy
ships, was announced on
August 21, 1969, just two
weeks before the battleship
was scheduled to depart
on its second Vietnam
deployment.

RIGHT: The caption for this
North Vietnamese propa-
ganda photograph reads:
"The guerrilla detachments
and the masses in central
South Vietnam develop
destruction warfare to cut
the surface supply line of
the U.S. and puppet armies,
isolating them and placing
them beyond reach of
reinforcements."

involved in the war. It asked them a number of questions, some of them simple, others complex, about the war and its conduct. Before they had a chance to evaluate the answers, however, the North Vietnamese launched widespread, unexpected attacks throughout South Vietnam. On February 22, officials of the Communist Headquarters, Central Office, South Vietnam, in Directive No. 71, ordered units to attack U.S. installations and to disrupt the increasingly viable pacification program in South Vietnam.

Another purpose of the Communist attacks was to create "body counts" of their own, bleeding the American public of its resolve to support the continuation of the fighting. The enemy knew that the killing of large numbers of American soldiers would infuriate the antiwar dissidents and demonstrators in America, called doves by their opponents. The dissidents had been agitating to get the Nixon administration to bow out of the war, which they believed was immoral and unjustified. The North Vietnamese politburo was aware of the American dissenters and tailored some of its actions and much of its propaganda with them in mind.

The Communist fighting forces that perpetrated the February attacks were a combination of regular NVA soldiers and those VC still able to fight after their disastrous battles of the previous year. On February 22, enemy sappers attacked 125 targets and bombarded 400 objectives in South Vietnam. While the attacks were fended off without great trouble, they were still costly. Some 1,040 Americans lost their lives. The attacks, however, did as much to wound VC morale as they did that of the dissenters in America; some 20,000 VC surrendered during and immediately after the attacks. The Viet Cong movement in South Vietnam appeared to be disintegrating.

Nixon was infuriated by the February attacks, believing that the enemy had violated a negotiated agreement between the United States and North Vietnam in which America promised to stop its air bombardments if North Vietnam scaled back its aggressions in the South. Nixon now sought revenge for the offensive, but in such a way that it would not inflame dissidents in the United States. Just the opportunity occurred in late February when a captured VC defector revealed that he knew the exact location of the Communist headquarters of the Central Office, South Vietnam (COSVN), which the CIA and others knew was now located somewhere in Cambodia and was

My Lai Massacre

On March 16, 1968, in a little village named My Lai in Quang Ngai Province, a VC stronghold, U.S. troops of Charlie Company, 1st Battalion, 20th Infantry Division, 11th Brigade, Americal Division, were on a search-and-destroy mission hunting for Viet Cong guerrillas of the 48th VC Battalion, known to occupy an area called Pinkville, near the village of My Lai. The VC, the U.S. soldiers were told erroneously, were hiding in My Lai. Charlie Company had been in Vietnam for only three months but had already lost five men dead in action and twenty-eight wounded, some from mines and booby traps during the Tet Offensive.

Two Charlie Company platoons entered My Lai that morning, and not long thereafter, shooting erupted. Some of the soldiers, it appears, had psychologically exploded in an orgy of violence, shooting men, women, and children—even babies. The horrified villagers fled into their huts or into bunkers, but no one was safe. Soldiers pulled them from their hiding places and began executing them. Even when the villagers raised their hands in surrender, they were gunned down. While many of the soldiers present did not participate in the killing, their platoon leader, First Lieutenant William Calley Jr., and others did. When some of his men refused to execute sixty rounded-up villagers, Calley unloaded his own weapon into the huddled mass of people. Meanwhile, according to the U.S. government's Peers Commission report, women were raped and men bayoneted in other parts of the village. A GI, Dennis Conti, later explained: "We were all psyched up, and as a result, when we got there the shooting started, almost as a chain reaction."

Later that morning, descriptions of the situation had spread up the chain of command, and the men of Charlie Company were told to cease firing. But by then, 175 to 200 dead Vietnamese lay scattered throughout their village. Captain Ernest Medina, Charlie Company's commander, reported to his superiors that only 20 to 28 civilians had been killed. Colonel Oran K. Henderson, in his report submitted a month later, said that 20 civilians were killed but failed to specify how they died. Because information concerning the atrocities failed to surface in the American news media until November 16, 1969—more than a year and a half after the killings—there was an immediate suspicion that the U.S. Army had attempted to cover up the crimes.

The story of the massacre came out only inadvertently, when a young GI, Ronald Ridenour, a member of the 11th Brigade, heard one of Calley's men bragging about the carnage. Ridenour was appalled at the tale and questioned other men from Calley's platoon to see whether the story could be corroborated. Yes, he learned, a large massacre had taken place. At the end of his tour, when Ridenour returned to the United States, he composed letters about the atrocities and sent them to thirty prominent people in Washington. One of the letters was received by General Westmoreland, who asked that an inquiry be made, although he did not believe the allegations. Lieutenant General William R. Peers, who conducted the inquiry, questioned four hundred witnesses. The result of the inquiry was a twenty-thousand-page document of testimony. The Peers Commission suggested that there was sufficient evidence to charge thirty soldiers for the crimes at My Lai.

The inquiry led to the criminal investigation of Lieutenant Calley by the U.S. Army's Criminal Investigating Division (CID), which ordered him sent back to the United States to stand trial for murder. Charges were made against sixteen other soldiers, but only five faced courts-martial, and only Lieutenant Calley was convicted. Calley was sentenced to life in prison at hard labor, but his defense lawyers appealed the case. Meanwhile, Calley spent three years under house arrest, after which time his sentence was commuted to ten years. Eventually, he was paroled, having served a little more than three years in prison. Many thought that Calley had been made a scapegoat for the many others also involved in the atrocities and for those who sought to conceal the crimes.

Most of the soldiers in Calley's platoon did not participate actively in the killings, and a helicopter pilot, Warrant Officer Hugh Thompson, who was hovering over the village while the carnage was taking place, landed his helicopter in the village, dismounted, and stopped some of the killing, saving several villagers. He also took a Vietnamese child to a field hospital and later complained to his superiors about the outrages.

designated Base Area 353. Intelligence experts examined the defector using a lie detector, and he appeared to be telling the truth.

Word was passed on to Nixon and his advisors about the informant, and, after much haggling and several canceled attack orders, on March 18, 1969, B-52s tumbled tons of bombs on Base Area 353 in a tremendous aerial assault. When Special Forces troops from MACV's Studies and Observation Group (SOG), a clandestine operations unit, tried to examine the area afterward to see if it was truly the Communist headquarters, they described the scene as being "like somebody had kicked over a hornet's nest," and they narrowly escaped the attack site with their lives. While it was not easy for anyone to learn of the attacks— unless the Cambodians or North Vietnamese complained about it, which they didn't—the

New York Times learned about the secret attack from its informants and printed a detailed report. This article inflamed the dissidents.

Two weeks before the secret bombing of Cambodia, Warrant Officer Millard Craig Rushing, a UH-1 gunship pilot working for SOG, was on his own perilous operation into Cambodia to extract a SOG reconnaissance team.

We were on a cross-border mission to extract a recon team that was in trouble and had called for aid, and I was responding to cover the initial pickup aircraft. We arrived first and expended our ammunition but had not gotten the team out yet, so we withdrew to rearm and refuel. I had probably taken two or three hits in the cockpit area. A second fire

team came in to replace us while we went back in and rearmed and refueled. By the time we had done that, we got word that the second fire team was shot down. So we went back to the scene of the LZ and ran into a helicopter ambush. To be honest with you, they had us pretty well pegged.

They showed us an automatic-weapons position, and when we bore down on it, two or three more positions came up on the sides. They knew they could easily stand us off if they had machine guns firing broadside fire.

Frankly, what happened was that I went in and stayed just a little bit too long, and I got shot up pretty bad. We weren't able to get the pickup aircraft in because they were in such heavy contact they had to orbit while we went in, and prep a little bit, and as I said, the enemy had more to prep with than we had. When I landed on the LZ, the aircraft engine was going, but the hydraulics were out, so that was about the size of it. I got it down without crashing, but if I had stayed airborne a little longer, I probably would have had no choice but to crash, and there would have been a crash with no hydraulics.

Finally, we were picked up, really within a matter of minutes, by our command-and-control aircraft. Other aircraft in the orbit area picked up the other two crews. There were two U.S. personnel and four indigenous personnel, probably Cambodians, on the team we were attempting to extract. Both the Americans were dead by the time I got out there the second time.

An indigenous guy on a radio "talked in" the initial pickup aircraft. As it turned out, he was an NVA operative. They were using one of the team's panels to talk on the radio to us.
— Colonel Millard Craig Rushing, U.S. National Guard

At about the same time as the secret bombings in Cambodia, Corporal Walter L. Sudol, a Marine machine gunner, was headed into the A Shau Valley to destroy enemy staging areas there as part of Operation DEWEY CANYON. Sudol had just arrived in Vietnam; his combat christening would occur on his birthday, February 26, 1969.

Marine recon teams reported a large enemy arms cache in and around Hill 1044. At approximately 1330 hours on February 26, we approached this objective along a well-made NVA dirt road. My gun team was with the point squad. We had just turned left at a bend in the road when there was a huge explosion that lifted me off my feet and threw me onto my back. I had a hard time catching my breath. Through all the smoke and noise, I saw Lieutenant James W. Simms, my platoon commander, holding a .45-caliber pistol and shouting at our Marine scout, who had a German shepherd dog and was directly in front of me. We followed Simms, along with the rest of the 3d Platoon, on a frontal assault up the hill. There were several bunker positions, machine guns, and automatic-weapons positions, all over the slope of the hill.

It was moonscape-type terrain, denuded by B-52 air strikes, with really no cover; the trees had been blown away. Almost immediately, the scout and his dog were hit by machine-gun fire. The Navy corpsman attached to our platoon, HM3 [hospitalman third class] George Collins, and I ran over to him. He was already dead. The corpsman handed me a battle dressing and told me to place it over the wound. To this day I still can't figure out why, except the medic was in great fear and in somewhat of a state of shock. The machine-gun rounds and AK-47 rounds were going past my head so close that I could hear the snap of the rounds as they barely missed me. I didn't realize it then, but an NVA soldier had me sighted in. I lay the battle dressing on the dead Marine's chest and looked up to see Lieutenant Simms being hit by AK-50 machine-gun rounds.

Doc Collins saw him hit at the same time. The corpsman was approximately ten meters in front of me, and I saw him get hit by the same gunner that had shot Lieutenant Simms. He had a portion of his right ankle shot away, and he was sitting down and holding his

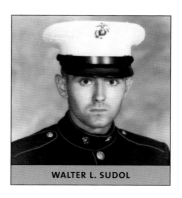

WALTER L. SUDOL

BELOW: As part of Operation DEWEY CANYON, Corporal Walter L. Sudol (pictured here at Camp Lejeune, North Carolina) engaged in one of the last major U.S. Marine offensives in Vietnam. In a deadly game of hide-and-seek played out in the remote mountain highlands of the A Shau Valley, far from allied support, the 9th Marine Regiment advanced on a major NVA base area with the objective of severing the enemy supply line from Laos. Five Marines would receive the Medal of Honor following the costly 1969 operation, four posthumously: Lance Corporal Thomas P. Noonan, Lance Corporal Thomas E. Creek, Corporal William D. Morgan, and Private First Class Alfred M. Wilson. For his combat action as a first lieutenant in command of Alpha Company, 9th Marines, Captain Wesley L. Fox received his medal at the White House on March 2, 1971.

BELOW: U.S. Marine infantrymen of the 3d Battalion, 9th Marine Regiment, move up a battle-scarred slope during Operation DEWEY CANYON in the northern A Shau Valley complex. Leathernecks advancing against the enemy-held mountaintop near the Laotian border dubbed the hill Tiger Mountain. The photograph was taken on February 20, 1969.

I tried to dig a hole into the ground with my hands, trying to get away from the intenseness of the death around me. A kid from New York City . . . shot the NVA gunner with an M79 round, hit him directly in the face, blowing the front of his head off. All the time, I could not get the thought out of my mind that I was going to die on my twentieth birthday.

—Walter L. Sudol

ankle, screaming in pain. I had just started to get up to run over to him, when I saw a burst of machine-gun fire hit him in the head and chest area, and the blood and parts of his body were blown directly onto me. I've never felt fear like that before or since. The corpsman was killed instantly.

I tried to dig a hole into the ground with my hands, trying to get away from the intenseness of the death around me. A kid from New York City, I can't recall his name, shot the NVA gunner with an M79 round, hit him directly in the face, blowing the front of his head off. All the time, I could not get the thought out of my mind that I was going to die on my twentieth birthday and of the pain my parents would have to go through. We continued our assault up Hill 1044, killing thirty-five NVA troops while losing five KIA and suffering several WIA, just from our platoon alone.

—Corporal Walter L. Sudol,
3d Platoon, Delta Company,
1st Battalion, 9th Marines

LEFT: The 3d Marine Division's 1st Battalion, 9th Marines, pinned down by NVA fire in the northern A Shau Valley during Operation DEWEY CANYON, February 1969.

BELOW: UH-1E Hueys of Marine Light Attack Helicopter Squadron 367 land among 105-mm howitzers at full elevation at Fire Support Base Cates to pick up recon grunts for a mission near Khe Sanh, spring 1968. Cates was located on a high ridge above Highway 9 in the I Corps area near North Vietnam.

BELOW: Specialist 4 James
P. Ducy, of Hartford City,
Indiana, carefully cleans
his M16 rifle during a
reconnaissance mission
conducted by elements
of the 101st Airborne
Division in the A Shau
Valley. As Ducy and his
buddies knew all too well,
the M16 needed to be
cleaned frequently or it
could jam during combat.

Invasion of Cambodia:
May 1, 1970

In 1970, the North Vietnamese abandoned large-scale operations, learning from experience the high cost of such actions in the face of overwhelming U.S. firepower from the sky and ground. Small-scale attacks by NVA sappers, mortar teams, and artillery formed the enemy's current military menu. The Viet Cong, after Tet, were too weak in most cases to mount serious threats. The North Vietnamese, meanwhile, decided to wait for the large U.S. troop withdrawals to be effected, after which they planned to strike the weakened U.S. and ARVN forces with renewed intensity.

By early 1970, a crisis had developed in Cambodia, on the western frontier of South Vietnam. Up to this time, the Cambodians had ignored the North Vietnamese occupation of the eastern part of Cambodia, an area the Communists had been using for base camps

and supply depots for their operations in South Vietnam. When Prince Norodom Sihanouk, the ruler of Cambodia, left the country for France on March 10, 1970, however, Lon Nol, the prime minister of the country, encouraged by anti-Sihanouk sentiment in the country, seized power. Unhappy over North Vietnam's occupation of eastern Cambodia, the new ruler threatened to throw the NVA out of the area and closed the port at Sihanoukville to underscore his intent.

The North Vietnamese, with forty to sixty thousand crack troops in Cambodia, answered this rash challenge by sending an attack force toward Phnom Penh. This invasion sent tremors all the way to Washington, D.C. The Americans feared that Cambodia was about to be turned into a Communist camp that would increase the threat to South Vietnam. As the NVA invasion advanced into central Cambodia, President Nixon believed that Cambodian resistance was about to collapse. Consequently, on April 28, Nixon ordered U.S. troops to attack the NVA in Cambodia. On May 1, U.S. forces were to strike

the "Fish Hook," a base complex near the Vietnam border. Two days earlier, on April 29, the ARVN had kicked off the attack by seizing the "Parrot's Beak," another NVA stronghold. The objective of the attacks was to destroy the men and supplies at these bases and to distract the NVA from its conquest of Cambodia.

In a typical U.S. operation, the enemy area was blanketed with bombs dropped by B-52s and fighter-bombers. In addition, U.S. heavy artillery pounded the area. As U.S. armor advanced northward into the Fish Hook, infantry units moved west and south. The 1st Cavalry, meanwhile, dropped into the enemy's

TOP: U.S. troopers of the 1st Cavalry Division (Airmobile), happy to be leaving Firebase Bronco in Cambodia, aboard a Huey that will transport them back to South Vietnam, June 24, 1970.

BOTTOM: President Richard Nixon announces in a televised address on April 30, 1970, that an "incursion" into Cambodia has been launched by U.S. forces to thwart a growing threat to South Vietnam by NVA units in "neutral" Cambodia. Despite favorable public opinion polls, student demonstrations immediately followed. Two days later, on May 2, demonstrations had turned violent and the ROTC building was torched at Kent State University in Ohio. Nixon commented to reporters, "You see these bums, you know, blowing up the campuses. Listen, the boys that are on the college campuses today are the luckiest people in the world." Then, on May 4, four Kent State students were killed when fired upon by National Guardsmen. Protests escalated, and two more students were killed by Mississippi State police at Jackson State University. Strikes were declared at some 450 colleges and universities around the country, with varying degrees of success, and the National Guard was called out in sixteen states, principally as a deterrent. Some universities simply closed for the semester. Later, Nixon said that the days following the Kent State massacre were among the darkest days of his presidency.

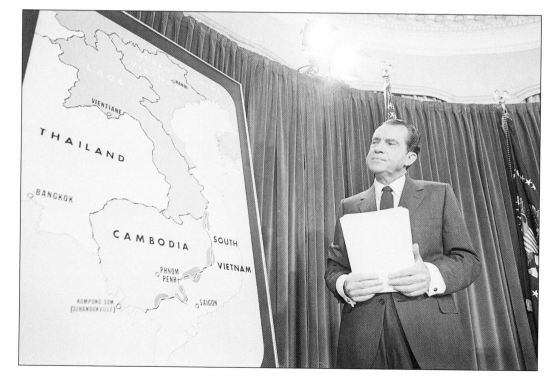

rear to create havoc. The ARVN, in its sector of the front in the South, with 8,700 men composed of three task forces, attacked Base Areas 706 and 367. In both instances, the enemy weakly resisted and melted away into the jungle, leaving their camps behind and losing as many as 11,000 dead and 2,500 captured. A vast amount of equipment and supplies were captured: 23,000 small arms; 16,700,000 rounds of small-arms ammunition; 143,000 rocket, mortar, and recoilless rifle rounds; and 200,000 units of anti-aircraft ammunition. In addition, a large number of enemy documents, some of high intelligence value, were captured.

Because Nixon had pledged in April 1970 that he would withdraw 150,000 American troops from Vietnam, the U.S. drive into Cambodia was necessary to stave off powerful NVA attacks into South Vietnam that likely would have occurred as a result of the U.S. withdrawal. The United States also won time for the Vietnamization process to thrive. The enemy, considerably weakened by this raid, failed to attack South Vietnam from Cambodia for more than two years, and the port of Sihanoukville remained closed, American casualties decreased, and the morale of the South Vietnamese increased.

The successful invasion of Cambodia in early spring 1970 was not the only military action by the United States in countries peripheral to Vietnam. In Laos, the CIA organized a clandestine force of volunteer elite U.S. Air Force forward air controllers, called the Ravens. William E. Platt, a first lieutenant in the U.S. Air Force at the time, describes his participation.

I heard them mention the word *FAC* [forward air controller, Platt's specialty], so I joined them at the table, and it was Craig Morrison and Carl Polefka. They proceeded to tell me stories about the "Steve Canyon Program" and what it was like to be a Raven and to be working in a place that they couldn't tell me about, doing things that they couldn't tell me about, but with the full assets of airpower available and with none of the delays for fighter aircraft.

It was an actual situation where we were supporting people who deserved supporting [the Hmong rebels in Laos, an ethnic minority], who were fighting for their freedom in their invaded homeland [invaded by North Vietnam]. I have to say it was romantic, almost passionate, to be part of that.

I didn't have the hours [to qualify to be a Raven]: you had to have a total of 750 hours of [flight] time, which equates to about 500 hours of combat time, in order to enter the program. So I continued to build my flying time and made it known that, when the time was right, I would like to be considered for the Raven program.

Later, in the midst of other operations, I got a wire from Seventh Air Force telling me to come for an interview. I had an interview, and within a few days I was on an airplane for Thailand, and from Thailand to Vientiane, Laos. One more day and I was on the plane flying as a forward air controller, without my uniform and my ID card, but really supporting the same type of operation as I had with Mike Force [his previous job working with the Montagnard tribesmen].

I was a first lieutenant, twenty-four years old, and I didn't understand the politics and the different borders and where the Air Force

TOP: Master Sergeant Richard Land, of Cartersville, Georgia, inventories an NVA arms cache discovered north of Song By during a 1st Cavalry Division sweep, May 1970. Because of their poor logistical capabilities, the NVA continually created and laboriously built up dispersed supply caches in South Vietnam, Laos, and Cambodia to support their ongoing operations. Land was a member of the 99th Ordnance Detachment.

BOTTOM: As his buddies back him up, an ARVN soldier throws a grenade during an attack on enemy positions in mid-1969 near Dak To. Both South Vietnamese and U.S. troops were involved in the action.

> **[The Ravens] were consummate professionals. . . . It was clandestine. People didn't like to have their pictures taken. People didn't talk about what their names were. Everyone had a handle or a different euphemism that they would answer to.**
> **—William E. Platt**

could operate and where it couldn't. But the men of the Raven program were forward air controllers who had had their mettle tested in Vietnam and then were employed in Laos, working with the indigenous peoples to interdict the activity on the Ho Chi Minh Trail running through Laos. The Ravens were located in four or five different locations, working with the local company. Actually, we were working with and for the air attaché.

An air attaché works for the embassy, and the embassy works for the State Department, and the State Department works for the chief. All I knew was that I was on loan and that I was no longer under the umbrella of the Air Force and that I took my directions from people in civilian clothes who were case officers [CIA operatives] who had been working in Laos for a number of years.

So all of our directions came from one source as far as clearances to strike were concerned. There were no time delays when you needed to put in a strike. You had tactical air available within minutes instead of tens and twenties of minutes.

They were consummate professionals that we worked with. It was clandestine. People didn't like to have their pictures taken. People didn't talk about what their names were. Everyone had a handle or a different euphemism that they would answer to. I guess that was part of the romance of it. It was never explained to me exactly why they needed to be this secret, and it wasn't until really after the war that I realized that there had been treaties signed and agreements made between governments that there would only be so many American military advisors allowed in Laos.

I'm not sure, even to this day, that I understand all of the reasons why it had to be kept as clandestine as it was. But the reality was that we were helping an indigenous people in their own homeland to defend their land—a freedom-loving people, a people that deserved our respect, who had suffered great losses.

The Hmongs were gentle, but consummate warriors in the field. They have a different belief system, but they've existed in those

BELOW: A U.S. Army machine gunner (left) peers cautiously around milling cattle and a cart, attempting to catch sight of a Viet Cong guerrilla. His ammo bearer (right) uses an uncomfortably thin palm tree for cover.

LEFT: South Vietnamese marines conducting an air assault in the I Corps area are ferried to their LZ in Navy CH-46 Sea Knight helicopters. Aggressive and highly motivated, the Vietnamese marines could be depended on to hold up their end during combat operations.

mountains for hundreds and hundreds of years. They were a minority in Laos and had been oppressed by one government after another, and they were worthy of support for their fight to maintain their way of life.

—First Lieutenant William E. Platt, Raven, U.S. Air Force

 Bill Deacy, recon team member, SOG, describes his harrowing experience in Cambodia on one of his missions.

One night I was out with a Montagnard team, and I remember going through agony that night as the mosquitoes set upon me and started biting me everywhere: my face, my head, my neck, and my lips. I remember trying to bring up my jungle fatigue jacket over my head, but they bit right through it. The next day, my head looked like a basketball. A short time after that, a friend of mine, my hootch mate, a great fellow named Jack Daneth, said, "Bill, you should go up to the dispensary." I'd just been sitting in a chair, with no energy whatsoever. He took me there, and they discovered that I had malaria.

I spent about a week or so in the hospital. When I got out, someone said, "All right, Bill, to get you back into the feel of things again, we're going to put you with two fellows." One was named Bob Malone, the other Ernie Massey. We were to do an area recon around the Parrot Beak area [of Cambodia], I think, which was not a friendly, receptive place to be going. I said, "Sure, I'll go in with you two fellows." We were inserted one afternoon and did a very slow area recon of this particular region. We stayed in our recon area that night, and the next morning, we continued examining the area.

Around noon, we were walking on the side of a ridgeline, and we saw some buildings below us, in a kind of shallow area. Even with the camouflage, it was obvious that it was an NVA bunker site.

We descended a slight slope and noticed NVA moving around in the area. They immediately turned and looked up at us, and we did an immediate I-A drill [fired automatic weapons at a continuous, rapid rate], and then we started moving quickly, running up the hill, then sideways along this ridge. They pursued us, and the chase was on, accompanied by a running firefight.

We finally ran a couple hundred meters and came upon a semi-clearing on the side of a hill. We had called for a helicopter extraction, for the slicks [helicopters used for transporting troops], when we had started running. Meanwhile, we set up a defensive perimeter around this clearing and waited for the ships to come to our rescue. The gunships, we thought, were going to be Cobras with some heavy ordnance on board.

When the slicks came in, they couldn't set down. It was a sloping area, so they dropped rope ladders for us. We let the Montagnards go up first, then Bob Malone ascended the ladder and was getting into the chopper. Rope ladders are very difficult. When you're climbing up them, they want to swing underneath the chopper. So I was coming up at an angle with about seventy pounds of equipment on my back and a rifle. I was the last one ascending the ladder, and Ernie Massey was ahead of me. In the meantime, I was putting down some covering fire into the immediate wood line where I saw muzzle flashes.

As I was halfway up the ladder, the chopper started to lift off. He naturally wanted to take off, so my intention was to just snap on to the rope, like we often did in crisis situations. When you're under fire, you wanted the chopper to leave as quickly as possible. I intended to ride back to the camp, just snap-linked on to the ladder. Unfortunately, when I was about halfway up, as I was starting to snap-link on to the ladder, I heard a loud boom.

Immediately, the chopper started twisting, doing 360-degree spins, just flailing all over the place. My only thought was to hold on to the ladder and try to get out from underneath the chopper. I knew that you couldn't be underneath it when it hit. The next thing I remember, I was laying on the ground, with the chopper some feet away. I remember the tremendous heat when I came to. I'd been knocked unconscious. Part of the chopper hit my skull, jammed my head down, and slammed me on my right side. This fractured

my skull and knocked all my right teeth out, screwed up my spine, damaging some of my vertebrae. They told me later that it was an axial-compression fracture.

So there I was, lying next to a burning helicopter with a tremendous heat searing me. I said to myself, "I've got to get out of here." I didn't stop to think that the chopper was on fire. I just knew something was drastically wrong. I wasn't thinking coherently. I tried to get out and move, but I was entangled in the rope ladder. I was partially underneath the chopper, so my legs were pinned underneath it.

Two of the fellows came down from another chopper to try to get me out, to untangle my legs, but it was too hot for them, and they were forced to move twenty yards away. One of the fellows said, "We're going to have to shoot him." He referred to putting a bullet in my head rather than letting me burn to death. But another fellow said, "Let's try one more time." One of the men was a door gunner by the name of O'Kelly, the other, Ernie Massey, my team member. Finally, they got me untangled and moved away again, quickly, because it was very hot. I remember crawling away from the chopper.

The gunships were coming in now and putting down suppressive fire all around us, especially in the wood line near the bunker complex. A helicopter dropped down hundred-foot ropes so that we could snap-link on to them. Once attached to the ropes, the helicopter could pull us up over the tree line—and hopefully move out. They dropped three ropes, and I remember them screaming to me: "Wrap your arms around that fella's neck." What happened was the door gunner, O'Kelly, snap-linked on to one of the rigs, but I didn't.

In desperation, I put my arms around O'Kelly's neck and straddled him, wrapped my legs around his hips. I was going to come out like that, so the chopper lifted off, and we were extracted. Another chopper came in and dropped more ropes, and the rest of the team came out.

As we were heading back to the launch site, I believe it was an A camp, the closest

ABOVE: "Mike Force" first sergeants Joe Lopez (left) and Asa Ballard coordinate information on enemy dispositions as the 1st and 2d "China Boy" companies try to break through to cut off the 3d Company of the 3d Nung Battalion (Chinese mercenaries) during Operation ATTLEBORO. Recon platoon leader Lopez was awarded a Silver Star for his actions during this November 1966 engagement, in which the 272d Viet Cong Regiment overran the 3d China Boy Company's position but was in turn decimated by the U.S. 1st Infantry Division. The "M.F." beneath Lopez's skull-and-crossbones shoulder patch stands for "Mike Force." As the war in 1965 progressively became more and more of a "big unit" fight with the infusion of NVA formations into the South, the isolated Civil Irregular Defense Group (CIDG) camps operated by U.S. Special Forces in remote border regions became increasingly vulnerable—particularly to artillery, which was used with devastating effect. Camps Duc Co and Cai Cai underwent prolonged sieges, while others, like

continued on next page

camp back in South Vietnam, I remember my head was on O'Kelly's chest, and I was losing blood. I started slipping down his body; I was losing my strength. I remember looking down at the jungle, and it was a terrible feeling thinking I was going to fall a thousand feet or three thousand feet, maybe.

So on the ride back, we were doing about ninety knots, maybe a hundred miles an hour. The wind was thrashing my body around, and I was slipping. My hands were on O'Kelly's neck, and my head was down by his belly or his abdomen. I said to him, "Please don't drop me." I heard him grunt a little bit, and I think the tremendous weight of my being on him, the pressure of my harness on his abdominal region, was causing him a lot of distress, a lot of pain. I don't remember him saying anything, but I remember tremendous arms underneath my armpits, holding me.

I remember touching down on the A camp and being laid out. The medics put an IV in me, and I remember one of the men in a group of faces staring down at me. One of the fellows was smoking. I think it was Bob Malone, and I asked him for a drag. That was the last thing I remembered until I wound up in the 24th Med Evac hospital.

—Bill Deacy,
recon team member, SOG

SOG chief Stephen Cavanaugh describes his men.

[The SOG recon teams] were tremendously self-confident and felt confident in their weapons, also, and that made a big difference. There was no hesitancy about what they felt about themselves in terms of capability. There was a lot of audaciousness involved in their actions, and that carried them a long way; I'm sure of that.

We tried to send them in as clean as possible. We had our own uniforms, simple black uniforms with no insignia. They could carry any weapon that they wanted, and a lot of them carried AK-47s, some of them M16s. We had various weapons, some made in Sweden, that we carried.

The team leader, nearly always a sergeant, had a lot of freedom of action. We tried to keep everything "sanitary," in terms of having no U.S. stamp on it. We tried to avoid giving any indication that we were a U.S.-supported team.

One of the problems we had was footwear, because to a guy on the ground, the proper foot equipment was important. We used an awful lot of U.S. boots because they were durable. Of course, when you went into an area like that and you left tracks behind— U.S. tracks—it identified we'd been there. So we started to collect old boots from the troops going back to the States, and we'd get packages of twenty or thirty boots, and we'd drop them along the Ho Chi Minh Trail.

The North Vietnamese would put them on, of course, and give us a cover [leave their tracks with U.S. boot prints]. We had tried going in with teams wearing the same kind of sandals as the North Vietnamese, which mainly looked like rubber tires, but they were very difficult to move in, run in, and fight in. They just wouldn't stand up to the kind of abuse they were taking. So, we went to airdropping boots like our own, and it worked fairly well.

Our men didn't wear helmets or berets. They usually wore a scarf or a black hat of some kind. The main thing that they wore was a rig, a harness that had been devised by a Special Forces guy. It had special rings attached to it. We lowered ropes down, and they attached their rings to it, and we pulled them up through the trees in these rigs. They worked beautifully. We'd pull the guys out with the chopper, yank them sixty or seventy feet in the air, and they'd be flying underneath the helicopter, maybe three or four of them at a time, as a way of escaping. A chopper couldn't get through the canopy, so we'd drop the "strings" down to them, a number of strings, and pull them out.

But other than the black uniform, or camouflage uniform, it was up to the team leader to do about what he wanted. I guess, in their minds, what they did was commonplace. Really, their actions were heroic in every case. I had a deep respect for them, and I still do, for what they did.

—Stephen Cavanaugh,
chief, Studies and Observation Group

When SOG recon teams were on the ground, they kept very tight security, according to J.D. Bath, a recon team member and chief.

If we were talking on the radio, we tried to stay as brief as we could because, being in the territory we were in, you didn't have time to spend a lot of time lollygagging around. In fact, if the bird [plane or helicopter] came over and he wanted to talk to me, he'd race his engine. He'd call me, and I wouldn't answer; I'd just click the hand mike twice, signaling that the team's okay, we're still moving, and he'd roger me and keep going. So that way, we didn't have to stop and talk with him and make up messages [and perhaps give up the team's position].

—J.D. Bath,
recon team leader, SOG

According to Bill Deacy, recon teams operated in a stealthy manner to avoid detection and to get the drop on the enemy, when that was their intention.

You know, you might spend a day or two in there and you haven't seen anything, haven't crossed any trails that looked like they were actively used. You haven't seen any bunker complexes. This would make you complacent if you didn't have some experience behind you or some savvy about you.

When you assume that the bad guys will see you, you move very slowly. You move maybe four or five minutes and stop. And when I say move slowly, I'm talking about very deliberately lifting your feet and putting them down in a precise manner. You walk

Song Be and Bu Dop, were overrun in vicious fighting as enemy lightning strikes simply overwhelmed the camps' defenders. The Ia Drang Valley battles of the 1st Cavalry Division forced the North Vietnamese to lift their siege of Plei Me, but this was hardly the norm, because the newly arrived large conventional units seldom could be spared to dash from one threatened site to another.

LEFT: Viet Cong guerrillas march to a soldier's tune as they proceed to an interrogation point. Constant surveillance of the area in the An Lao Valley, a VC-infested section of South Vietnam, kept the enemy at bay.

For the Montagnards, [Army life] beat the hell out of . . . digging roots. . . . When it's their turn to die, that's it, they go. . . . They don't really get jacked out of shape about dying.

—J.D. Bath

where the other man's footprints might be on the ground also. When you come across a trail, you may back off that trail, not traverse that trail. Before crossing the trail, you might want to observe it a while.

You'd listen for sounds; that was another key thing. You wanted to hear the natural sounds of birds or maybe the monkeys in the trees or insects. Normally, if you didn't hear that, there was something going on. There may be an ambush being set up. People might be in place for it, which frightened the animals. If you heard super quiet, normally something was amiss.

Another thing, you had to be careful not to go to sleep at night. You would go into a kind of a semi-coma type of state. You would relax and just lie there. And your rest for the night period was normally, and deliberately, in the most difficult terrain that somebody other than you might try to get to.

You wanted to be able to hear them. That was the key to it. Make them trigger some

kind of a sound trying to sneak up on you. But you would never take off your rucksack. You'd just loosen it and lie against it. You never put away your weapon, never put it on the ground. You always had it across your lap. And you would listen. Before you went to sleep, your backs would be in a semi-circle. You would put out your claymores and your defensive perimeters. You might fall asleep for a little bit, but the entire team was never sleeping or completely relaxing.

—Bill Deacy

Recon teams operating in Montagnard territory usually had a number of tribesmen on them, led by U.S. team leaders. The Montagnards were skilled woodsmen, especially in a jungle setting, but their culture was vastly different from that of the Americans, and U.S. soldiers had to adjust to it, as J.D. Bath recalls.

The Montagnards were born and raised in the jungle, so they could see things out of the ordinary that you and I would never see out there. They could spot troop movements through the trees before you'd ever see them. If they didn't know how to count, we'd teach them: "Yeah, beaucoup VC."

For the Montagnards, [Army life] beat the hell out of going out and digging roots out of the ground and picking bananas or whatever you needed to make a few dollars and enjoy life. Because, you know, life is a daily thing with them, and when it's their turn to die, that's it, they go. Maybe they'll come back tomorrow as a buffalo or something. They don't really get jacked out of shape about dying.

They have their own language, but they can speak basic Vietnamese, and they just about all speak French, so we worked with them and developed a team and made them competitive against each other. They learned

Studies and Observation Group (SOG)

Among the less publicized operations conducted by MACV during the Vietnam War were those performed by the Studies and Observation Group (SOG), an innocuously titled organization that performed cross-border ground reconnaissance operations in Laos, Cambodia, the DMZ, and, in some instances, North Vietnam. Its ground component, Operations 35 (OPS-35), was involved in strategic intelligence gathering as part of clandestine operations.

OPS-35 field elements were Command Control North (CCN), Command Control Central (CCC), and Command Control South (CCS), in Da Nang, Kontum, and Ban Me Thuot. SOG also had other secret arms, OPS 31, 32, 33, and 34, which were involved in psychological operations (PSYOP), maritime operations, and the insertion of agent-operatives into North Vietnam. Navy SEALs and U.S. Army Special Forces were included in SOG. MACV-SOG was not a Special Forces element, however, but a part of General Westmoreland's command that used Special Forces as required. In recent years, more SOG operations have come to light as secret documents have been declassified. Some of the activities SOG was involved in included the identification and freeing of captured personnel; the capture of prisoners outside of South Vietnam for interrogation; and psychological operations.

Some of the SOG components were affiliated with the U.S. Army's 5th Special Forces Group as an administrative cover. SOG's indigenous Asian mercenary forces were realigned from the Civilian Irregular Defense Group (CIDG).

From 1964 to 1972, SOG had some two thousand to twenty-five hundred U.S. personnel and some eight hundred indigenous members, including Montagnards, Nungs (North Vietnamese tribespeople of Chinese origin), and Khmer Kroms (Cambodian tribesmen from the isolated mountainous and border regions). SOG operations sometimes tapped NVA telephone lines and imbedded acoustic and seismic sensors along the Ho Chi Minh Trail to monitor enemy activity. SOG teams invariably were composed of U.S. and indigenous soldiers, in a mix of three U.S. to five to six indigenous mercenary soldiers/sailors, working together toward a common cause. Team leaders were usually U.S. noncommissioned officers or, in some instances, a lieutenant or captain. All units were highly trained elite Special Forces.

A series of operations into Laos by SOG from 1965 to 1969 was called SHINING BRASS and, later, PRAIRIE FIRE. Composed of "Spike" teams, six to twelve men in number, they operated in Laos to monitor the growing scope of NVA troop movements down the Ho Chi Minh Trail. Cambodian operations were performed under the code name DANIEL BOONE and, later, SALEM HOUSE. During this period, operating out of Khe Sanh, Kham Duc, and Kontum, SOG conducted more than fifteen hundred reconnaissance patrols and several hundred platoon-size operations into Laos. With a well-established communications center in Laos, SOG could call for fighter-bomber raids against the NVA anywhere in their area of operations. Sometimes, in SLAM operations, NVA forces were lured into areas where fighter-bombers, directed by FACs, annihilated them in large numbers. When questioned about SOG operations, the Department of Defense first denied knowledge of them, then reported that they were merely intelligence-gathering reconnaissance efforts.

RIGHT: By the late 1960s, NVA manpower was so abundant along the Ho Chi Minh Trail that the Communists could afford to provide personnel to directly monitor hundreds of potential LZs twenty-four hours a day and effectively position antiquated anti-aircraft weapons, of little value against jets, for effective use against helicopters. SOG's answer was to equip each of its Hueys with a pair of thirty-four-foot coiled aluminum ladders. These simple, sturdy devices allowed for immediate extraction from any location with a tiny clearing and no surrounding jungle canopy taller than twenty-eight feet. Since recon teams were frequently exhausted after evading or outrunning their pursuers, they had only to grasp tightly to the ladders to be pulled up and away from certain death.

to trust us and we learned to trust them, and from that humble start we started going out on the ground and running and doing local things to make sure we all understood our immediate-action drills and everything.

These guys weren't new to war; it's been a part of their lives all their lives. I wasn't able to go out on the first mission they went out on, but the second one, I went out with them, and the chopper went in, sat down, and these guys bailed out the door. When they were almost ready to get on the ground, they were giggling. My knees were so weak, I didn't want to get up. I wanted to go on sick call.

They had their beliefs, their taboos, their traditions, and we had to learn to live with those. Sometimes it really took a lot out of us. They had these big urns, and they filled them full of water all the way to the top, with rice fermenting in the bottom of them. They would say to you, their guests, "You come here. You got to have nonpai." They've got these long straws that go to the bottom. They expect you to drink clear to the bottom of that thing, and this stuff is kind of sweet tasting. So we sat up there and we drank this stuff. These guys just suck a quart of it down and pass the straw around, and I wasn't really happy about using the same straw. Think about all the bugs I'm going to get.

1st Aviation Brigade

The 1st Aviation Brigade was activated in Vietnam on May 25, 1966. While it began its operations with the assets of a provisional unit, the brigade ultimately became one of the largest commands in Vietnam, being comprised at its peak of some 641 fixed-wing aircraft, 311 CH-47 cargo helicopters, and 44 Cobra AH-1G attack helicopters. With these assets, it held air superiority over the battlefields of Vietnam. The brigade conducted tactical combat assaults, air reconnaissance, troop lifts, direct fire support, medical evacuations, cargo hauling, and assisted the evacuation and relocation of civilians as part of the Rural Development program. Tan Son Nhut was the brigade's headquarters until December 1972, when it was moved to Long Binh. After relocating its headquarters back to Tan Son Nhut on March 28, 1973, the brigade was redeployed to the United States.

By this time, I've got three quarts of this stuff in my body, and it's got to go somewhere. It was so sweet my body began to… I went out and threw up. They laughed and rolled around on the floor and thought that was cute, so we went to the store, and we got some Jim Beam. We came back and we popped the lids off, old American custom, and gave them a big swig and passed it around. Now, they could handle that rice wine, but they couldn't handle Jim Beam. So, we had kind of a Mexican standoff; you know, we could do things together.

—J.D. Bath

When helicopter pilot Spike Eskins arrived in South Vietnam, he was unsure of what he wanted to do. He ended up participating in a number of dangerous, challenging missions as part of SOG.

I came into Cam Ranh Bay [a U.S. base in South Vietnam] from San Francisco. I was assigned to the 1st Cavalry. Once I got there, I met one of the officers, and he said, "Well, we're going to put you in the 1st Aviation Brigade." We sat in his office—he was a friend of a friend of mine from high school—and he said, "We have these companies, which one would you like to go to?"

One of the companies he mentioned was the 195th. He said, "The unique thing about them is they're on a classified mission; it's voluntary only, and they get a lot of medals." So, with the guy that I was with, I actually ended up in the "thunder chickens," the gun[ship] platoon. He said, "Oh yeah, let's do that!" Maybe it was stupid, but that's how we did it.

When I first got there, one of the bigger missions that we had was a several hours' firefight. That's the first exposure I had in the platoon. When I first got into the company area, the crew that I flew with, the 1st Platoon, showed up. They had just come back from a mission into the Fish Hook [on the Cambodian border], where they had been in contact with the enemy for fourteen straight hours. It had been pretty intense. At that point, I said to myself, "Wait a minute. What did I do to myself?" But once I went out on the mission and found out how close they were, it was really a cool mission; then it was, Oh boy, this is kind of neat stuff. And you felt safe because it was such a professional operation.

I was an aircraft commander. My role was to put a team on the ground and extract the team. There was extensive training tied up in that. The extractions would be so tight that you could just barely get the helicopter in, and sometimes you'd take some trees with you. You had to sort of gauge it sometimes. I went through six rotor blades while I was there. If you lost too much of the rotor blade, you weren't coming out. But in some situations, there was no option at all.

We flew a UH-1H, and they were a bit unique because the governors were removed. We could overrun the engines if we had to, and we often needed the extra power just to lift the loads we had. Sometimes we took a lot of hits, so we needed the extra power for those kinds of things. In addition, we spent six months training people to handle the rope ladder and the McGuire rig used in extractions. [The McGuire rig was a long rope with a ring hanging from it, usually attached by a recon team member to a hook on his harness; the soldier was left dangling in this position until he got to his destination, where he was lowered carefully to the ground.]

When I first got in-country, we used the McGuire rig. It was basically just a rope. It had a loop on the end of it so that a team member could sit in it, and a nylon bag that gave it some weight so that it would penetrate the jungle. You would spend time training

because the helicopter had some unique anomalies when you had people in any of those rigs. For example, any time you're on a rope ladder and you had people coming up, every step would cause the helicopter to rock, and, as I told you, the landing zones were so tight, you had to offset that. Then, the next guy would come up on the other side, and the aircraft would rock the other way. So the helicopter was constantly going back and forth.

The way the mission worked was that we would all stand by at a remote location, all the gunships. That would be all the aircraft armed with 60-mm machine guns. We also had a command-and-control [CNC] ship, and we got calls from FACs when we were needed to do an extraction.

We had a routine. The aircraft commander would run to the ship and start the engine. The crew member and crew chief would untie the rotor, and nobody waited for anybody else: it was a timed event. And the right-seater would start putting on his "chicken plate" [bulletproof vest] immediately.

A lot of times, we were sitting there with no shirts on or anything else, sunbathing, just killing time. So we would get ready, get our helmets on, and get hooked up so we could communicate. The aircraft commander would just take off, bare-skinned, nothing else—just go! We'd scramble, probably be off the ground in about four or five minutes. The first ship out would be the CNC ship, and the FACs would already have been there, and we would know the location. So, the CNC ship would go on-station, locate the team.

Then, we would form up the slicks, three slicks each, and begin a rotation pattern. They would be called in to a reporting point, which was pre-agreed upon. We would hit that point, at a low level, and the CNC ship would be at an altitude to direct the ships from below. So you basically flew at normal air-speeds, and you would be told, maybe, to turn right ten degrees, turn left ten degrees, and vector right to the landing zone. Once you got to the LZ, the CNC ship slowed you down, held your airspeed back, and you'd hover over the

BELOW: A U.S. Air Force
Skyraider drops napalm on
Viet Cong structures south
of Saigon. Like the opposition to the use of Agent
Orange, napalm attacks
caused an outcry in some
quarters.

LZ, out the left door, which is where the aircraft commander sat, so he had a perfect view
of the LZ.

Normally what would happen is the team
[to be extracted] would pop smoke [throw a
smoke grenade to signal for an aircraft] to
identify for you where the team's location
was. If it was a hot LZ [surrounded by the
enemy], we came in blazing, and you needed
to make the determination: how are you
going to get into the LZ? What were your
options? You'd go to the McGuire rig if you
couldn't get down to the ground. You'd go to
a rope ladder if you could get to within sixty
feet or all the way to the ground. You just
had to make those decisions along the way.
The aircrew was very coordinated, and the
aircraft commander would move the ship in,
and the door gunner and crew chief would
look down the tail bone and see that the tail
rotor was out of the trees, check the rotor
on their side, and you would get constant
communications: "Move right"; "Move left";

"You can't go down any farther on the left-
hand side; move a little bit to the right." They
were constantly feeding you information
about what was going on, and, by the way,
they're shooting M60s as this is going on,
so it was hectic.

In our particular case, we used Charlie-
model [the faster UH-1C] gunships, the
"thunder chickens," so we could put fire
down within thirty feet of the friendly forces.
Their rockets [long, thin 2.75-inch] were just
grease pencils; you just made an X on the
windshield and that aircraft commander
would punch them off. You just flew your
ship, which is a full plate in itself. It took
100 percent concentration just to hold that
aircraft steady. Your right-seater would help
you monitor the gauges and help you identify
fire from different directions. He was there
also in case you were disabled, shot, whatever, and he could take over the aircraft.

But the bottom line is your full concentration: you just sit there and "think small," hold

that aircraft in position; the crew is feeding you information, and the team to be extracted is coming; they're on the rope ladders or whatever; the last man is on, and we can take off. There's just a field of fire everywhere, with rockets going off and smoke and all that good stuff.

—Spike Eskins,
helicopter pilot, SOG

In a program called ELDEST SON, *a psychological operation, SOG attempted to undermine North Vietnamese confidence in weapons the Chinese were providing to them. There had always been considerable animosity between the North Vietnamese and the Chinese, including mutual distrust, and this program was meant to aggravate that normal rift, according to SOG chief Stephen Cavanaugh.*

We felt that if there was some way we could lead [the North Vietnamese] to believe that the weapons themselves or the ammunition [they got from the Chinese] were inferior, they would lose confidence in them. So ELDEST SON was designed to plant doctored ammunition [in NVA ammunition dumps] that would explode in NVA gun barrels, and when it exploded, of course, it would destroy the weapon and perhaps injure the guy firing it.

So one of the things our teams targeted were ammunition caches they found in Laos or Cambodia. They would pull this ammunition out, usually small caliber, sometimes mortar rounds, and bring it back [with them]. The CIA had an operation to doctor them for us. Then, we would send a team in to reinsert this ammunition, properly muddied up, as though it had never been moved. Then, hopefully, the enemy would pick the ammunition up from their dumps, or wherever they happened to find it, and use it. We did find some weapons that had been peeled back, so we knew the ammo had caused damage. How effective it was over the long pull, in terms of making the North Vietnamese feel that they had inferior weapons, I don't know, but it was a good program.

—Stephen Cavanaugh

Antiwar Demonstrations

While the Cambodian raids had a salutary effect on South Vietnamese morale and the general conduct of the war in Vietnam, the impact of the invasion in the United States, especially on college campuses, was exactly the opposite: it caused a furor. After the raids, thirty Reserve Officer Training Command (ROTC) buildings at colleges across the nation were put to the torch. Wild demonstrations were held, and an intense excitement held sway. On May 4, 1970, on the Kent State campus in Ohio, two days after antiwar protesters had attacked the ROTC building, National Guardsmen ordered to the area by Ohio governor James Rhodes fired into the unruly crowd, killing four and wounding nine people. When Nixon's press secretary, Ron Ziegler, said the deaths demonstrated that "when dissent turns to violence, it leads to tragedy," many considered his remarks insensitive. At about the same time, in a riot at Jackson State in Mississippi, two more students were killed. In more than twenty-two schools of higher education in the United States, the National Guard had to be summoned to quell threatening demonstrations. Some four hundred colleges

ABOVE: Members of the military police cut off an antiwar demonstration at the mall entrance to the Pentagon. Such confrontations sometimes resulted in violence if the authorities lost control of the situation or the mob became overly aggressive and obstreperous, as it did at Kent State.

Protecting the Convoys

One of the first images that comes to mind when the Vietnam War is mentioned is that of a helicopter, the ubiquitous Huey dropping fast into a hover over a hot LZ in the Ia Drang or perched atop the U.S. Embassy during the final, desperate fighting for Saigon. Throughout the conflict, however, it was the rubber-wheeled vehicles on Vietnam's old French roads and highways—all virtually rebuilt by U.S. Army engineers—that sustained the war effort by transporting troops, food, fuel, munitions, and all manner of supplies in the thousands of tons each and every week.

ABOVE: An M113 of the 25th Infantry Division engages in "reconnaissance by fire" of the woods along the road between Tay Ninh to Katum, February 1968. Sweeps like this were a common feature before a convoy would pass through close terrain.

ABOVE: Although still terribly exposed, these MPs were fortunate to have half-inch sheets of armor plate welded to the front, back, sides, and floor of this jeep (officially an M151 quarter-ton reconnaissance utility truck).

BACKGROUND: An M55 quad .50-caliber machine-gun system in the shallow bed of a 2.5-ton M35 truck. Although the driver's compartment on such ad hoc weapons platforms often received armored doors and additional plate behind the seats, the need for the absolute maximum field of fire trumped gun crew protection. Aside from a generous supply of .50-caliber ammunition boxes at the front of the bed, there is probably an M60 machine gun available for close-in security.

BACKGROUND: Staggered roughly fifty yards apart in case of ambush, a 173d Airborne Brigade patrol moves through a village north of Saigon after overrunning a Viet Cong tax-collection point in Long Khana Province.

ABOVE: An ARVN V100 Commando armored car speeds past a series of cargo trucks near Phan Thiet on Highway 1.

ABOVE: A jeep-mounted M40A1 106-mm recoilless rifle with M-8C .50-caliber spotting rifle provides overwatch for a convoy of 1st Cavalry Division engineer vehicles heading out to work on the bridges on Route 1.

The Press

The Vietnam War was the first war in American history reported on television. Every evening, almost without fail, TV screens were filled with violent images of fighting, bombing, machine-gun fire, blood, death, and destruction. In an industry in which ratings were often measured by the high drama of the nightly fare, the tendency was to excite, to titillate, then to provide easily digested explanations for the violent images on the screen—images heretofore experienced only by fighting men on bloody battlefronts.

In order to compete with television news, magazines, newspapers, and radio stations sometimes began to report on events in a similar fashion, allowing their journalists in the field, like those of the TV networks, to create quick, spontaneous explanations for events rather than to intensively research the ongoing situation and report the hard facts.

In 1968, during the Tet Offensive, when widespread Viet Cong attacks occurred all over South Vietnam, television commentators and other news media representatives, in line with this loose manner of reporting, quickly jumped to the totally erroneous conclusion that the United States and its ally, South Vietnam, had suffered a stunning, critical defeat in the war and broadcast that seriously flawed message for several months. So pervasive was this false "story" that it affected and influenced the American public's perception of the war, and also that of the president of the United States and the Joint Chiefs of Staff.

General Earle Wheeler, chairman of the Joint Chiefs of Staff, said, "I guess I

was influenced by those newspapers I read. Those newspapers colored my thinking. They said [Tet] was the worst calamity since Bull Run." Thus, an incorrect interpretation of the impact of the Viet Cong's Tet Offensive by the news media may have become a self-fulfilling

prophecy influencing subsequent U.S. conduct of the Vietnam War.

Newsman Peter Braestrup wrote: "Rarely had contemporary crisis-journalism turned out, in retrospect, to have veered so widely from reality. Essentially, the dominant themes of

the words and film from Vietnam . . . added up to a portrait of defeat for the Allies. Historians, on the contrary, have concluded that the Tet offensive resulted in a severe military-political setback for Hanoi in the South. To have portrayed such a setback for one side as a defeat for the other—in a major crisis abroad—cannot be counted as a triumph for American journalism."

But the coverage of the Tet Offensive was only the most flagrant example of the distortion of the conduct of the war by the news media. For some time previous to Tet, the fighting had been misrepresented. Renowned journalist Howard K. Smith maintained, "Viet Cong casualties were one hundred times ours. But [the news media] never told the public that. We just showed pictures day after day of Americans getting hell kicked out of them. That was enough to break America apart."

TOP: Using a jeep for a dolly, a *CBS Evening News* cameraman is rolled along at walking speed by helpful Marines to provide some "action" during anchorman Walter Cronkite's interview with Lieutenant Colonel Marcus J. Gravel, commander of the 1st Battalion, 1st Marine Regiment, during the Battle of Hue, February 20, 1968. Cronkite was accused of dropping all objectivity late in the Vietnam War to campaign against it, using his important position to influence public opinion.

BOTTOM: Young war correspondent Dan Rather in Vietnam, circa 1966. Always alert to get a "story," the now-famous newsman probably got one on this occasion in Vietnam.

and universities closed down during the rioting, as students and their professors staged demonstrations and sit-ins against the war's conduct.

Regular troops had to be called to Washington, D.C., where the White House and other government buildings were encircled. The presence of troops was necessary to stabilize the city when one hundred thousand people marched in protest. Some ten thousand demonstrators were ejected from a camp along the Potomac. On May 3, the mob began blocking traffic and littering the Capitol with trash. More than twelve thousand protesters were arrested before the demonstrations could be contained. Nixon was so unnerved by the disturbances that he went to the Lincoln Memorial one evening with his valet and talked with some of the demonstrators, attempting to show them that he was sensitive to their feelings. Possibly in response to the demonstrations, the Senate repealed the Tonkin Gulf Resolution, which President Johnson had used as the basis for U.S. military involvement in Vietnam. President Nixon argued, however, that the resolution was not his only empowerment, that as president of the United States, he was also Commander in Chief of U.S. forces, with all the rights expressed and implied by that title.

This turmoil produced a number of negative developments. One of these was President Nixon's formation of a secret team of spies led by Tom Huston, an ex-Army intelligence officer. Their mission was to place Nixon's critics under surveillance and to inform the president of any activities by his enemies that might have adverse consequences on his presidency. Even Huston warned Nixon that this program was illegal. In the meantime, Henry Kissinger, Nixon's national security advisor, encouraged Nixon to resist the dissidents, saying that the executive branch of government "had to make it clear that our foreign policy was not made by street protests." The violent agitation reminded Kissinger, a Jew, of the terrifying Nazi mobs he had witnessed in Germany when he was a youth.

Congress, meanwhile, passed a variety of bills and resolutions limiting the president's future powers. Through these actions, the

BELOW: A mortar crew of the 196th Brigade, Americal Division, conducts a fire mission north of Dong Ha, May 20, 1968. The men shield their ears from the loud blast, which, over time, without protection, can injure a soldier's hearing.

president was not allowed to use U.S. advisors in Cambodia. On June 30, 1970, U.S. military aid to Cambodia was constrained by the Cooper-Church Amendment (although this prohibition was later eliminated). Military funds also were made unavailable for U.S. ground troops in countries outside the boundaries of Vietnam. In addition, the raid into Cambodia accelerated the withdrawal timetable for troops operating in Vietnam; monthly draft calls were scaled back; the defense budget was reduced; and some members of the House of Representatives even called for a unilateral withdrawal from Vietnam, although their initiative failed.

While a large number of Americans supported the president, many newspapers

23D (AMERICAL) INFANTRY DIVISION

General William C. Westmoreland reactivated the 23d Infantry Division and organized it in Vietnam on September 25, 1967. The division was deployed adjacent to the Marines, initially, in the northern coastal sector of Vietnam, making its home in the southern part of I Corps, with headquarters at Chu Lai. The terrain in the area varied from coastal, marshy lowlands to rugged mountains and triple-canopy jungles. From autumn 1967 to autumn 1968, the division fought the enemy in Quang Nam and Quang Tri provinces, and in early 1968 one of its brigades was sent to Quang Ngai Province. In 1969 and 1970, the division battled the enemy in the Duc Pho, Chu Lai, and Tam Ky areas. In November 1971, after 1,526 days in Vietnam, the division was inactivated.

At that time, 1969, there was still favor for the war back home. But by April of 1970, there was Kent State, so that's when things really started going sour. . . . But prior to that, everybody was more favorable. Jane Fonda's movie, *Barbarella*: everybody loved that. . . . But now, she's not a favorite.

—Bill Townsley

regularly attacked him. A *New York Times* writer accused Nixon of renouncing his pledge to end the Vietnam War. Walter Hickel, Nixon's secretary of the interior, publicly criticized the Cambodian invasion and may have been fired later for his lack of loyalty. Nixon, while shaken by the attacks issued by clergymen, professors, businessmen, and lawyers, held his ground, saying: "If, when the chips are down, the world's most powerful nation, the United States of America, acts like a pitiful helpless giant, the forces of totalitarianism and anarchy will threaten free nations and free institutions throughout the world." Many agreed with Nixon, but just as many dissented.

As the war progressed, U.S. soldiers became increasingly aware of antiwar sentiment in the United States. A few, too, brought some of that dissent with them to Vietnam. Soldiers were puzzled and offended by the increasing lack of support by the American press, the agitation against the war by celebrities like Jane Fonda—who even hobnobbed with their enemies in Hanoi—and, of course, the campus demonstrators, who were considered slackers by many GIs.

At that time, 1969, there was still favor for the war back home. But by April of 1970, there was Kent State, so that's when things really started going sour for the notion of our being in Vietnam. But prior to that, everybody was more favorable. Jane Fonda's movie *Barbarella*, everybody loved and wanted to see that fifteen times, just the first reel, fifteen times at the club. But now, she's not a favorite.

—Bill Townsley

Declining Soldier Morale

Starting in 1969, U.S. forces in Vietnam began to exhibit a steady decline in morale. Such deteriorating morale can sometimes result when an army is subject to high casualty rates or repeated defeats, or when operating conditions become unbearable. None of these factors seemed to be the case with the U.S. Army in Vietnam, however; no more than in other wars fought by the United States in its history. One of the things that might have eroded morale, though, was the U.S. no-win policy in the war after 1968. Why should soldiers die for a cause, they asked themselves, the issue of which was already decided and was to be an American failure. The elusiveness of the enemy also

BELOW: Jane Fonda sings an antiwar song while sitting behind a North Vietnamese AZP-57 optical-mechanical computing site at the fire-control position of a 57-mm towed anti-aircraft gun (Soviet S-60/Chinese Type 59) in July 1972. During her two-week visit to the Hanoi area, Fonda taped as many as ten propaganda messages, some broadcast live, for her North Vietnamese hosts. She also told seven POWs that "Americans are fighting for Esso, Shell, and Coca-Cola" during a photo op staged principally for the Communist press. (An eighth captive, USAID worker Michael Benge, was tortured for three days when he refused to cooperate.) The photo op at the three-gun anti-aircraft battery, however, was well attended by the Western media, and dozens of photos exist of Fonda smiling, clapping, and laughing. She later expressed regret at having her picture taken and that her actions caused pain to many vets, but clarified that "I did not, have not, and will not say that going to North Vietnam was a mistake."

BELOW: Low morale and lax discipline can have a negative effect on survivability. For example, after a hard slog through rough terrain, circa 1969, these 9th Infantry Division soldiers took a break before cleaning the mud from their M60 machine-gun ammunition. This photograph invariably elicits a range of responses, from groans to outright anger, from enlisted, NCOs, and officers alike. A former 25th Division corporal who served in 1967 to 1968 blurted out, "Where's these guys' sergeant? But, really, they shouldn't have to have anybody tell them to get this stuff clean." Exhausted or not, the first thing these men should have done in this situation is to use clean stream water, or better yet, the water in their canteens, to rinse the mud off of their ammunition before it starts to dry and harden. It would be absolutely useless now if they came under fire, and it will only get tougher to clean as the seconds tick by in the hot climate. Said another vet: "There is a reason for ammo boxes and bandoliers."

exasperated the soldiers. They witnessed their comrades being killed by unseen enemies who fired at them with automatic rifles from behind a curtain of jungle. Moreover, a casual step forward, or a cautious one for that matter, could result in the explosion of a camouflaged mine or booby trap that killed or maimed the soldiers, leaving them crippled for life.

The difficulty of identifying the enemy was also frustrating. Anyone they encountered—a man, woman, or child—could be the enemy, so an unnatural paranoia gripped some of the soldiers. A villager who stared at them as they passed by on a patrol might be setting them up for a rendezvous with death. Drugs increasingly became prevalent among the soldiers, and inci-

dents of "fragging"—attacks on junior officers and NCOs by their own men—increased to 126, including 37 deaths, in 1969. In addition, search-and-destroy operations, as the war ground on, became desultory "search-and-evade" excursions, in which patrol leaders often sought safety for themselves and their men and returned to base camps with phony reports of their supposed activities.

The erosion in morale that began in 1969 became more pronounced in the following years. By 1970, some 65,000 American soldiers indulged in drugs, and more than 11,000 arrests were made that year for drug violations. More than three times as many fraggings occurred that year compared with the

year before. By 1971, the instances of courts-martial had increased 26 percent per capita over 1969, while the instance of fragging rose more than 500 percent. Desertions and absences without leave also rose dramatically. Arrests for heroin offenses rose from 1,146 in 1970 to more than 7,000 in 1971. Drug abuse had become epidemic. This behavior was the result of a number of causes: the ready availability of drugs, the general permissiveness of the times, failures in leadership, and a war that led to no positive good the soldiers could envisage.

Morale among black soldiers suffered under these conditions, also, but it was further eroded by the inequities of the draft, which fewer blacks than whites were in a position to avoid through college deferments. In 1969, the Nixon administration attempted to make the draft system fairer by putting in place a lottery system that eliminated a large number of exemptions, but the damage to morale had already been done. The fact that casualties were sometimes disproportionately higher for African Americans than for enlisted whites only made matters worse. In his book *The 25-Year War*, General Bruce Palmer states that black casualties in Vietnam "amounted to almost one-fourth of the U.S. Army enlisted losses at a time when blacks composed approximately 11 percent of the U.S. general population between nineteen and twenty-one years of age." This disparity likely represented the disproportionate representation of blacks in frontline infantry units—those who take the biggest hits in combat.

When First Lieutenant Brian M. Thacker, the son of a military man, joined the U.S. Army, he noticed that an antimilitary attitude had evolved in draft-age young men.

We knew the wheels were off, and we knew we were getting out. We already knew that we had a racial problem and issues, that the armed forces were no different from our regular society. There was an incredible antiwar sentiment in the age group that I was with that was very divisive. A lot of people just couldn't understand why we didn't just get

out. Why don't we just leave, pull the troops out now? Why go? That's one of those questions we'll be arguing about for a long time to come. And the answer is, you just can't leave and pull out that quickly.

—Brian M. Thacker

Jerry D. Morelock, the commander of an artillery battery of the 196th Light Infantry Brigade, viewed U.S. soldier morale during the Vietnam War differently than many. For him, it became a personal leadership challenge.

From November 1971 until November 1972, I served as an artillery battery commander supporting the 196th Light Infantry Brigade. We operated outside of Da Nang, and later we were moved to Phu Bai, south of Hue, during the 1972 Easter Offensive. U.S. soldiers during this period are often portrayed in films and other media as either drug-crazed killers or having extremely low soldier morale. Some commentators have suggested that the soldiers spent their idle hours figuring out ways to murder their officers.

That image, to officers like myself who were there during this difficult period, is patently false and does an incredible injustice

ABOVE: Americal Division cannoneer Sergeant Michael Ruibal, of Bellflower, California, raises a flag given to him by his father. The event informally celebrated the September 4, 1970, recapture of the Special Forces camp at Kham Duc, which had been overrun two years earlier by the NVA.

BELOW: The U.S. Army set up "Kick the Habit" centers both stateside and in Vietnam to give soldiers with drug or alcohol dependencies a safe channel to get effective medical attention. The centers were affiliated with the Army's medical system—not its criminal justice system—to ensure that soldiers could seek help without fear of reprisals. Personnel from the centers gave seminars and classes on how to spot and deal with drug and alcohol abuse within a given command or unit.

to the men who, for the most part, served honorably. Over 96 percent of Vietnam-era GIs, for instance, received an honorable discharge. Significantly, the overwhelming majority of U.S. Army troops who served in Vietnam were volunteers, not draftees, and had chosen to serve. Of the 2.5 million soldiers who served in Vietnam during the period of U.S. involvement, only about 25 percent were draftees and ordered into the service. Nearly all of our soldiers served honorably.

Post–Vietnam War studies have shown that, despite the popular stereotype that most of the soldiers serving in Vietnam were from American society's lowest economic strata, the socioeconomic makeup of the majority of our forces in Vietnam was upper working class and middle class, although all classes of society were represented, from top to bottom. Another myth about the war, the claim that African Americans suffered casualties disproportionate to their representation in American society, has been proven false by renowned sociologist Charles Moskos. African Americans accounted for about 12 percent of all Vietnam casualties, which is about the same proportion as their representation in the overall population. Another exploded myth is that Vietnam veterans suffered more psychiatric problems after the war, more than soldiers in other wars. In fact, the rate of psychological disorders for Vietnam veterans is about half that experienced by World War II and Korean War veterans.

Nonetheless, like the rest of American society in the late 1960s and early 1970s, drug use in Vietnam was a problem, but not to the extent usually claimed. The real issue with drug use among troops boiled down to leadership failures in individual units. For example, in my own artillery battery of about one hundred soldiers, in January 1972, we had exactly two soldiers who tested positive for drugs

RIGHT: U.S. Army officers presiding over a general court-martial in Vietnam. MACV intelligence chief, Lieutenant General Phillip Davidson, later wrote: "The caseload was staggering. Key witnesses either rotated back to the United States or were unavailable due to death or operational requirements. The military lawyers themselves frequently rotated before their cases came to trial. Many offenses were committed in isolated combat areas, and getting the accused, the witnesses, and the court together required Herculean coordination. Frequently, offenses involved Vietnamese witnesses who were difficult to locate and interrogate. Finally, the mass of paperwork required to protect the rights of the accused had to pass laboriously up and down the chain of command…. Military justice was neither swift nor certain and transgressors have been comparatively free to repeat their acts with impunity."

in unit testing. However, when the 101st Airborne Division stood down and went home in late January, many soldiers from the 101st were sent to other units to serve the remainder of their one-year tours. We received about twenty of these ex-101st soldiers. Every one of them tested positive for drug use. This included a young sergeant who I had personally promoted when he was in my unit back at Fort Sill and had been "clean" before he deployed to Vietnam. In this instance, leadership failures in the 101st in controlling drug use in its units led to my own unit going from approximately 2 percent of troops having a drug problem to over 20 percent in that category—literally overnight. So I ended up spending a great deal of time and effort dealing with this imported drug problem during the remainder of my combat tour. The real issue was not drugs. It was basic leadership.

—Jerry D. Morelock

Lam Son 719

After the U.S. invasion of Cambodia in May 1970, the NVA, hampered by its losses in men and supplies, conducted small, desultory attacks the rest of the year. This lull in the tempo of enemy operations allowed MACV to further heighten training in the ARVN and to improve the South's combat capability. By 1971, a more assured ARVN appeared ready to conduct its own large-scale combat operations.

Throughout late 1970 and early 1971, the NVA had been transporting troops and supplies to bases along the Ho Chi Minh Trail into southern Laos. They were to be used for new planned attacks into South Vietnam. Because the United States was planning to evacuate much of its air support from South Vietnam in the near future, MACV urged the ARVN to conduct a large-scale operation into Laos to destroy this NVA buildup while U.S. air support was still available.

NVA Base Areas 604 and 611, near Tchepone, were chosen as the targets of the attack for an operation called Lam Son 719. Two ARVN

divisions and a U.S. Marine division would compose the assault force. If successful, the operation would take military pressure off South Vietnam for another year, much as the 1970 attack into Cambodia had stalled future Communist attacks. Protecting these base areas, though, was critical to the North Vietnamese, especially after the closing of the port at Sihanoukville in 1970. The Ho Chi Minh Trail was their only logistical pipeline into South Vietnam, and the base areas and supplies stored along it were crucial to the NVA's future operations in South Vietnam. Thus, a desperate defense of these bases should have been expected. Because of the Cooper-Church Amendment passed by Congress, U.S. forces were prohibited from attacking these bases, so only the ARVN could invade Cambodia. But U.S. forces could support the ARVN, and they planned to do so.

When Henry Kissinger suggested the operation, General Abrams ordered some of his subordinates to plan it in detail. The South Vietnamese, on their part, eagerly agreed to participate. Virtually everyone in the U.S. chain of command was aware of what was being planned and approved of it, including President Nixon, Secretary of Defense Melvin Laird, and the chairman of the JCS, Admiral

BELOW: During Operation Lam Son 719, February 1971, South Vietnamese forces cross over into Laos in a personnel carrier. Without close coordination, advice, and support from the U.S. Army and Air Force, the ARVN operations did not go well.

ABOVE: The ARVN forces that invaded Laos in 1971 as part of Operation Lam Son 719 captured this Soviet 37-mm anti-aircraft gun. ARVN troops also seized five thousand individual weapons and two thousand crew-served weapons. But the ARVN's unsteady operations against NVA forces did not bode well for the future of the conflict.

Thomas H. Moorer. Before the operation began, however, the North Vietnamese had learned about it in detail from their agents and through press leaks.

The North Vietnamese had for some time considered an attack on Tchepone likely, and they had taken a number of precautions to render an assault on their staging and supply bases costly. Defensive positions were prepared, ambush sites created, and artillery preregistered to fire accurately on likely helicopter landing areas. After their spies informed them that an attack was imminent, critical supplies were moved to nearby secure locations.

Operation Lam Son 719 began in earnest on January 29, 1971. As the operation got into full swing, bad weather prevented allied air assets from neutralizing the potent NVA anti-aircraft positions around Tchepone. Soon, as part of the operation, an ARVN airborne division landed in the area around A Luoi, fifteen miles from Tchepone. Its mission was to screen the ARVN 1st Armored Brigade when it reached that village on February 10. By February 11, though, the ARVN forces appeared to be frozen in place. This caused consternation at Abrams's headquarters. Inactivity was a dangerous thing for an army surrounded by its enemies. During the lull in the fighting, the NVA pushed more of its

artillery forward and bombarded the ARVN with increasing intensity. Soon, enemy T-34 and T-54 tanks appeared.

Before the operation began, President Nguyen Van Thieu had warned his commanders to take no more than three thousand casualties. This was the cause of the ARVN's cautious, indecisive behavior at Tchepone. The result was disastrous. The NVA, with four divisions, tanks, and artillery units in the area, began attacking the ARVN aggressively. Soon, a number of ARVN units were overrun, and a brigade commander was captured. Anti-aircraft fire became intense. In desperation and to save face, President Thieu ordered the ARVN to capture the village of Tchepone, a position with little military and only symbolic value by this time. Once the village was captured, the ARVN began withdrawing its soldiers by helicopter. Meanwhile, it had abandoned any hope of destroying the two NVA bases, the primary objective of the raid. During the frantic ARVN withdrawal, NVA artillery rained shells onto its positions, creating chaos in the ranks. In response, U.S. B-52s and fighter-bombers fiercely pounded the NVA positions, but the NVA refused to budge.

The operation was a disaster for both sides. The NVA is said to have lost half of its 40,000-man force, most of them killed by U.S. B-52s, which were extremely lethal against massed troops. In addition, it lost 106 tanks—versus 54 tanks lost by the ARVN. The terrible attrition suffered by the NVA hampered its operations for some time, but the loss was far from critical.

The ARVN situation was equally imperiled. Its mission had been to capture NVA Base Areas 604 and 611 and to disrupt enemy operations along the Ho Chi Minh Trail. It had failed to accomplish these objectives. But it was the poor performance of the ARVN that was most unsettling. Its command and control had been miserable; its various commanders had worked at cross-purposes with one another; and its armor was misused or not used at all. All in all, the ARVN appeared to be incompetent to conduct the sort of complex, modern operations that would be necessary to defeat the North Vietnamese Armed Forces when the United States withdrew from the war.

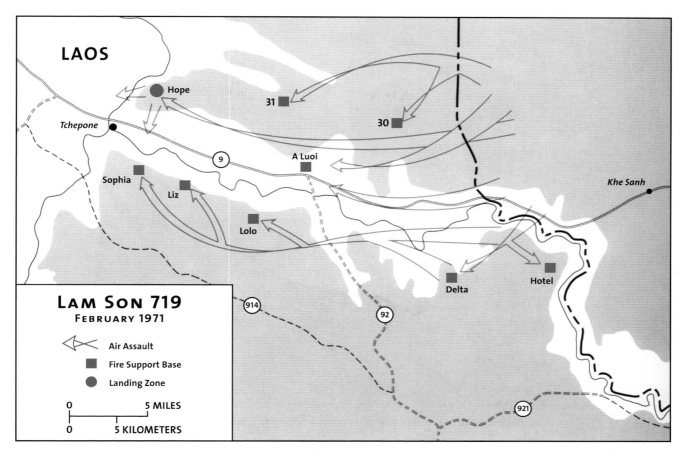

LAM SON 719
FEBRUARY 1971

LAOS

Hope

Tchepone

31

30

9

A Luoi

Khe Sanh

Sophia

Liz

Lolo

Delta

Hotel

914

92

921

Air Assault
Fire Support Base
Landing Zone

0   5 MILES

0   5 KILOMETERS

LEFT: One of XXIV Corps'
175-mm guns fires deep into
Laos from the old Special
Forces base near Lang Vei
during Operation LAM SON
719, February 1971.

After Quang Tri fell, Hue appeared vulnerable. The intensity and style of combat practiced by the NVA was completely different from that previously practiced by them in Vietnam; in fact, [it was] like World War II all over again.

—Colonel Jerry D. Morelock, Ph.D.,
U.S. Army, Retired

Chapter Five

WITHDRAWAL FROM THE FIGHT

By 1971, drug abuse was up and soldier discipline and the general morale of U.S. forces in Vietnam had reached an all-time low. Morale in the United States languished also. A massive antiwar demonstration in San Francisco drew 150,000 protesters; 200,000 angry people poured into the streets of Washington. Meanwhile, the Mansfield Amendment, passed by the Senate, called for the exit of U.S. troops from Vietnam "nine months from passage," later changed to the "earliest practicable date." A formal, legitimate way out of the war had to be discovered, and it had to be found via the ongoing, but to this point totally unsuccessful, negotiations with the North Vietnamese Communists, who were playing a waiting game, biding their time until we capitulated.

NVA Easter Offensive

Periodically throughout 1971, North Vietnam's chief negotiator, Le Duc Tho, met with Henry Kissinger, ostensibly in an attempt to arrive at a peace settlement. Most of the concessions made during these talks, however, were by the Americans. In a proposal at a meeting on May 31, 1971, in return for an immediate POW exchange, Kissinger promised to establish a deadline for complete U.S. troop withdrawal and authorize a cease-fire; he also pledged to bring no new forces into Vietnam or the countries bordering it.

The Communists, however, refused this offer. The POWs were one of North Vietnam's principal negotiating tools, and once turned over to the United States, the North's negotiating leverage would be greatly weakened. Kissinger's offer, moreover, did not address the dismantling of the Thieu government, one of North Vietnam's nonnegotiable demands, so the rest of the year was spent sparring over this last issue. From a cynical perspective, it appears that the Communists were merely buying time with these feigned negotiations while they geared up for another big offensive in 1972. What was the use in negotiating seriously when they could play for time and win everything they wanted on the battlefield once most of the American forces had pulled out of the country?

As Le Duc Tho talked of peace and quibbled endlessly over terms and terminology, the Soviet Union was sending North Vietnam huge quantities of military supplies: T-34, T-54, and

T-55 tanks; surface-to-air missiles; MiG-21 fighter jets; long-range 130-mm guns; trucks; shoulder-fired SA-7 anti-aircraft missiles; tons of ammunition; 120-mm mortars; and petroleum products—but, alas, no olive branches. By the end of 1971, well-equipped North Vietnamese Army units had surged into the area just north of the DMZ. Now, with the NVA poised on the northern border of South Vietnam, Le Duc Tho refused to talk to Kissinger any longer.

When the attack came, President Nixon ordered the resumption of bombing in North Vietnam's confined border region between the DMZ and the 18th parallel, hoping to disrupt the passage of some twenty divisions of NVA troops into South Vietnam. War protesters accused Nixon of widening the conflict, but in the president's view he was protecting South Vietnam and the remaining sixty-five thousand U.S. soldiers still in South Vietnam. The Communists, meanwhile, were convinced that Nixon was incapable of calling in further U.S. troops because of the political situation he faced at home. They hoped, in fact, that their invasion of South Vietnam would seal Nixon's fate in the upcoming American election.

By late March 1972, some 125,000 NVA troops and hundreds of tanks and artillery pieces were poised for the Hguyen Hue, or Easter Offensive, a charge into South Vietnam to defeat the remaining allied forces. General Giap's operational plan consisted of three invasion thrusts. The first, by the 304th and 308th NVA divisions and three infantry regiments with two hundred tanks, would attack Quang Tri across the DMZ. The 324B Division would simultaneously attack Hue. These two spearheads of the Northern offensive were to clear the northern provinces of ARVN troops.

Meanwhile, in the South, the 5th, 7th, and 9th VC divisions, with two hundred tanks, would attack Loc Ninh and An Loc. If successful, they would continue on to Saigon. A third invasion, by the 2d, 3d, and 320th NVA divisions, would strike the belly of South Vietnam, around Kontum, and the coastal area of Binh Dinh Province. The objective of the three-prong invasion was to damage the ARVN's fighting power and to seize control of key Southern cities. Giap planned to practice modern,

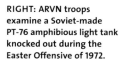

RIGHT: ARVN troops examine a Soviet-made PT-76 amphibious light tank knocked out during the Easter Offensive of 1972.

conventional warfare and to score a knockout punch. His forces' critical weakness, however, was their vulnerability to U.S. airpower.

The NVA attack was to begin in late March. This was to avoid the monsoon season, which would begin around June and render resupply difficult, if not impossible. General Abrams understood that an attack was coming, but he did not know its exact date. When the offensive occurred, he was out of the country. President Nixon agreed that an NVA invasion was imminent and had U.S. airpower increased to include six available aircraft carriers and two hundred B-52s at the ready at bases on Guam and in Thailand.

The South Vietnamese forces by this time numbered more than 1 million men, and U.S. aid had provided them with more than a million M16 rifles, two thousand heavy mortars, forty thousand M79 grenade launchers, and twelve thousand machine guns. They also had nine tactical air wings. In addition, some 5,300 U.S. advisors were attached throughout the various commands, but only a fraction of them were used to advise combat units. Thus, while

a few U.S. Army combat units were available to support ARVN operations, massive U.S. tactical airpower, including helicopter gunships, remained a threatening presence.

Although most U.S. Army units had retired from Vietnam by 1972, some units, like Jerry D. Morelock's artillery battery of the 196th Light Infantry Brigade, were still in the thick of the worst combat.

When the NVA Easter Offensive began in the spring of 1972, my artillery battery was conducting limited combat operations from a firebase located outside of Da Nang, Vietnam's second-largest city. At the time the offensive occurred, U.S. military forces in Vietnam had been drawn down to only two combat brigades: our 196th Light Infantry Brigade in the north and a brigade of the 1st Cavalry Division farther south.

This latest NVA offensive was a complete departure from previous NVA tactics in that it featured an all-out assault by massed formations of troops supported by field artillery

BELOW: North Vietnamese 130-mm guns on the Kontum front, April 1972. The NVA marched aggressively across the DMZ and eastward into the Central Highlands, and finally attacked An Loc, the gateway to Saigon. The Communists, nonetheless, failed to topple the South Vietnamese government.

and large numbers of tanks, mostly Soviet T-54s. The NVA attack hit two general locations. Part of the forces crossed the DMZ and headed for Quang Tri and then proceeded south to Hue. The other attack was farther south in Vietnam, in Military Region 3, and focused on An Loc.

The powerful attack in the north hit the ARVN 1st and 3d Infantry divisions with a massive surprise attack. The ARVN 1st Division was a veteran outfit and held its ground well; however, the ARVN 3d Division, a recently formed, inexperienced unit manned by castoffs from other units, crumbled almost immediately.

The NVA offensive rolled over the firebases in the north and captured Camp Carroll, then Quang Tri. It was only through the heroic efforts of an American Chinook helicopter pilot, Captain Harry Thain, that the U.S. advisors were rescued from Camp Carroll. Thain was awarded a Distinguished Service Cross for his heroic actions in landing his helicopter at the camp under intense fire to take off the advisors. Meanwhile, the NVA marched into the opposite side of the large camp. Tragically, Thain was killed a month later, flying a combat mission for my own artillery battalion. As his Chinook landed to deliver barrier

materials to our firebase, an NVA mortar round hit the cockpit and exploded the helicopter, killing all aboard. Harry was one of seventeen of my West Point classmates [USMA class of 1969] killed in Vietnam; many of them were helicopter pilots.

After Quang Tri fell, Hue appeared vulnerable. The intensity and style of combat practiced by the NVA was completely different from that previously practiced by them in Vietnam; in fact, [it was] like World War II all over again. The first word we had that something big was occurring was when we received a late-night notification to prepare the battery for removal to the U.S. Air Force base at Da Nang. We were to move north to a location south of Hue, the ancient imperial capital. This news sent us into a frenzy of activity preparing the guns for transport and packing all of our equipment. After working all night to get the battery ready for redeployment, we road-marched to the air base and loaded troops, howitzers, and all other equipment and supplies onto U.S. Air Force C-130 transport aircraft. The flight to the U.S. air base at Phu Bai, around fifteen kilometers south of Hue, was a short one. After landing, we moved all of our equipment to an abandoned ARVN artillery base not far from the

RIGHT: Vietnamese paratroopers of the 2d Airborne Battalion caught five NVA T-54/55 tanks and an infantry company crossing this river during the Easter Offensive. All five tanks were destroyed during an air strike called in by the paratroopers' U.S. advisors, and fifty-seven NVA soldiers were killed during the subsequent firefight. It must have taken an awfully big bomb to flip over this 36-ton brute.

The CORDS and Phoenix Programs

Impressed with the effectiveness of the Viet Cong's "action militia" groups that worked at the hamlet (village) level, the South Vietnamese government began forming their own "Revolutionary Development" cadres in 1966 to serve as a direct link between the government and people in select areas that would be expanded over time. The 59-man and, later, 30-man cadres lived in the hamlets they served and their members were responsible for specific political, economic, social, and security functions. Local self-defense platoons organized by the Revolutionary Development Teams soon became known as the Popular Forces (PF) and, together with the Regional Force (RF) companies, were known as Ruff-Puffs by American forces.

The cadres greatly enhanced the pacification program and were given added impetus when the wasteful rivalry between the U.S. government's various civilian agencies in Vietnam was ended by integrating them more closely with the military's counterinsurgency effort. In May 1967, the Agency for International Development, the U.S. Information Agency, the State Department, many Army, and most Central Intelligence Agency projects were placed under the Civil Operations and Revolutionary Development Support (CORDS) program, administered by Robert W. Komer as the deputy to the commander of MACV for CORDS (DepCORDS). The unified military-civilian advisory effort quickly showed results and operated in all of Vietnam's 250 districts and 44 provinces.

A unique opportunity opened up for the CORDS program after the

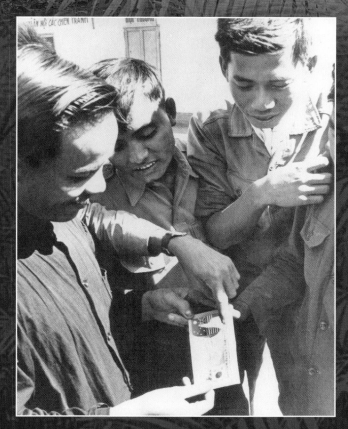

LEFT: Former Communist fighters examine the pass that allowed them to surrender voluntarily. Expanding village by village, the CIA-sponsored CORDS Revolutionary Development Teams offered a first chance for surrender and amnesty, and would then ferret out remaining Communists with the help of rewards, informants, and a number of other "unspecified but effective means" to sweep targeted localities free of insurgent and underground resistance to the government.

BELOW: An early example of the safe-conduct passes that were distributed as the opening gambit during pacification operations.

Communists—and particularly the Viet Cong—suffered grievous losses during the Tet "Great Uprising-Great Offensive" of 1968. Openly exposing themselves for the first time to massive American firepower, more than 32,000 enemy were killed and 5,800 captured, figures that included an exceptionally large number of local and regional political and operational leaders. The decimated Viet Cong were given no time to recover. On July 1, 1968, the South Vietnamese announced the beginning of Le Loi (Accelerated Pacification), which

included the Phung Hoang (Phoenix) program. The goal of Phung Hoang was nothing short of the eradication of all leaders and operatives in the Communist infrastructure, principally through encouraging defections and capturing the maximum number of cadres in order

ABOVE: William E. Colby, the CIA station chief whose cover designations were officially MACV Deputy for Pacification and then DepCORDS, is seen giving a final personal inspection of an elite, handpicked Revolutionary Development Team that has been deployed to help clean out Kien Hoa Province. The team members, as well as Colby, are distinguished by the traditional peasant "black pajamas," which reflected their grassroots, unorthodox methods. Before going operational, this cadre had received extensive instruction at the Revolutionary Development Training Center at Vung Tung.

to gain valuable information and speed further operations.

MACV, through its CORDS assistance structure, lent direct material support and approximately 450 advisory personnel, as well as energetic guidance in the form of one William Colby, a former CIA station chief in Saigon who was sent back to Vietnam after Tet, at Komer's request, to serve as his deputy. Of the remaining 80,000 Viet Cong who survived Tet, roughly 1,950 defected, 2,250 were killed, and 10,800 captured by the end of the year. Colby succeeded Komer as the DepCORDS in November of 1968, and by the end of 1971, the number of "neutralized" VC had grown to 17,000 who accepted amnesty, 20,000 killed, and 28,000 captured, with many thousands more fleeing to sanctuaries in Cambodia.

Large swaths of Vietnam were now completely free from Viet Cong attack and the NVA were forced to turn to conventional warfare. The North Vietnamese also managed to keep a few VC "main force" battalions in the field, in order to retain at least some pretense of an active "people's revolution" in the South, by packing them with large numbers of "volunteers." The Communists, who had worked effectively to turn their military defeat during Tet into a political victory, now staved off complete destruction of organized Viet Cong resistance by orchestrating denunciations of Phoenix "assassination squads" in the international press. The murder of 61,000 village officials, civil servants, and family members at the hands of the Viet Cong between 1958 and 1966 did not figure into these articles, and neither did the 5,800 civilians murdered by Communist death squads in Hue during their monthlong seizure of the city in 1968.

The antiwar movement in the U.S. quickly took up the drumbeat, which ultimately led to congressional investigations of the CORDS and Phoenix programs in February 1970. Colby was pulled back to Washington to provide testimony, and, in a rather transparent effort to soften CORDS' now tarnished image, the word *Revolutionary* was replaced by *Rural* in the organization's title the month before the hearings were set to begin. Although assassinations had been specifically prohibited in writing by Colby, some had undoubtedly occurred, and the shoot-first-and-ask-questions-later aspect of a combat raid's opening seconds led to deaths of VC who might—or might not—have surrendered.

Funding cuts that followed in the wake of the U.S. hearings sent the Revolutionary Development cadres into

a steady decline, and they were disbanded altogether in 1971. William Colby continued on in Vietnam, then rose to the CIA's executive director-comptroller post in 1972, and was director of Central Intelligence from 1973 to 1976. As for the Viet Cong, with their power broken throughout most of the South they took little part in the armor-heavy conventional offensives of 1972 and 1975, but they had a conspicuous presence among the victors during the brutal reprisals that followed the fall of Saigon.

ABOVE: Revolutionary Development Teams were the cutting edge of the CORDS program to eliminate Communist influence or control over rural areas in South Vietnam. During an initial village sweep, these teams were often reinforced by "Amnesty Teams" made up of specially trained psychological-warfare troops that would broadcast appeals to surrender. The program's gathering reputation for ruthless effectiveness caused many Communists to surrender or defect upon hearing the warning from such broadcasts. Once the detainees were questioned and removed from a populated locale for further interrogation, the Revolutionary Development cadre would establish itself in a village as the national government's representative on all matters, and would assist a Phung Hoang (Phoenix) program's Provisional Reconnaissance Unit in methodically tracking down and eliminating remaining Communist resisters and "die-hard" cell leaders through the use of ingenious intelligence ruses, locally obtained intelligence, and brutally effective tactics that concentrated on "fighting fire with fire."

air base. We found out soon afterwards that President Nixon had made a televised address in which he stated that no American ground troops were involved in opposing the NVA offensive. Our presence in the fighting area belied that assertion.

Another disturbing sight that greeted us as we off-loaded equipment from the C-130s was dozens of Vietnamese civilians pressed against the chain-link fence on the perimeter of the air base. At first I didn't know what they were doing there and suspected they were trying to get on a plane to leave the area. However, one of my sergeants soon found out their intentions and told me: they were narcotics dealers, hoping to sell us heroin and other drugs. It seems they were suffering economically because their main source of customers—soldiers of the 101st Airborne Division, who had been stationed at Phu Bai before the unit had stood down—had left the drug dealers high and dry when they departed in late January. The dealers were so desperate to make a sale that they were tossing "caps," small, round, plastic capsules containing a modest amount of heroin, over the fence on approval, hoping we'd throw money back to them. I sent a section over to run them off, and we were soon rid of them— for the moment.

We immediately occupied the position and began improving it. Specifically, we had the troops enlarge and strengthen the bunkers we'd need in case of a rocket or mortar attack. It was good that we did so because beginning that night, rockets began to fall on the camp every night for the next several days. Our position was a particularly vulnerable one because we were located near a critical air base, an air cavalry base, and a Special Forces training camp. We guessed the enemy was trying to hit those more important targets, but he kept hitting us instead. The knowledge that we were not the enemy's intended target gave us small comfort.

I was sleeping in the Fire Direction Center that first night when we got rocketed. One of the sergeants came in to wake me up, and I moved outside to find a nice, thick bunker. The first one I found looked good to me, but

RIGHT: Two U.S. paratroopers of the 3d Battalion, 503d Infantry Division, rush forward to oppose an enemy sniper who has impeded the forward movement of the 173d Airborne Brigade during a patrol in the An Loa Valley near Bong Son.

Within the image: SONG MIEU GIANG RIVER, DROPPED SPAN, DROPPED SPAN, N

within a few seconds, four of my soldiers rolled inside, and it got so crowded I left and tried to find another refuge. The same thing happened in the next bunker I was in, so I gave up and just walked the perimeter, "enjoying" the fireworks.

For the next two months, we were engaged in fire support of the U.S. task force sent to Phu Bai, our express purpose being to protect that vital air base. The U.S. warplanes and TOW-firing helicopters from that base were absolutely critical in stopping the NVA offensive, which they did by destroying tanks, artillery, and troop formations. Clearly, the air base had to be protected at all costs. We were, therefore, part of Task Force Lafayette, composed of our artillery battery and a battalion of the 1st Infantry Regiment, which had also been operating around Da Nang. Our task force commander was 1st Infantry's Colonel Fred Mitchell, an outstanding combat leader. We fired missions all day long and sometimes throughout the night as well. The best thing about the situation was that we did not have to "clear" our fires with any Vietnamese civilian or military authority, as we had at

Da Nang. It had gotten so bad in Da Nang that even when we could see NVA rockets being set up and readied to fire, the Vietnamese civilian authority would not let us fire: "Too close to village," they usually said—which is why the wily NVA had chosen to set up their rockets there in the first place, of course.

That all changed at Phu Bai, however. I could "clear" my own fires, meaning we could get "rounds on target" within thirty seconds, plus time of flight, after receiving a call for fire from one of our forward observers with the infantry. One of the most notable fire missions we conducted in this regard occurred shortly after we got to Phu Bai. It was a "contact fire mission," i.e., the unit to be supported, an infantry platoon, was getting mortared right then. Our first rounds were on their way within seconds and were adjusted onto the suspected mortar location in a short time by the platoon's forward observer. The mortar fire quickly stopped, and when the infantry moved to clear the position they found two dead NVA, the remains of a mortar base plate, and a pair of Soviet binoculars— with an artillery shell fragment blasted right

ABOVE: A blown bridge over the Cua Viet River. The photograph was taken on April 6, 1972, from an aircraft attached to the USS *Kitty Hawk*. The plane was flown by Navy pilots Lieutenant Commander McKay and Lieutenant Commander Travis.

Individual and Crew-Served Weapons

BELOW: Although Communist armored fighting vehicles were not a significant factor in the war until the 1970s, the M20 3.5-inch bazooka rocket launcher saw steady use as a bunker-buster until replaced by the LAW in the mid-1960s. Here, in the midst of an August 1964 firefight, a U.S. advisor carefully removes a bazooka rocket that he had rammed too far forward into its launcher.

RIGHT: As with the bazooka rocket launcher, the M72 66-mm light antitank weapon (LAW) with fin-stabilized rocket produced a considerable back-blast when fired, but the weapon could be handled easily by one soldier, then discarded after ignition. To fire a LAW, the rear component containing the rocket, held by this MP's left hand, is pulled out until it locks in place at full length. This action automatically cocks the weapon and pops up the aiming sight. Although the 66-mm warhead could burn its way through twelve inches of steel-plate armor in controlled test conditions, effective use against even obsolescent tanks required pinpoint marksmanship gained through regular, repetitive training, which few U.S. or South Vietnamese troops ever received. Skilled anti-armor teams of ARVN soldiers at Kontum and An Loc, however, proved themselves to be quite adept at tank killing during the NVA's Easter Offensive of 1972.

ABOVE, LEFT AND RIGHT: The M29 81-mm mortar (left) and, beginning in 1970, the improved M29A1 (not shown) were envisioned to be the "mobile artillery" of U.S. Army infantry companies, but at 106 pounds apiece they were seldom lugged through the bush or jungle by the heavy-weapons platoon, which relied instead on Hueys for the heavy lifting. A handier mortar was the highly portable M19 60-mm (right), which the Marines had wisely kept in service but otherwise could be found only in the Army's National Guard formations since they had been phased out of "active" units. Mysteriously, within a short time after arriving in Vietnam, many Army rifle companies were found to possess the M19 and even the older M2 mortar on which it was based. Although obtained through a variety of means, most company M19s were weapons recaptured from the Viet Cong, with the ones in the best shape quietly retained for U.S. troops' use. A combination of wheeling and dealing with ARVN units and, eventually, direct acquisitions from U.S. stocks ensured an ample supply of mortar rounds. In 1970, the Army decided officially that it needed to have the 60-mm back in its inventory, and development began for a lightweight company mortar that became available years after the last U.S. troops departed Vietnam.

RIGHT: The heavy M30 rifled mortar could fire its 4.2-inch (107-mm) high-explosive (HE) round some 7,400 yards, compared with a maximum of 5,000 yards for the M29A1's HE round. A very useful indirect-fire weapon during the defense of firebases, this hefty 671-pound monster, as well as the 81-mm, were given a high degree of mobility when installed on mortar-mountable variants of the M113 APC.

LEFT: Early photographs from Vietnam often show a .30-caliber Browning automatic rifle (BAR) in the hands of a Special Forces soldier or other U.S. advisor. Because the rifle weighed more than twenty pounds, the "BAR man" of a Vietnamese patrol was frequently an American, while the weapon would be operated by the Vietnamese themselves when in static positions.

BELOW: Weapons-platoon members of a South Vietnamese Regional Forces company are briefed before going out on patrol from their village near Nha Trang, May 1967. In the foreground are .30-caliber M1919A6 Browning light machine guns. Although ruggedly constructed, the weapon was generally disdained by American troops because of its low rate of fire (400-500 rounds per minute), and was even less popular with the Vietnamese because its weight, with bipod and metal stock, exceeded 32 pounds. The soldiers at left are armed with the venerable .30-caliber M1 Garand rifle while those at center have .30-caliber M1 Winchester carbines. A significant number of Vietnamese had trouble accurately shoulder-firing the Garand, particularly after a long march, because, at more than 10 pounds with 8-round clip and sling, much of that weight was well forward down the rifle's 43.5-inch length. Even after the appearance of the light, modern M16, many ARVN troops preferred the M1 carbine, which, with clip and sling, was almost half the weight of the Garand and had an adequate range for most combat settings. At center right facing the camera are BARs.

TOP, LEFT AND RIGHT: For automatic fire, ARVN soldiers prized the legendary Thompson sub-machine gun (left) because of its compact dimensions, comparatively light weight, and the stopping power of its large .45-caliber slug. Seen here being disassembled by a South Vietnamese cadet (right), who wears a blindfold, is the M1911A1 automatic pistol. Despite its relatively small size, this .45-caliber sidearm had great stopping power and dependability in harsh jungle environments.

BELOW AND RIGHT: At the opposite end of the size and firepower spectrum is the powerful M2 .50-caliber Browning heavy machine gun (below), which pumps up to 600 rounds per minute at a range of 1,530 yards with great accuracy. The .50 caliber formed the cornerstone for the defense of virtually all allied camps and firebases. Still, the .50 caliber in combination with its lightest tripod weighed nearly 100 pounds, so the rugged M60 general-purpose machine gun (right), only 2 pounds heavier than the BAR, was the weapon carried into the field. Served by a crew of two, the M60, even in the hands of a skillful gunner, could use up a considerable amount of bullets in a firefight, and it was not unusual to see as many as half a dozen soldiers in a platoon draped in extra belts of the weapon's 7.62-mm NATO-standard ammunition.

AMBUSHERS

TOP, LEFT: The low-caliber, high-velocity round of the M16 was not suitable for the family of grenade launchers that were attachable to the muzzles of the M1 and M14 rifles. Fortunately, the U.S. Army had already fielded the M79 grenade launcher, a shotgunlike, shoulder-fired weapon that shot aerodynamic, exploding projectiles as far as 320 yards from its 40-mm barrel.

TOP, RIGHT: The M79 filled the need for a weapon that could cover the ground between the reach of a hand-thrown grenade and the shortest range of a mortar—and was loved by the troops. Any infantryman issued the M79, however, had to carry both it and his rifle, and switching from one weapon to the other meant that a target had to be, in effect, disengaged and then reacquired before it could be fired upon. A combination rifle/grenade launcher was clearly called for, and the XM148, shown here being test-fired by the 101st Airborne Division's 1st Brigade commander, Brigadier General Salve Matheson, was issued to the 101st.

BELOW: Following its successful introduction to the 101st Airborne Division, a growing number of other units were issued the XM148 until the M203 began replacing both launchers on a one-for-one basis in 1969.

BELOW: The M14 was essentially the same size and weight as the M1 Garand but used the 7.62-mm NATO round for semiautomatic and automatic fire from a larger and more efficient 20-round magazine. Although a fine weapon, it nevertheless lacked the firepower of the Communists' AK-47, and, beginning in 1966, the M14 was replaced in American units by the M16 yet saw continued use in several variations as an extremely effective sniper rifle.

ABOVE, LEFT: Fully five inches shorter and two pounds lighter than the M14, the M16, developed by Armalite and manufactured by Colt, was handled more easily in confined jungle conditions, and its small, high-velocity 5.56-mm (.22-caliber) bullets were actually more lethal than larger, slower bullets because, as wound ballistics long demonstrated, smaller, faster rounds would tumble as they passed through a body instead of tending to pass straight through. A series of early teething troubles centering chiefly around the power used in M16 cartridges had to be rectified before many U.S. soldiers and Marines felt comfortable with the weapon. Soon after the M16 proved its effectiveness, calls for an even shorter version prompted the design and fielding of the Colt Model 733 Commando, or CAR-15, assault rifle, a weapon fully ten inches shorter than the M16.

ABOVE, RIGHT: Although it was purchased in quantity for U.S. Army Special Forces and other special elements, the Colt Commando rifle was never approved for general use by the Army but nevertheless made its way into the hands of many "conventional" soldiers, like this 1st Infantry Division point man (at right), near Tan Hiep, who, lacking web gear, can travel much more lightly than the other 1st Division infantrymen in the photograph.

through them! When they rotated out of the field, the infantry platoon treated our gunners to a whole pallet of beer in gratitude. Undoubtedly, we'd saved some of them.

Hue was saved when U.S. advisors serving with the embattled ARVN forces blew up the strategic bridges that crossed the Cua Viet River just north of the city, preventing the NVA from advancing any further. The NVA offensive eventually fizzled out by the end of May, when U.S. airpower and TOW helicopters had blasted and eliminated many of their tanks and artillery. The NVA, however, had learned a valuable lesson: they would not again try to overrun South Vietnam until all U.S. military forces—especially American airpower—had been withdrawn and Congress had tied our hands, preventing any U.S. military action to enforce the treaty the NVA had signed.

When the NVA treacherously broke the treaty in 1975 there was nothing to prevent them from overrunning the entire country. In June 1972, because my battery was slated to deactivate, we ended up turning all our howitzers and small arms over to an ARVN artillery battalion, and we road-marched by truck back to Da Nang.

—Jerry D. Morelock

General Phillip B. Davidson, a general officer who has analyzed the Vietnam War in as much depth and breadth as anyone in the services or in academia, offers his assessment of Giap.

"Limited War" is the brainchild of a group of academic theorists who believe war can be fought by limited means for a limited objective. Its style is to apply force skillfully along a continuous spectrum…in which adversaries would bargain with each other through the medium of graduated military responses. This gradualism played into the hands of Giap and his strategy of revolutionary war.…Giap's whole strategy after Tet 1968 was aimed at one decisive objective—to attack the greatest American vulnerability, its will to continue the struggle.

—Lieutenant General Phillip B. Davidson, U.S. Army, Retired, in *Vietnam at War: The History, 1946–1975*

There's Always Hope: Bob Hope's 1971–1972 Christmas Tour

By the Christmas season of 1971, the number of U.S. troops in Vietnam had dropped by nearly 400,000 men, and those that remained were coming home at an average of more than 11,000 per month. But while, for many Americans, the war was quickly becoming something to put behind them, it was unlikely that Bob Hope would forget that 156,000 men were still in Vietnam, and, as he had done on twenty previous Christmases, he put together a tour that would bring his show to these troops and others in Thailand, Okinawa, Guantanamo Bay, and other spots around the globe.

Hope's variety show, headlined by comedian Jim Nabors and country-western singer Charlie Pride, included a wide assortment of entertainers and celebrities: Les Brown, whose Band of Renown had provided the music for nearly every previous Christmas show; the 1971 Miss World-USA, Brucene Smith; Oakland A's pitcher Vida Blue; teenage soul group Sunday's Child; the Blue Streaks, a roller-skating duo; and "Bob's Girls," who mingled with the wide-eyed grunts. These eight young professional actresses had either been spotted and recruited by Hope during his travels or were suggested to him by friends in Hollywood. Starlets of past years had included Jill St. John, Raquel Welch, Anne Francis, and Susan Saint James.

Hope began his tours, sponsored by the USO and military services, in 1941, and he presented shows in the South Pacific and Europe throughout World War II. His annual Christmas tours began in 1948 and continued each year through the Persian Gulf War, 1990–1991, except for a short period during the 1950s when health reasons prevented him from traveling.

LEFT: Bob Hope brightens the stage in Vietnam, Christmas 1968. Looked upon as "one of our own" by many in the military, Hope was designated an honorary veteran by Congress in 1997 for his "humanitarian services to the U.S. Armed Forces."

BELOW: Bob's Girls brought a little Christmas cheer to servicemen still in Vietnam. Prominently displayed in Hope's publicity materials and the Army's news releases were the names, weights, heights, and bust measurements of each of the young starlets on the tour.

Leslie Dalton   Kathy Baumann   Patricia Mickey   Brenda Dickson   Jayne Kennedy   Leslie McRay   Leana Roberts

marks, and how were they going to suck out the poison? I could almost hear the reaction of my airborne friends: "Well, Lieutenant, I guess you're just gonna die!"

—Terry A. Griswold, senior advisor, ARVN 2d Airborne Brigade recon company

An Loc and Loc Ninh

SOUTHERN FRONT. In the South, the NVA invasion force targeted An Loc, the capital of Binh Long Province, which lay along a route leading to Saigon. The attacking force included the 5th, 7th, and 9th VC divisions, including the 69th VC Artillery Command, a total of thirty-five thousand troops. While the units were designated Viet Cong, they were manned by NVA soldiers armed and organized like main force units.

In the first phase of the attack, Loc Ninh, some fifteen miles north of An Loc, was struck. Crossing the border from Cambodia, the 5th VC Division attacked Loc Ninh on April 4, showering the town with artillery, mortars, rockets, and tank fire. Despite their determined resistance, the ARVN 9th Infantry Regiment was soon cornered in the northern and southern parts of the town. The next day, some thirty T-54 and PT-76 tanks attacked Loc Ninh from three directions. The American advisors within the town called in tactical air support from aircraft carriers, Bien Hoa Air Base, and from Thailand, which pounded the NVA forces for the next two days. One AC-130 Spectre gunship caught NVA troops in the wire surrounding one of the ARVN compounds and ground up an entire regiment.

On April 6, human wave assaults supported by twenty-five to thirty tanks and artillery and rockets overwhelmed the ARVN forces and their U.S. advisors. Only one hundred men escaped the town. The troops at two firebases located between Loc Ninh and An Loc now came under attack and were ordered to retreat before they were overrun and captured. By this time, it was clear that An Loc was the principal target of the operation and held the key to the capture of Saigon. Major General James F. Hollingsworth, commander of the Third Regional Assistance Command, ordered the advisors at An Loc: "Hold them and I'll kill them with airpower."

By April 7, the enemy had encircled An Loc and seized its airfield (which was on high ground good for their artillery), and a siege lasting two months commenced. All supplies into the town had to be air-dropped. Meanwhile, one of the fiercest bombardments of the Vietnam War began to rain down on the city, creating peril for the soldiers and the helicopters and crews who descended into the town to drop supplies and evacuate the wounded. Two battalions of the ARVN 3d Ranger Group were soon sent into the town as reinforcements, followed by two more from the 8th Regiment. The ARVN now had three thousand troops in An Loc, but the NVA outnumbered them six to one.

On April 13, the NVA fired more than seven thousand rounds on An Loc. At dawn on that day, Soviet-made T-34 and PT-76 tanks foolishly attacked without supporting infantry, which made them vulnerable to handheld M72 light antitank weapons (LAWs, 66-mm in size) wielded by ARVN infantry. In addition, the tanks moved hesitantly, allowing the defenders plenty of time to knock them out. Swarming like eagles over the city were American A-6s, A-7s, F-4s, A-37s, AC-119K Stingers, and AC-130 Spectre gunships, as well as South Vietnamese A-1s and A-37s. Guided to targets by U.S. advisors in An Loc, the pilots made more than twenty-five hundred strikes, dropping bombs on the massed NVA forces.

The NVA, desperate by April 15, braved all odds and advanced their tanks to within two hundred meters of the allied command bunker and fired into it, killing three staff officers before being destroyed. The NVA now brought in greater anti-aircraft assets to suppress the air armada over An Loc. The town, once one of the most beautiful in the area, was studded with shattered trees, pocked with mounds of rubble, and strewn with garbage. The bodies of soldiers and domestic animals lay everywhere in contorted heaps.

After midnight on May 11, a seven-thousand-round barrage blasted the town for four hours. Leaving a bunker at this time meant death. Finally, the barrage ended and silence reigned for a short time. Then, another ten thousand rounds began falling on the besieged soldiers. Supported by tanks and artillery, the NVA now advanced on the town from all sides. The skies overhead buzzed for the next five days as thirteen hundred sorties rained death on the city. Anti-aircraft missiles and guns fired back, and the sky was filled with fiery traces. On May 12, the NVA infantry attacked again, in a last-ditch effort, only this time they advanced at night and during bad weather, hoping to thwart the swarms of attacking aircraft. But some thirty B-52s dropped their deadly loads regardless, causing one NVA regiment to literally vaporize. After continued sporadic fighting during the next month, the siege of An Loc was declared broken on June 18.

James H. Willbanks was a young captain in Vietnam recently assigned as an advisor to an ARVN regimental task force, when his unit became involved in the Battle of An Loc.

ABOVE: Private First Class Lawrence Rasnick, of Cincinnati, carries a pair of 40-pound shells to his 155-mm howitzer battery of the 11th Artillery, near Saigon, September 1968.

Major Raymond Haney and I had joined the regimental task force after the original advisory team members had been wounded and subsequently evacuated during the withdrawal from their positions along Highway 13 to the north of An Loc. We arrived in the city by helicopter on April 12 [1972] to find a grim situation. Artillery rounds and rockets were falling steadily, and the helicopter that brought us into the city hovered only long enough for us to jump off the aircraft into a freshly dug hole in the city soccer field as artillery rounds impacted near the landing zone. During the evening, the South Vietnamese soldiers prepared for the inevitable North Vietnamese attack, and they were up early for whatever the day would bring.

Early the next morning I was installing a radio antenna on the roof of the building the regimental commander had established as his command post, when I heard a tremendous explosion and ran down the stairs to the front of the building. Frantic South Vietnamese soldiers ran by shouting, "Thiet Giap!" I had never heard this phrase before, but as the soldier ran around the corner of the building, it became all too apparent that the cry meant "tank." Advancing down the street from the north was a line of North Vietnamese T-54 tanks! So began the Battle of An Loc....

The Soviet-made T-54s and several PT-76 tanks moved down Ngo Quyen Street, the main north-south street in An Loc, toward the ARVN 5th Division command post in the southern section of the city. The South Vietnamese troops, who had never faced tanks in battle before, were panic-stricken; the forces in the north of the city that took the initial brunt of the tank assault quickly fell back in the face of the NVA attack.

The Communist armored thrust was finally halted when Private Binh Doan Quang, a soldier from the local territorial forces, destroyed one of the lead tanks with an M-72 light antitank weapon (LAW). This was a galvanizing act that demonstrated that the enemy tanks could be stopped and greatly enhanced the confidence of the badly shaken defenders. Word spread quickly and the ARVN soldiers began to emerge from their holes and fire at the tanks.

—Lieutenant Colonel (then Captain) James H. Willbanks, U.S. Army, Retired, in *The Battle of An Loc*

The NVA attack on An Loc exhibited the normal ruthlessness associated with the Communists' attacks in South Vietnam.

The fighting raged on for nearly two more months as the North Vietnamese continually shelled, and made repeated attempts to take, the city. The ARVN defenders and their U.S. advisors used B-52s and tactical air support to hold the enemy at bay.

The civilian citizens of An Loc were not immune to the death and destruction going on all around them. One of the NVA T-54 tanks made it into the center of the city, where it rolled into a Catholic church. Huddled inside were old men,

U.S. Army Engineer Command, Vietnam

One of the NVA T-54 tanks made it into the center of the city, where it rolled into a Catholic church. Huddled inside were old men, women, and children who had taken refuge. The tank fired its cannon and machine guns, killing over 100 of the innocent civilians.

—James H. Willbanks

JAMES H. WILLBANKS

LEFT: Soviet-made T-54/55 tanks destroyed in An Loc by ARVN soldiers armed with the M72 light anti-tank weapon, April 1972. The NVA armor had moved through the city streets with virtually no infantry protection, making them easy prey for teams of tank-hunting South Vietnamese.

women, and children who had taken refuge. The tank fired its cannon and machine guns, killing over 100 of the innocent civilians....

[Days later] the civilians merely wanted to get away from the fighting, but the North Vietnamese forces had the city encircled, and there was no way out. Still, the refugees tried to escape; some were successful, but many suffered the same fate as a group of 200 refugees who made a run for it on April 15. Led by a French Catholic priest and a Buddhist monk, they went through the barbed wire and concertina that surrounded the city and tried to move south down [Highway] 13 toward Lai Khe and Saigon, and safety. They made it to the southern edge of An Loc before the NVA opened fire with rockets and artillery, driving those that survived back into the city. The abortive attempt left dead and wounded lying in ditches like cordwood all along the highway.

This was not an isolated incident. Almost every time a large group of refugees tried to escape from the heavy combat, the NVA's artillery forward observers targeted the fleeing columns and devastated these innocents. This pattern also prevailed in Military Region I and the Central Highlands: President Thieu claimed on May 9 that enemy guns had killed a total of 25,000 refugees trying to escape the three major battlefields in the previous seventy-two hours.

The human toll inside the city was ghastly; the streets and rubble were littered with bodies, both military and civilian. The smell of death permeated the air. Under these conditions, innumerable diseases, including cholera, soon ran rampant through both civilian and soldier ranks. To avoid a full-fledged epidemic, bodies were buried in common mass graves, some containing 300 to 500 corpses, by soldiers operating bulldozers during the infrequent lulls in the shelling. Many bodies had to be reburied after exploding shells churned up the original graves.

—James H. Willbanks,
in *The Battle of An Loc*

Cargo, Engineer, and Utility Vehicles

LEFT: U.S. soldiers take a break from guard duty at an M43B1 ambulance converted by a 9th Infantry Division signal battalion for use as a MARS (Military Affiliate Radio System) mobile relay station for soldiers' calls to home. Note the soldier on watch with a grenade launcher atop the nearby bunker.

BELOW: The other end of the size scale was occupied by the M274 "Mechanical Mule" (or simply "Mule") light weapons carrier, which was highly portable, used very little gas, and could operate effectively whether on narrow jungle paths or rocky hilltops. The infantry loved them, and it was not unusual to see Mules turned into heavy-weapons platforms.

LEFT: An M522 GOER 8-ton cargo carrier twists its way across a deep ditch near Pleiku. Because its front and rear sections are connected by an "articulated joint" allowing a lateral oscillation of 20 degrees and a steering angle of 60 degrees, the GOER quickly developed a reputation for dependability and the ability to pull big loads where no other wheeled vehicles could even travel.

BELOW: A Vietnamese woman is dwarfed by a BARC (barge amphibious resupply, cargo), capable of easily transporting 70 tons (110 tons in an emergency) of supplies or two hundred troops between ship and shore. The name of this amphibious lighter was later changed to LARC-60.

ABOVE: A 5-ton dump truck of the 116th Engineer Battalion, Idaho National Guard, spreads gravel on a section of Highway 20 northeast of the Saigon area. By the summer of 1969, the U.S. Army had some 2,105 M51, M342A2, and M817 5-ton dump trucks in Vietnam.

BELOW: A 937th Engineer Group (Combat) Model 12 heavy road grader works on camp improvements for the ARVN 2d Ranger Battalion. The Model 12 has all-wheel power and steering and is essential to the building of roads and airfields.

ABOVE: David Chardlen (left) and Stanley Prevost, 538th Engineer Battalion, move earth with a D8 bulldozer near Korat, Thailand, in support of operations in Vietnam and the Thai government. The Army had 1,417 D7- and D8-series bulldozers in nearby Vietnam by the summer of 1969.

RIGHT: A Playboy Bunny logo adorns the front bumper of an M52A1 5-ton diesel tractor pulling a loaded M127-series 12-ton trailer. By the summer of 1969, the U.S. Army had some 3,299 of these 5-ton tractors in Vietnam.

BELOW: Specialist James E. Silks, of Norwalk, California, pumps JP-4 aviation gas (jet fuel) into an M131-series 5,000-gallon semitrailer tank at Long Binh as Specialist Dennis L. Anderson, of Corpus Christi, Texas, checks the fuel level. This 48th Transportation Group rig is typical of those used by medium-petroleum truck companies.

The Christmas Bombing

The Easter Offensive was the end of Vo Nguyen Giap's tenure as commander of the North Vietnamese Army. After the offensive, his chief of staff, General Van Tien Dung, replaced Giap, who now became minister of defense. The change was hardly a promotion and expressed the dissatisfaction of the politburo with the Easter Offensive. In many respects, the campaign had been a failure. Entire NVA regiments had disappeared in the conflagrations resulting from B-52 bombardments, and NVA tank hulls littered the provinces. Now, the diplomats stepped forward to joust with one another over the final settlement of the war. The United States had been negotiating with the North Vietnamese since 1966 but with little success. Both sides wanted diametrically opposed end states for the war. The United States wanted to preserve South Vietnam; North Vietnam wished to absorb it and thereby more than double its size and vastly increase its material resources. The North Vietnamese used negotiations with the United States as a cheap, bloodless tactic to obtain their strategic goal: the reunification with South Vietnam.

Since the beginning of the war, the United States had dropped bombs on North Vietnam in an attempt to compel the Communists into some sort of equitable settlement of the war.

These attacks had been punishing but gradually applied and interspersed with cease-fires that allowed the North Vietnamese periodic respites. Now that the Communist forces had been bloodily repulsed once more in the Easter Offensive, U.S. diplomats stepped forward again to see whether the United States could find some honorable way out of the quagmire in Southeast Asia. In early May 1972, in a meeting with Le Duc Tho, the North Vietnamese chief negotiator, Kissinger called for a U.S. withdrawal of its troops in four months, a supervised election in South Vietnam, and Thieu's removal as president of South Vietnam. Tho rejected the proposal out of hand. The next day, President Nixon reiterated the terms and stressed an immediate standstill cease-fire, an exchange of prisoners, and the same four-month withdrawal time mentioned by Kissinger. But there was no mention by Nixon of removing Thieu, and the Communists ignored him.

By July 1972, though, things were getting tougher on the NVA, and on July 19, Le Duc Tho initiated a meeting with Kissinger, followed by meetings in August, September, and October, in which a draft agreement was hammered out. As a final gesture of goodwill, Kissinger advocated a bombing halt north of the 20th parallel. Finally, North Vietnam demanded that a settlement be signed by October 31. At this

point, Kissinger went so far as to say, "Peace is at hand," perhaps a political statement for American consumption during Nixon's reelection campaign. The draft settlement agreement, though, when it was carefully perused, was seen by many to be just one more minefield in the Vietnam War: its text was filled with all sorts of ambiguous and unworkable details and pitfalls. Thieu opposed the document, demanding sixty-nine changes in it. Finally, all sides were suggesting changes until the situation became chaotic. By mid-December, it was clear to Kissinger that Le Duc Tho and his associates were trying to scuttle the negotiations.

Before Congress reconvened on January 17, Nixon decided to use force once again to get the North Vietnamese to negotiate an end to the war. In mid-December, Nixon wrote Hanoi officials demanding that they resume negotiations within seventy-two hours or suffer the consequences. They refused, and the result was Operation LINEBACKER II, the Christmas Bombing—eleven days of around-the-clock bombardments of the sixty-mile corridor between Hanoi and Haiphong.

In this operation, nearly all stops were removed as the air forces of the United States raided military posts, docks, shipyards, radio transmitters, electric power plants, steelworks, bridges, roads, and railroad yards in the Hanoi area, dumping more than twenty-thousand tons of explosives. From December 18 to 29, the Air Force and Navy mounted 729 B-52 sorties and approximately 1,000 fighter-bomber sorties,

BELOW: How Haiphong Harbor in North Vietnam looked to a bomber pilot late in the war (1972). The U.S. Air Force gave the Communists the full treatment during the Christmas Bombing. It brought them to the conference table and created the atmosphere for a settlement, but it did not end the war, except for the United States.

R&R and China Beach

RIGHT, TOP: Cameras in hand, U.S. soldiers enter a Buddhist cemetery during a "Cross-Cultural Understanding Tour" that also includes a visit to an orphanage in Qui Nhon and a trip to the local fishing fleet as a means of understanding the customs and way of life of the Vietnamese, December 1971. Although unevenly promoted at middle and lower command levels outside of Special Forces, this type of "sensitivity training" is an example of U.S. Army efforts to keep its soldiers informed and appreciative of Vietnamese society; these efforts were greatly intensified after General Creighton Abrams took command of MACV in July 1968. On the whole, the dividends were well worth the work. Not only did many obscure cultural signals come to be understood by U.S. troops in the field, but also to this day the Vietnamese people remember Americans not as the murderous fiends portrayed in some postwar films, but as polite and cordial people who were, and still are, welcome in their country.

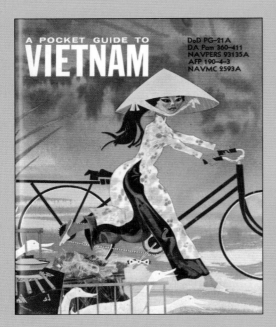

ABOVE: The U.S. Department of Defense *Pocket Guide to Vietnam* that was to be provided to all military personnel deployed to the country after the spring of 1966. In addition to a language guide, "Do's and Don'ts," as well as descriptions of the nation's peoples, land, cities, and culture, the guide contained a brief account of Vietnam's two-thousand-year history and a brutally honest, yet ultimately upbeat, look at its current situation.

RIGHT, BOTTOM: New arrivals in Vietnam shop for cameras, watches, and other goodies at the 50th Replacement Battalion's well-stocked PX in Long Binh, May 1967. The extensive network of U.S. post exchange stores did an excellent job of supplying for soldiers' needs and also helped keep some of the pressure off of Vietnam's overcrowded cities.

ABOVE: U.S. soldiers match skills at the Qui Nhon putt-putt. Besides miniature golf, the men were also provided with the opportunity to surf, scuba dive, water-ski, and take part in a variety of other activities. Concern for soldiers' welfare and cognizance of how hard it was to serve so far from home in a troubled land led to troops in Vietnam being provided with as many aspects of traditional Americana as possible. The small print beneath the number 2 post notes that this is a "par 2" hole.

LEFT: A U.S. Army lifeguard scans the surf as military personnel relax at Qui Nhon's "Red Beach"—more popularly known as China Beach—where a battalion of the 7th Marines first came ashore in 1965. Qui Nhon was designated as one of several seaside rest and recreation (R&R) areas, and soldiers from units in the vicinity would be assigned a slice of sand that they could rotate through at set intervals. On Sundays, thirty lucky paratroopers of the 173d Airborne Brigade could head for the beach and the twenty Quonset huts at the local post exchange (PX), containing a post office, barbershop, snack bar, and large shopping area. One suspects, however, that nurses and "Red Cross girls" from the nearby hospital were the main attraction for these 173d paratroopers in July 1968.

as well as almost 1,400 sorties by support aircraft, including the Wild Weasels (SAM suppression units). After twelve days, North Vietnam's industries, airfields, and military installations were reduced to ashes. The *New York Times* referred to the attacks as "Stone Age barbarism," which coincided perfectly with North Vietnam's view of the matter. Fifteen B-52s were shot down in the attacks, as well as eleven other aircraft. Ninety-three U.S. pilots and crewmen were killed, and thirty-one more ended up in Hanoi's jails for POWs, which were hellholes where no international rules or laws applied.

The Christmas bombings were a momentary cessation of frustration to some military men, as Major General Thomas S. Swalm confirms.

Linebacker I occurred in 1972, and over a considerable period of time. It consisted of the bombing of selected targets in North Vietnam. That happened when President Nixon decided to engage many of the targets that we had been bypassing before. We had been flying right by them and didn't bomb them because they weren't on the list. Linebacker II, I think, lasted only eleven days. It involved a massive raid of B-52s going up North, something the North Vietnamese thought could never be done.

Typically, we used B-52s in-country for most of the war, and we took the tactical airplanes, the fighter airplanes, up North. It was just the opposite of the name *strategic* and *tactical*. But when we got to Linebacker II, during those eleven days we were flying a hundred-plus B-52s, almost two hundred B-52s, up there on a daily basis. Of course, they lost a number of B-52s to SAMs. Some of those aircraft, incidentally, were lost to SAMs where those airplanes did not have good radar-warning systems or jamming systems. So that was a tragedy, without question. But Linebacker I and Linebacker II, like Rolling Thunder and other attacks, were specific-time-frame attacks and deployments.

Well, there was frustration [about the lack of strategic objectives]. What we saw, of course, was a graduated escalation. Every time the North Vietnamese would do something [we didn't like], we would generally ratchet up [the attacks] a notch. The sad thing is, we could've ratcheted up twenty notches and ended the war, in our opinion, much, much sooner. Certainly it was a mistake to stop the bombing after the eleven days of Linebacker II. If we wanted a military conclusion to that battle, they were clearly brought to their knees, the North Vietnamese. I think that it wouldn't have taken too much more. They didn't have any more SAMs to launch, incidentally, until we had the bombing halted after the eleven days. Then they got a lot more SAMs, and they were ready to go again.

So that was a mistake—again, in my judgment—if we wanted a military conclusion, and, of course, most military officers do. But during the battle itself, flying past airfields was the one thing that bothered us most. You were going after some legitimate strategic target, but you were allowing their MiGs to take off. You could even see them taking off, and you could not bomb their

But then you got to the point where they said you could not turn right over some targets because that would take you near Hanoi, and a bomb might fall off an airplane near Hanoi. Some of these silly restrictions were just so prohibitively dangerous for us, as if no one cared about our lives.

**—Tom B. Wilson,
electronic warfare officer, Wild Weasel**

RADAR

BAMBOO MATTING

ABOVE: A SAM site as seen from the air. The area shown in the inset photo at upper left bears one of at least three missiles visible in this photograph. The missile site's radar equipment and supporting buildings are shown at the upper right of the photograph.

airfields. If we could've taken those out early, as we did in Desert Storm—that operation was done properly. Desert Storm was a war that was fought by the entire U.S. defense system. I'll include the president, who was obviously involved.

—Thomas S. Swalm

EWO Tom B. Wilson, back-seater in a Wild Weasel duo, had this to say about the Christmas Bombing of 1972.

I sincerely feel we could've won the war in any two weeks. We could've forced the North Vietnamese out of the South. This was proven, of course, during the twelve days of Christmas in 1972, when, after twelve days, the North Vietnamese came to the table and

gave us anything we wanted, released our POWs. I've always felt that any two weeks we could've won it. And if we'd have done the same thing in 1966—or 1965, the first time— there wouldn't have been a long seven years' war. There would have been a short police action. I think that's frustrating.

But then you got to the point where they said you could not turn right over some targets because that would take you near Hanoi, and a bomb might fall off an airplane near Hanoi. Some of these silly restrictions were just so prohibitively dangerous for us, as if no one cared about our lives. But they wanted to make sure they didn't give any kind of a show that we were bad guys.

—Tom B. Wilson

The Hanoi Hilton

From 1964 to 1973, the air war over Vietnam had resulted in the capture of a large number of American pilots. Some twenty-six planes were downed over Hanoi in the Christmas Bombing of 1972 alone. From the time pilots were captured in the field—often with broken bones and other serious injuries from the effects of the ejections from their planes—until they arrived in a jail, they were beaten by their captors; jeered at by the North Vietnamese in real and staged demonstrations; paraded through villages where they were struck by people's fists and spat on; and generally humiliated. Many of the pilots were taken to Hoa Lo Prison in downtown Hanoi—referred to, ironically, as the Hanoi Hilton. Hoa Lo was Hanoi's central prison and was built of twenty-foot-high concrete walls surmounted by live electrical wires. Imbedded in the tops of the walls were glass-bottle shards to dissuade escape attempts. Guard towers ringed the prison complex. In the nine years the prison was used to hold American POWs, no one escaped this chamber of horrors.

Once inside the jail, a prisoner was placed in a tiny cell and given a rusty can to use for a toilet. The prisoner was then brought before an interrogator who demanded U.S. military secrets from him. When the pilot refused, he was kicked and beaten by his tormentors until his eyes swelled shut, his body was bruised thoroughly, and he was covered with blood.

During the initial stages of imprisonment, the North Vietnamese systematically tortured a prisoner. These sessions began by tying the prisoner's feet and hands together, then pulling them together forcibly with a rope until he was bent into a bowed position that scarcely allowed him to breathe. The prisoner was then hoisted off the ground and the rope around him attached to a hook suspended from the ceiling. He would be left dangling for hours—sometimes days—in this position, in excruciating pain. During this time, his hands swelled up and turned purple. Once the prisoner was brought back to earth, he discovered that he had lost feeling in his arms and legs, sometimes

LEFT: Master Sergeants Daniel Pitzer and Edward R. Johnson, U.S. Special Forces, at a Viet Cong camp in the U Minh area. Pitzer was captured in October 1963, and Johnson, called *da den* ("black skin") by the Viet Cong, was captured in July 1964. Their November 11, 1967, release in Cambodia, to demonstrate the "humane and lenient" treatment afforded American POWs, was arranged by antiwar activist Tom Hayden, who subsequently turned them over to U.S. officials in Lebanon.

BELOW: A Viet Cong release ceremony near Tam Ky, South Vietnam, January 1969. The soldiers seem unimpressed by the china-and-flowers treatment from their captors.

for weeks afterward. After a number of these sessions, some of which deliberately pulled arm joints out of their sockets, the prisoner, in order to stay alive, generally revealed either credible lies or information that had little or no military value.

Once the initial interrogations were concluded, a new form of real and psychological torture began in the form of political

ABOVE: Lieutenant Commander R.A. Stratton, U.S. Navy, sits glumly in his prison cell in North Vietnam. This was one of the more "luxurious" suites. Cells in the "Hanoi Hilton" were described by their inhabitants as "tombsized."

The most ingenious attempt to communicate to the world outside about what was happening in the Hanoi Hilton was accomplished in 1966 by Captain Jeremiah A. Denton, a U.S. Navy A-6 carrier attack pilot. After undergoing seventy-two hours of continuous indoctrination and intimidation, Denton was dragged before a Japanese television crew, where he parroted a stilted script concocted by his captors. Unknown to the Vietnamese, during silent intervals in the interview, Denton deliberately blinked his eyelids at the cameras, forming the Morse code symbols, T-O-R-T-U-R-E.

When these preliminaries were finished, the prisoners were taken to their cells—tiny, rat-infested compartments that swarmed with mosquitoes. The cells had concrete bunks on two side walls, leaving only two feet of wriggle room between the so-called beds. At the ends of the bunks were leg stocks, used for extra disciplining. One Air Force pilot said the cells were about the size of a tomb. Collectively, the chambers were called the Heartbreak Hotel, a sign that military men seldom forsake their sense of humor. The prisoners' food was usually a cup of rice and pumpkin soup, often shared with the rats. Other prisons in the Hanoi area served even more pitiful fare: animal hooves, chicken heads, and rotten fish. These prisons were given suggestive names by the prisoners also: Alcatraz, Zoo, Dirty Bird, Briarpatch, Skid Row, Dogpatch, and Rockpile. Some 771 Americans were imprisoned in North Vietnamese prisons during the war. One hundred and thirteen of these valiant men died in captivity.

Pilot Leo Thorsness discovered that being shot down by the enemy at supersonic speeds, which often left the pilots' limbs mangled or broken, was only the beginning of an exceedingly long ordeal of fear, torture, and deprivation as a prisoner in a North Vietnamese jail run by Communists.

Harry and I had briefed many times that, if we ever took a direct hit, that we would eject no matter what our airspeed was, because we'd seen airplanes hit, and the guy, we thought, tried to stay with it till he slowed down and could get out safer, and the airplane just came

questioning and indoctrination. During these sessions, the prisoner was told that he was a war criminal and therefore not protected by international law and would soon be tried by a people's court and executed. The interrogator followed up this threat with a demand that the prisoner write a letter or record a tape attacking his country's war policies in Vietnam, to be used by the Communists for propaganda. If the prisoner refused to cooperate, he was given no water or food until he complied. Finally, after suffering extreme deprivation, some 80 percent of the prisoners cooperated in creating these extorted tapes and letters. Some of those who did not cooperate, it is believed, were killed or died.

When writing these letters or dictating tapes complaining about U.S. war policies, the prisoner usually attempted to twist the wording to make it obvious to Americans back home that it did not express his true beliefs.

apart, or he never made it out. So we briefed about it many times. I said, "Harry, if you ever hear me say the word *go*, and you'll know the context, don't question it, and just pull the ejection trigger, and I'll be right behind you." The back seat is supposed to go before the front seat because you'll burn him with your rocket if he's got his canopy open.

When we took this severe hit, it felt like somebody hit the airplane with a big sledgehammer. The controls were instantly gone. The controls were all smoky. I put my visor right against the cockpit. I couldn't see out it was so thick. I was starting to feel smoke in my lungs, and the airplane was starting to do gyrations. That took a lot longer to say than the decision to say the word *go*. Harry said "Shit," and went.

I heard the rush of sound, and I went right after him, and we were doing 600 knots—675 miles an hour—about 525 is the fastest you're supposed to be able to escape without injury. Both of us had some minor injuries. My legs went straight sideways at my knees when I hit the airstream, and so both of my inside knees were torn up badly. But the system worked. We got out of the airplane.

As we were floating down, there were two thoughts that were going through my mind.

I don't know why, and I hadn't thought that I'd think about it, but it went over and over and over in my mind: Leo you're going to make it. You're going to make it. It was a very comforting thought. The second thought was how will my family take it. I had a wife and a daughter, and I was close to being home [near the end of his tour of duty], and we had gonna-get-home-itis. They knew about when I finished my missions. But that was frightening. I looked down and there was a pretty good wind, and I was drifting across the jungle, but maybe two thousand or three thousand feet below me were the trees, and I saw an opening.

I saw muzzle flashes, rifle flashes, men shooting at me in my parachute. It's hard to hide in a parachute, but they were lousy shots, and I was moving fast. But that was the apprehension: some people are killed when picked up. Some people are skinned alive, I know. That's the fear of becoming a POW. That was not a good day.

I couldn't walk when I got on the ground. My parachute got hung up in a tree. I had a rope with me, a lanyard, and I got down. But I couldn't walk because my knees were out. So I was crawling up this mountain, and I knew there were rescue airplanes en route. About ten minutes afterward, I was captured. Our

BELOW: A North Vietnamese guard keeps close watch on the proceedings as Major Leo Thorsness is put on display for the cameras, circa late summer 1967. Said Thorsness: "A dozen or so of we POWs were taken to a 'visiting delegation' off the prison compound. We were led to believe they were friendly, or neutral at best, toward the U.S. Turns out the lead delegate was a hardcore Communist, and the entire event [was] not a pleasant experience, to say the least." During the last years of the war, 1970–1973, the North Vietnamese eased up on their systematic torture of American POWs that had left many prisoners permanently injured and had killed others. Upon his arrival at the "Hanoi Hilton," Thorsness met two F-105 crew members that he had tried to rescue just a few weeks earlier, and the officer who put Thorsness's name up for a Medal of Honor was himself shot down and brought to the same prison two years later.

ABOVE: A Communist cage for POWs that was hastily evacuated before a Bright Light program rescue attempt is examined by SOG personnel. The face of the indigenous SOG team member at left was blacked out by an MACV censor. While SOG teams rescued dozens of U.S. airmen from almost certain capture in the Communist-infested border regions and freed as many as 492 ARVN soldiers held by the Communists, only one American POW was rescued during a Bright Light mission. Specialist 4 Larry D. Aiken was snatched from a camp in Laos on July 10, 1969, after he was attacked with a machete and left for dead by his escaping captors. Aiken died ten days later at Bethesda Naval Hospital. Some 37 other American military personnel successfully escaped on their own from Communist forces, and one, Specialist 5 William B. Taylor, 221st Aviation Company, was inadvertently "found" and rescued when the Chau Doc Province camp where he was held was attacked by Cobra gunships on May 6, 1968.

men were overhead, but they were too late. There were probably twenty young enemy guys, all young males. A couple of them had real rifles, and others, old rifles. A couple of them had training rifles, I assume. They all had machetes.

They caught up with me as I was crawling up the hill, up the mountain. The first thing they did was cut my clothes off. They'd never seen a zipper. This was in the mountains, some of the tribes there. My boots had zippers on them, but they were very good at using machetes, and they didn't care if they nicked you a little, so I ended up pretty well bloodied up in a set of underwear. They set me down, and I'll never forget this feeling. They put like a pillowcase, a bag, over my head. Just as that was happening, I saw the man in front of me, a young man with a machete, and he was pulling it back and pointing it right at my stomach. There was no question in my mind but that was the end of it.

The thought that went through my mind is: I wonder if my family will ever find out how I died. But he didn't attack me, and they carried me in a net because I couldn't walk, and we made it down to the flatlands. We spent a night and day there because they

didn't travel with trucks during the daytime because my buddies were bombing them. Harry and I were interrogated, literally, in a pigpen that first day. I got by with name, rank, and serial number, like you're supposed to. I thought I could handle it. It was kind of tough, getting knocked around in a pigpen with the manure and so on, but that was just the beginning.

I was there [in the Hanoi Hilton] about six years. Three years were brutal. Torture was normal. Three years were boring. Ho Chi Minh died, and our wives, the families, started to campaign: letters, letters, you know, the bracelets, "Hanoi, release my father" bumper stickers and billboards. The Communists finally realized that we were expected to come home alive. That was after about three years, and then treatment got quite a bit better.

Then we lived in big cells, and we got to talk out loud. It was now a matter of waiting it out instead of wondering if you'd survive because of brutality or being shot or something, which was the case for the first three years. But I'd gladly say that I wasn't strong enough to make it on my own. I had some help from outside: faith. I'm a Christian. My back-seater, Harry Johnson: I'm not sure if he was an atheist or agnostic, but there were very few atheists in the prison camps. Harry became a pretty devout Christian. But most of us would admit that we needed some additional help and some strength. There were times when you'd pray, you'd pass out, and try to get through the next day.

Sometimes, it wasn't just the next day; sometimes, it was the next hour, next minute, next few seconds, and it was pretty brutal for some time. Beatings, torture, shoulders being torn out of their sockets because they've got your shoulders, your elbows strapped behind you with wire, and with their foot up, they're pulling it, and they'll pop your shoulder; or they'll hang you upside down with shackles on your feet and a bar through it, and hang you in Room 18 or one of those cells with a hook up in the ceiling. It was very difficult.

—Leo Thorsness

First Lieutenant George Petrie, a newly commissioned Army officer, formerly a sergeant first class, was recruited by the Studies and Observation Group for a super-secret mission: the recovery of U.S. POWs from a North Vietnamese prison—an incredibly risky operation. He was to discover that the operation's planning meshed poorly with the reality on the ground.

We didn't find out what the mission was until the night we went. By that time, there was no backing out. They kept it secret, even from us. They initially told us the code name was IVORY COAST. That was to lead everyone astray, including us, into thinking that we were training as an antiterrorist team or a hostage rescue team to be used in the Middle East.

When we really got into rehearsals, when we saw the mock-up and everything like that, it was pretty obvious that we were going to bust open a prisoner of war camp; however, we didn't know where it was. We assumed it was going to be in Laos or North Vietnam [actually, near Hanoi]. Even if they told us the first day, though, it wouldn't have made any difference. No one would've backed out.

The training was hard, physically demanding, particularly if you were in Dick Meadows's [U.S. Army Special Forces] platoon. We had three platoons that actually were to go into the POW compound to break the prisoners out. Our training schedule, while we were in rehearsals, normally consisted of us having the morning off and going to work at 1:00, doing all afternoon training, then night training until we finished.

The ground-action part of the operation was relatively straightforward, but it was difficult getting there because of North Vietnam's radar windows. The Air Force had to really plan the raid in minute detail. You had to fly a heading of 180 degrees for eight miles, then turn right on another heading, fly that way for three miles at a certain altitude, then turn right: they practiced that scenario extensively over the southern United States during training.

The basic plan was pretty simple, but things would get complicated if we were forced into alternate plans. What happens if one of the platoons doesn't get there, the command platoon, maybe? Who has to do this? Who has to do that? So we had various alternate plans, and we had to rehearse them all.

We carried AR-15s, which is a Commando, short-barreled version of the M16, with a folding stock. We did have a couple guys that carried M16s. We also had M60 machine guns and M79 grenade launchers. We even had antitank weapons, and every man was armed with a .45-caliber automatic.

But our marksmanship was gross, horrible. At night, at fifty meters, we were getting maybe 25 percent hits on the silhouette targets. There were only a few exceptions, guys that were exceptional marksmen.

One day, the colonel was looking in a *Field & Stream* or *Gunsmith* magazine and saw an advertisement for a single-point aiming sight. It was like a scope, except you couldn't see through it. It had a red dot in it and a blue dot. It was an aiming device and could be mounted on the handle of the AR-15. It had to be zeroed in, and your eye had to adjust to the sight. It was really strange because most shooters are used to closing one eye and shooting. With this sight, your right eye looked at the target, and it was instantaneous.

LEFT: Colonel Arthur D. "Bull" Simons discloses a SOG mission to raiders in Thailand to "thunderous applause."

Our marksmanship went up 95 percent, and we were very confident with that weapon. It took us about two weeks to get used to it, but once we got used to it, that weapon was magnificent.

Once the operation began, it was kind of unreal. Our biggest fear was that once we got to our launch site in Thailand or crossed over into North Vietnam, the politicians would call the operation off. Someone back in Washington would say, "Aw, now, we can't do this." That was our biggest fear.

Once we landed and got in the compound, particularly my platoon, we knew right away that there were no prisoners there. There were several construction workers there, and they were remodeling the camp; that's why they had moved the prisoners. Almost instantly, once we hit the ground, we noticed that there were no American voices, and we were expecting them. The only noises were the guns going off, but there were no American voices. We'd hit a dry hole.

Our landing had been very hard in the helicopters, one of which was a "Jolly Green." We had to crash because we had to land inside the walled-in area, and the helicopter was too big to land in that small an area.

We used the CH-3 helicopter [Jolly Green Giant] because we could load it with thirteen members plus extra gear. When we landed, the Air Force and our general manager didn't want the pilot jacking around trying to land it safely so he'd be able to take off again, the way pilots want to do.

The intention was to crash the airplane, just make a crash landing. When we landed, came in over the wall, the pilot accelerated and came in a little bit too low, because we'd had to do some gyrations right before we got in. When he landed, there were some big trees in the compound, huge oak trees. Well, hidden among the oak trees was this large, concrete pole. It looked like they were going to use it to make a volleyball court for the guys. Our roller-blade hit the pole, ran into the trees, and it just spun the helicopter around. Well, I was supposed to be the second man out because my team was at the right door. My team sergeant, Tom Kimmer, was supposed to come out in front of me and get into position to cover me when I knocked out the front gate guard tower.

Well, it didn't happen that way. When we landed I wasn't holding on, and the crash just catapulted me straight out the door, so it was a hard landing, with pieces of trees and limbs flying around the compound.

I hit the ground running. The only problem was that we'd rehearsed that thing like 165 times; everybody had a set route, and you knew exactly what your route was, and to get the benefit of that, you rehearsed it so many times that you did what you're supposed to do, so your mind didn't have to worry about it.

OPPOSITE, TOP AND BOTTOM: An eastern-aspect photograph of the Son Tay prison camp model (top) made for training the Son Tay raiders and a southern-aspect photograph (bottom) of the prison taken at low level by a pilotless drone.

ABOVE, LEFT AND RIGHT: Special Forces raiders with a satchel charge for breaching the Son Tay prison camp wall (left); the raiders aboard a U.S. Air Force HH-53 "Jolly Green Giant" helicopter.

ABOVE: The destroyed "secondary school" building that was assaulted by Colonel Simons's raiders when they landed in the wrong compound.

BELOW: Wreckage of the helicopter destroyed by a demolition charge detonated by Dick Meadows, U.S. Army Special Forces.

Your mind, then, was available to deal with the unexpected. So when I hit the ground running, I was actually going in the wrong direction! It took me a few seconds to get oriented because I said, "Nah, this ain't right, I'm supposed to be here," and I got confused, but I managed to get over to the front gate guard tower, which was another mess, it turned out. We had agency and aero photographs of that tower, and the CIA and all the intelligence people said that the front gate guard tower was either just a shed or a small tower. Maximum security was supposed to be underneath it, either in a cellar or on the first little floor of it.

Fortunately, I had practiced throwing a grenade; I was supposed to throw a stun grenade into the tower to knock out any guards that might be there before anybody could really do anything inside the compound. So, I did a lot of training practicing at night, back in Florida, throwing dummy grenades through tires. I'd throw them at different angles, but I had never practiced putting one thirty-five feet high, and that's how high that sucker was; it was eighteen feet across at the base, a huge concrete thing. And I'm standing there holding the concussion grenade in my hand, and one of the guys covering me said, "Throw the grenade!" And I said, "I can't throw the damn thing that far. It'll come back on us." The guy said, "Throw it anyway." And I said, "Okay," and I popped it right in. I couldn't believe it. I stood there and looked for a couple of seconds. I said, "God, I did it." So once that got out of the way, everything went all right, except the fact there weren't any prisoners there.

We all came out okay. We had one man, Technical Sergeant Leroy Wright, who was the crew chief on our helicopter, an Air Force tech sergeant. His job, once the helicopter crashed, was to come support my team, to help me out. But he had a compound fracture of his ankle when a fireball broke off, a fire extinguisher broke off, and hit him in the ankle.

He didn't say anything to anybody, came out, did his job, did everything he was supposed

to do coming out. After we came through the Hanoi flak screen later and kind of settled down a little and everybody put piss in their pants, he kind of shook me and said, "You know," he said, "I think I'm hurt." I looked down and pulled his pants leg back, and there was a bone sticking straight out. I said, "God, Leroy!"

As we came into the camp, we could see southwest of the camp, about fifteen or twenty kilometers southwest, a compound lit up like a football field. It looked like one of those Friday night Plano, Texas, high school football deals. In fact, it was where the prisoners had been moved, and there were over two hundred prisoners in that camp that night. I found that out much later by talking to some of the guys that were there at the time. My first cousin was a prisoner up there; he and I were raised by my grandmother. But he was in that camp, that night, as were some of the guys who were from Dallas that were POWs. It would have been perfect if we could have gone there instead. We would have come out with two hundred prisoners instead of the sixty or eighty we had anticipated.

The scariest part of the whole mission was that ten-minute ride back out. I'd never seen anything like that in my life before. I don't know how those pilots did it. I wouldn't have done it. I was hoping the helicopter would crash so I could get out and get my feet on the ground. The SAMs were firing, and the anti-aircraft fire…you looked out the window and it was a solid wall of tracers and fire. When I got on the helicopter, like every GI that I've ever known, coming out, you take all your stuff off and look for a cigarette to light up.

—Major George Petrie,
U.S. Army Special Forces, Retired

American Withdrawal

After the Christmas Bombing of North Vietnam in 1972, only a month passed before Hanoi agreed on a cease-fire. A "peace" agreement was signed on January 23, 1973. President Thieu of South Vietnam bitterly referred to it as a

ABOVE: SOG raiders receiving awards at the White House, from left to right: Air Force brigadier general Leroy J. Manor, of Morrisonville, New York, who commanded the overall raiding force; Air Force technical sergeant Leroy Wright, of Little Falls, Minnesota; Specialist First Class Tyrone Adderly, of Philadelphia, and Colonel Arthur D. "Bull" Simons, of New York City.

"surrender agreement," not altogether a misnomer. The terms of the document enjoined the United States to remove all of its armed forces from South Vietnam within sixty days and to desist, meanwhile, from all military operations against the Democratic Republic of Vietnam. But stipulations allowed Hanoi to leave its forces in place in South Vietnam, where they could be supported from bases in North Vietnam and Laos. Military materiel and weapons replaced in the South were to be in kind and number, but there were virtually no safeguards, no supervision of the terms. In the meantime, North Vietnam was allowed to bring in arms and materiel from China and the Soviet Union, while the South Vietnamese were not given reciprocal rights to bring in similar American arms and supplies.

Once Hanoi officials realized that the United States would not mount reprisals for breaches of the cease-fire agreement, they cynically ran untrammeled over all the established rules and protocols of the agreement. In addition, they immediately began planning the complete military overthrow of the South Vietnamese government. As a result of the agreement, South Vietnam would have to wage war alone against its formidable enemy. Upon the United States' withdrawal from the war, President Nixon said, "We have finally achieved peace with honor." Not everyone was certain what was meant by "peace" or by "honor."

The cost of the war for the United States had been great. More than nine thousand helicopters and airplanes had been lost in the Vietnam theater since 1961. Moreover, the Communists had been holding more than six hundred pilots and crews prisoner, many of them for years. In addition, some two thousand pilots and crewmen had lost their lives in Vietnam, Cambodia, and Laos. Another thousand were missing in action, most of them presumed dead. On February 12, 1973, the first of the captured pilots and crew members were released. Some of the men had been in prison for more than seven years. Pilot James Stockdale complained that, after the POWs' great suffering, they found themselves in their native land, "stripped of all entitlement to reputation, love, or honor," an allusion to the sometimes scathing attacks some of the returning servicemen received from homegrown dissidents in the United States. Some servicemen had to wear civilian clothes on commercial airliners to discourage attacks by fellow Americans on their honor and persons. Some 46,498 American combatants would never return to their homeland: they were killed in the war.

But now the war was over, and the U.S. Congress had approved a bill by Senators Steven Case and Frank Church that blocked funds for further military use in Indochina. The House passed the bill also. By this time, the Watergate scandal had erupted, and President Nixon would soon lose most of his credibility with both parties, and resign. One of the United States' most unpopular wars was now history. But the war in Vietnam was far from over.

A number of veterans of the Vietnam War have returned to that country since 1973. Some of them have been surprised by what they found.

The first day I was there, I hadn't made up my mind whether I should be doing this or not. I didn't know. I started thinking, why am I here, really? I have nothing in common with these people except the war, and what is that to have in common with somebody? But our car broke down along the side of the road and beside a village. People somehow found out from the driver or interpreter or some way that I was an American. And, of course, I was the right age. They started kind of cautiously approaching me.

At that time, very few Americans—this was in 1992—had been back there, or at least veterans. Finally, this little kid came up to me with a cut pineapple, and put a piece on a stick, like an ice cream stick, you know. He just took it out like an olive branch and handed it to me. "Thank you," I said. Another little kid came along. The parents were watching them and telling them what to do. They weren't quite ready to come out themselves. The parents were young people in their twenties.

Then someone brought out a little chair, one of those little stools about so tall. I sat down. Another one brought out an umbrella and was holding it up. I was just so taken by that. I finally said, "Can I take your picture?" I had a Polaroid. For anybody that travels over

I think what I've gotten out of going back all these times [to revisit Vietnam] is that they've done a lot better job of putting the war behind them. . . . One of the reasons is that, when the war was over, it was just over for them.

—Gerry Schooler

there, take your Polaroid camera because they'll remember that forever.

It's something you can take of them, a remembrance. A lot of them have never seen a Polaroid, for one thing. You can take a picture, and you can give them that, and you can go back a year later, and it'll be on their wall. I took pictures of the family, and me with the family. Some of the old people even started coming out there. I started passing around the Marlboros. I don't smoke, but another guy who had been over there told me that that's a pretty nice icebreaker.

These people treated me really great. This was near Trang Bang, which was a hotbed of VC activity once. All those people there that I had dealings with had to be relatives of Viet Cong who had fought. Some of those people lost their whole families. In that area, the Cu Chi district, it was a hellhole for Viet Cong. I mean, it wasn't that great for us either, but most of them were killed. So the survivors, you would think, would have terrible memories of us.

I think what I've gotten out of going back all these times is that they've done a lot better job of putting the war behind them than we

have. A lot of vets still have trouble even contemplating going back over there. A lot of vets have blacked out all those years. Really, we could learn something from watching those people. One of the reasons is that, when the war was over, it was just over for them.

—Gerry Schooler

Except for the withdrawal of U.S. troops, the exchange of prisoners, the cessation of all U.S. war activities in Vietnam, and the de-mining of North Vietnam's ports, no other provision of the Paris agreement could be implemented, especially the cease-fire.
—General Cao Van Vien and Lieutenant General Dong Van Khuyen

Chapter Six

DEFEAT OF A BESIEGED ALLY

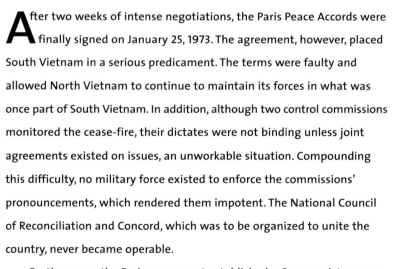

After two weeks of intense negotiations, the Paris Peace Accords were finally signed on January 25, 1973. The agreement, however, placed South Vietnam in a serious predicament. The terms were faulty and allowed North Vietnam to continue to maintain its forces in what was once part of South Vietnam. In addition, although two control commissions monitored the cease-fire, their dictates were not binding unless joint agreements existed on issues, an unworkable situation. Compounding this difficulty, no military force existed to enforce the commissions' pronouncements, which rendered them impotent. The National Council of Reconciliation and Concord, which was to be organized to unite the country, never became operable.

Furthermore, the Paris agreement established a Communist government in South Vietnam, a puppet affair manipulated by Hanoi, to compete with President Thieu's government. Finally, while South Vietnam had a million men under arms, an impressive number, only two hundred thousand of them were in infantry units. In short, South Vietnam found itself in an extremely vulnerable position. While the North Vietnamese and

PAGES 272–273: As North
Vietnamese tanks take position around the presidential
palace in Saigon, infantry fan
out to search the grounds
and building, April 30, 1975.
Although the palace was
thought to be deserted, the
new South Vietnamese president, Duong Van Minh, was
present, along with many
senior officials who waited
to hand over the govern-
ment. The highest-ranking
NVA officer on the scene
happened to be Colonel Bui
Tin (attached to the North
Vietnamese Army's official
newspaper, *Quan Doi Nhan
Dan*), who accepted South
Vietnam's surrender—the
first of several surrenders
that President Minh was to
perform that day—and
promptly filed a press dis-
patch datelined from "The
Puppet Presidential Palace."
Both men had been involved
with the Viet Minh in their
youths but had followed very
different paths. Duong Van
Minh, a former ARVN general
widely known as Big Minh
for his unusually large stat-
ure, had been a key fig-
ure in the overthrow and
assassination of Ngo Dinh
Diem in 1963 and, more
recently, was the principal
proponent of a nationalist
"third force" between the
government in Saigon and
the Communists. Minh was
appointed president because
it was mistakenly believed
that he might be able to
negotiate more lenient terms
from the North Vietnamese.
Indeed, the Communists had
been careful not to criticize
him, because they wanted to
encourage neutralist sentiment in the South and also
because his brother was
Duong Van Nhut, a high-
ranking NVA general. Colonel
Tin, when a member of the
NVA general staff, had made
dangerous trips down the
Ho Chi Minh Trail to conduct
inspections of operations
in the South, and two years
before riding onto the
presidential palace grounds
atop a T-54 tank had
achieved notoriety when,
as spokesman for the
Quadripartite Military
Commission supervising the
U.S. withdrawal, he wished

continued on next page

the VC were also in disarray following the
Easter Offensive, their organizational abilities,
morale, and capability to resupply were higher
than that of the South Vietnamese. This
spelled trouble.

Within weeks of the signing of the Paris
Peace Accords, the Communists, demonstrating
their true intentions, committed two hundred
violations of the agreement, infiltrating some
seventy-five thousand soldiers and equipment
into South Vietnam in 1973. The NVA quintu-
pled the number of tanks present in the South,
raising the number to five hundred. NVA anti-
aircraft defenses were expanded in the South
as well. In addition, the NVA created twelve
thousand miles of new road, enlarged and
improved the Ho Chi Minh Trail, and built a
major oil pipeline into the Central Highlands,
all the way to Loc Ninh, in the heart of South
Vietnam. Hanoi's intentions were obvious.
Meanwhile, Hanoi's propaganda ministry
churned out volumes of propaganda screaming
of South Vietnam's violations of the Paris
agreement—but nothing relating to its own
extensive subversive efforts. People around the
world believed much of this misinformation,
including many gullible people in the United
States. All the while, the North Vietnamese
cynically built up their war machine for the
final conquest of South Vietnam.

President Thieu, meanwhile, considered
his options and officially pronounced his
guiding principles, referred to as his Four Nos:
No territory or bases would be surrendered
to the North Vietnamese; no coalition government would be formed; no negotiations with
the enemy would be agreed upon; and no
Communist or neutral agitation would be tolerated in that part of South Vietnam occupied by
Thieu's government. The president concluded
that the only danger to his country was through
political infiltration, agitation, and subversion.
He believed, foolishly it appears, that a large
North Vietnamese invasion was unlikely
because of the likelihood of an American
intervention in the war. In this view, he was
completely out of touch with the mood in the
United States and guilty of wishful thinking.
When Henry Kissinger in March 1973 warned
President Nixon that the Communists were
infiltrating South Vietnam in huge numbers,
Nixon was so preoccupied with his Watergate
troubles that he was incapable of addressing
the problem.

At the same time, the U.S. Congress was
taking actions that would prevent either Nixon
or any successor from initiating combat operations in Vietnam. In June 1973, a bill was passed
cutting funds for any operations conducted in
Laos or Cambodia. In October, Congress went
further, enacting legislation that banned combat activities in the skies or on the ground in
Laos, Cambodia, or South and North Vietnam.
In addition, Congress passed a War Powers Act
limiting Nixon's use of troops in any military
conflict anywhere without the agreement of
Congress. Nixon vetoed the bill, but he was
overridden.

*The North Vietnamese used the Paris
Peace Accords to gain a military
advantage over South Vietnam. The
accords turned out to be a sham—not a peace
agreement but a blueprint for North Vietnam
to rid itself of its nemesis, the United States,
and to begin the war anew, on a stronger
footing, with its South Vietnamese enemy.*

The Paris agreement offered North Vietnam
the favorable conditions to pursue its conquest

of South Vietnam with success. No longer constrained by bombings and blockades, Hanoi devoted its efforts to reconstruction and development in order to better support its war efforts in South Vietnam. No obstacle now lay in the way of its continued infiltration through Laos and Cambodia. Hanoi simply ignored the restrictive provisions of the Paris agreement that did not serve its purposes.

In South Vietnam, the NLF was given a legitimate national status. It now had an official government, an army, and a national territory of its own. In all respects, the NLF had become a political entity equal in power to [the government of South Vietnam]. All the major obstructions that had prevented North Vietnam and its South Vietnamese lackeys from winning a military victory were now gone. U.S. and FWMA [Free World] forces had all left, while nearly 300,000 NVA troops still remained on South Vietnamese soil. Never since 1954 had the Communists enjoyed such a strong political and military posture.

The Paris agreement never restored peace to South Vietnam. The reports of gunfire continued to echo throughout the country even after the cease-fire day had passed. Except for the withdrawal of U.S. troops, the exchange of prisoners, the cessation of all U.S. war activities in Vietnam, and the de-mining of North Vietnam's ports, no other provision of the Paris agreement could be implemented, especially the cease-fire. This was because of the very ambiguity and impracticability of the agreement and the fact that North Vietnam never renounced [its] aggression.

—General Cao Van Vien and
Lieutenant General Dong Van Khuyen,
ARVN, in "Reflections on the Vietnam War,"
Indochina Monographs

South Vietnam's Decline

At the beginning of 1974, the Communists made a few conquests of bases in South Vietnam, mostly in the western highlands. Meanwhile, drastic cuts in U.S. military assistance began to take their toll on the armed forces of South

Vietnam, or RVNAF. The United States had organized the South Vietnamese Army and Air Force to fight a high-tech modern war, so when the United States bowed out of the war, it left South Vietnam unable to continue the only sort of war it was organized to fight or knew how to fight. But that kind of war was expensive in ammunition and materiel, and the South Vietnamese could no longer afford it. Their armed forces had also relied too heavily on U.S. military advisors, and they now lacked the expertise to fight the American kind of war that their U.S. advisors had urged on them.

For lack of sufficient funds, all military training was halted. Soon, the RVNAF's lack of spare parts forced it to cannibalize parts from existing weapons and machines to repair broken or faulty ones. This, of course, lessened its inventory of usable weapons and machinery. Soon, hand grenades were rationed, use of ammunition was restricted drastically, and mortar and artillery shells were cautiously distributed. Its hospitals lacked bandages, antibiotics, and the medical devices necessary to preserve the lives of its soldiers. Many ambulances were short on gas or lacking in parts. Sometimes, caravans of gasless ambulances were hitched together and pulled behind a single truck. In addition, soldiers' salaries were lowered to the extent that the troops and their families eventually lived in straitened circumstances. Even clothing was rationed carefully, which meant that fewer boots and socks were available. Some soldiers worked two jobs to make ends meet. Meanwhile, some twenty thousand soldiers deserted each month, and those who remained on duty often stole military equipment and sold it to augment their salaries. Many junior officers supplemented their salaries by engaging in graft and corruption.

The consequences of this tightening of funds affected morale and efficiency. ARVN commanders became convinced that the war was going against them, and some of them avoided combat situations whenever possible. Conditions for the South Vietnamese people were dismal also. The South Vietnam economy, accustomed to the millions of dollars filtering into it from U.S. aid and the presence of U.S.

good luck to the last American leaving Tan Son Nhut Air Base, Air Force sergeant Max Beilke, on March 29, 1973. (Beilke was later killed when a jetliner hijacked by Al Qaeda terrorists crashed into the Pentagon on September 11, 2001.) Duong Van Minh, unlike most other senior, mid-level, or even low-ranked South Vietnamese officials, was not arrested after "reunification"; he simply served eight years of house arrest in his villa before immigrating to the United States. He was followed by Colonel Tin, who defected in 1990 after becoming disillusioned with the repressive and vindictive policies of his government. Tin became a critic of the Communist government, in fact, which promptly erased his decades-long role in the conflict from the country's history books.

OPPOSITE: The strain of battle shows on the face of a heavily laden ARVN soldier. After the U.S. withdrawal, the South Vietnamese were left to fend for themselves as Congress progressively cut and then eliminated all aid.

troops, now nearly collapsed. Inflation soared. Manufacturing suffered, and unemployment was rampant. By 1974, one-third of South Vietnamese civilians were out of work, and the per capita income of those who did work shrank to one-third to one-half of what it had been previously. Farmers were affected by the high inflation in the cost of fuel and fertilizer, the result in part of corruption, some instances of which were linked to President Thieu him-self. In the meantime, Thieu's support from both Catholics and Buddhists deteriorated, leaving him with a throng of opponents within his own religion, people, and party. He was disheartened and felt deserted and betrayed. Clearly, South Vietnam as a political and military entity was on the verge of collapse. Thankfully for that country, the North Vietnamese were not yet aware of the fact.

 General Nguyen Cao Ky, former vice president of South Vietnam and a general in its air force, disparaged

the higher-ranking officers in the South Vietnamese armed forces, pinpointing their weaknesses. Ky infers that fundamental flaws in the conduct of the South Vietnamese officer corps became critical once the United States bowed out of the Vietnam War.

All those senior officers had served the French. They belonged to the era of colonialism, when the French promoted not those who displayed courage or initiative but those who served as their most loyal puppets. The French taught them that what was best for France was best for Vietnam, that white Europeans had a monopoly on brains, that the French way was the right way. A few of the brightest officers went to the military academy, but even they got no significant military experience. They were administrators, lower-level staff offi-cers—bean counters—most of whom dressed and acted like French officers. When the French went home, these Vietnamese officers became comic-opera generals: extraordinary

drinkers, graceful dancers, masterful chasers of girls. They spoke beautiful French, though some had trouble with Vietnamese, and few had any idea what it meant to be a fighter. The best would have struggled commanding a division or even a regiment. And they were, to a man, corrupted. From this group came Thieu and those in charge of his million-man armed forces!

—Nguyen Cao Ky,
in *Buddha's Child: My Fight to Save Vietnam*

The corruptness and incompetence of high-ranking South Vietnamese officers was not always the result of the South Vietnamese, according to Nguyen Cao Ky. Sometimes, self-serving U.S. officers helped perpetuate the corrupt system.

Each [U.S.] advisor prepared regular reports on his [monitored Vietnamese officer's] activities and sent them up his chain of command. American captains and majors learned that if the colonels and generals whom they advised were described as intelligent, cooperative, and eager to fight, these qualities would reflect, in part, their own performance as advisors. Advisors whose Vietnamese counterparts were brave tigers got medals and career advancement. If the commander they advised was stupid, corrupt and cowardly, however, those advisors [who honestly rated them] risked poor efficiency reports and being passed over for promotion.

When [American] advisors went home, they usually received the highest decoration, a medal that only their Vietnamese counterpart was in a position to recommend. Such decorations were important to careers, so many American advisors promoted their own interest by reporting that an ARVN general was terrific and ran a crack unit. Ninety percent of Vietnamese commanders were repeatedly lauded by their American advisors.

—Nguyen Cao Ky,
in *Buddha's Child: My Fight to Save Vietnam*

North Vietnam's Great Offensive

In 1973 and 1974, the U.S. Air Force in Thailand began to receive reports from its observers of a huge buildup of NVA forces in South Vietnam. Clearly, North Vietnam's politburo was organizing its forces for a major offensive. The signs indicated that NVA divisions were being reinforced and fitted with new tanks, artillery, anti-aircraft guns, and missiles. Meanwhile, the NVA began conducting strategic raids in South Vietnam to sharpen its units' performance. The operations around Saigon, directed by General Tran Van Tra, caused attrition and demoralization in ARVN troops and reestablished esprit and initiative in NVA soldiers. But the principal aim of Tra's strategic raids was to eliminate ARVN bases that obstructed the passage of NVA troops and their logistic trains in the direction of Saigon. Raids in the northern part of South Vietnam would open up passageways for attacks on other major target cities once the Great Offensive got under way. The Great Offensive was planned originally for 1976, which reveals how cautious the NVA had become after the failure of its two previous major offensives in South Vietnam. As the Great Offensive came closer to reality, though, the politburo, in coordination with its generals, moved up the attack time to 1975. The Communists were recognizing telltale signs that South Vietnam and its armies were crumbling. But they had no clear idea just how severe the deterioration was.

By late 1974, General Tra had destroyed the ARVN bases that impeded an attack on Saigon. Tra believed that he had a great plan for an offensive against the capital—contingent upon agreement by the politburo. He intended to attack the city along five fronts. The first prong of the attack would reach toward Saigon from the direction of Tay Ninh; the second spearhead would proceed from An Loc; a third thrust would advance from Bien Hoa; and a fourth attack would approach Saigon from the east, from a starting point south of Xuan Loc. A fifth and last spearhead would approach Saigon

NGUYEN CAO KY

directly from the west. The attacks would approach the capital of South Vietnam like the spokes of a wheel reach toward the axle. To further prepare the battlefield, General Tra planned for attacks on Don Luan and Phuoc Long, north of Saigon on Highway 1A. Eventually, his plan would be accepted, but another general would command the main attack. The NVA was ready now to begin its final, Great Offensive against the RVNAF.

🎤 *Once a cease-fire agreement was in place, the North Vietnamese began pursuing the same strategy they had previous to the cease-fire, only this time the goal was the destruction of South Vietnam in a main force battle in which its major ally, the United States, was no longer a factor.*

During this cease-fire period, the Communists progressed from pressures and sieges on outlying outposts, villages, and district towns [of South Vietnam], overrunning them wherever they could, to large-scale attacks, first against the provincial city of Phuoc Long, then against Ban Me Thuot. Their purpose was to occupy more land, control more population, and put pressure on our diminishing territory until the time was ripe for a final blow.
—Generals Cao Van Vien and Dong Van Khuyen, in "Reflections on the Vietnam War," *Indochina Monographs*

🎤 *After the Paris Peace Accords, and against all its stipulations, the North Vietnamese began building up their armaments with a flood of Soviet weapons.*

Just three months after the cease-fire, their armor forces had been augmented by 400 tanks, which brought the total to 500, and their 122-mm and 130-mm guns also increased to 250 pieces compared to 80 in 1972. By that time, NVA air-defense units were being upgraded into regiments and divisions equipped with radar-controlled 37-mm, 57-mm, and 100-mm guns and even SAM-2s. Infantry units also received improved SA-7s, which had an effective range of 15,000 feet. The NVA strategic communication system was modernized and expanded, which made vehicle traffic possible from the 17th parallel to the boundaries of Tay Ninh in MR [Military Region]-3. Our air reconnaissance had detected important convoys rolling on this route, sometimes as many as 300 vehicles at one time.
—Generals Cao Van Vien and Dong Van Khuyen, in "Reflections on the Vietnam War," *Indochina Monographs*

The Fall of Military Region 2

The attack on South Vietnam began with the assaults on Don Luan and Phuoc Long, north of Saigon. The assaults on these two cities were critical for two reasons. One, the cities held great tactical significance for the ultimate attack on Saigon. Two, the assaults would reveal how the United States was going to respond to North Vietnamese aggression, a question that

ARMY OF THE REPUBLIC OF VIETNAM AIRBORNE DIVISION

The ARVN Airborne Division's origins date back to 1951 during the French colonial period. Its initial two parachute battalions grew to become the five-battalion ARVN Airborne Group by 1955, and division strength was achieved in 1965. During the "Second Indochina War," this all-volunteer force fought mainly as infantry assault troops and earned a reputation as tough, determined fighters not timid about taking heavy casualties. Elements within the division received twelve U.S. Presidential Unit Citations, but the commendations were often poorly utilized by senior ARVN leadership. The later war years saw the division frequently employed as separate brigades to shore up developing crises, and its brigades were finally overwhelmed by armor-heavy North Vietnamese forces in 1975.

intensely interested the politburo. The first major attacks by the NVA, though, were centered on ARVN forces in Military Region (MR) 1 and 2, north of the capital in the northern two-thirds of South Vietnam. These attacks were meant to weaken the ARVN forces and, if all went well, to set the stage for the final assault on Saigon.

In early March 1975, the NVA began final preparations to attack cities in MR 2, some three hundred miles north of Saigon. The key to the area, the NVA believed, was Ban Me Thuot, situated astride Highways 14 and 21. The town provided access to the eastern (coastal) and western (mountainous) sections of the province. The six towns and cities in MR 2 on which the NVA focused were Kontum, Pleiku, and Ban Me Thuot, in the west, and Nha Trang, Tuy Hoa, and Qui Nhon, in the east. All were provincial capitals with airfields. The NVA had five main force divisions in MR 1 commanded by Senior General Van Tien Dung, while the ARVN had two divisions and seven ranger regiments led by General Pham Van Phu, II Corps commander.

On March 10, General Dung made several diversionary attacks near Kontum, Pleiku, and along Highway 19, a hundred miles north of Ban Me Thuot. His forces then interdicted Highways 14 and 21, which led to the town, blocking any reinforcements from the north, south, or east. After heavy fighting, the town was taken in a two-division attack on March 11. Soon thereafter, President Thieu commanded General Phu to make a counterattack against Ban Me Thuot. For that purpose, Phu had troops airlifted to Phuoc An, ten miles east of Ban Me Thuot, where he placed them under the command of Brigadier General Le Van Tuong, who would lead the counterattack. On March 15, the ARVN forces advanced on Ban Me Thuot, but when they arrived, many of the officers and men became so obsessed about their families' welfare in Ban Me Thuot that they broke ranks, gathered up their families, threw away their uniforms and weapons, and rushed eastward to Nha Trang on the coast.

On March 11, demoralized by the defeat at Ban Me Thuot, Thieu called his advisors together and told them that he had abandoned his "hold everything" strategy and was now intent

on holding only that part of his country that held most of its people and resources, that is, the country south of Tuy Hoa. The area north of that point would be held selectively, with only Hue, Da Nang, Quang Ngai City, and Qui Nhon on the list to be saved. General Tuong was told that he was to occupy Da Nang and a sufficient area around the port city to protect it. Meanwhile, Thieu ordered General Phu to withdraw all ARVN forces from Kontum and Pleiku and to lead them down Provincial Route 7B, a little used and dilapidated logging trail in the direction of Tuy Hoa. When Phu began his withdrawal, the civilians in the area and the soldiers' families joined his column in a disorganized throng. The column was forced to halt at Cheo Reo while engineers repaired the road ahead. At this point, the 320th NVA Artillery Division began bombarding them, soldiers and civilians alike. When the panicked ARVN soldiers finally advanced, tanks began running over people. Compounding what was already chaos, the South Vietnamese Air Force accidentally bombed its own people, knocking out four tanks, killing civilians, and wiping out a ranger battalion. Eventually, only one-third of the soldiers made it out alive to Tuy Hoa, their destination. This botched operation marked the defeat of the ARVN in MR 2 and set the tone for most of the ARVN's actions to follow.

ABOVE: During a near riot at Nha Trang airfield, a Vietnamese refugee aboard a transport aircraft tries to pry open the hand of a panic-stricken man as an American official lands a "hard right" in their effort to force him from the doorway of the severely overloaded plane, April 2, 1975. These and thousands of other refugees were seeking to flee the coastal city ahead of the NVA armored spearheads closing in from the north and west.

BELOW: U.S. Army Chinook helicopters dropping off supplies and airlifting refugees from Highway 1, approximately thirty-eight miles northeast of Saigon, April 14–15, 1975.

The ARVN throughout its history was encumbered by the families of its military personnel and by the civilians who followed in the army's wake as the soldiers performed their duties. This weakness exacerbated the attempt to safely evacuate Pleiku under threat of NVA assault and ultimately fostered chaos.

The element of secrecy that General Phu had desired and expected to achieve did not last very long. When the first convoy left Pleiku, the people were alerted to a possible evacuation. This was inevitable in the context of the Vietnam War. For years, our people had depended on army units for their security. Therefore, they monitored the activities of military dependents and units; if troops and their dependents left because of enemy action, so did they. As for the enemy, he was indeed surprised by this sudden redeployment. However, he immediately threw his units into the pursuit. Once again, NVA troops had turned Route 7B into another "Boulevard of Terror."

—Generals Cao Van Vien and
Dong Van Khuyen,
in "Reflections on the Vietnam War,"
Indochina Monographs

The Fall of Military Region 1

General Ngo Quang Truong had between four and five divisions scattered throughout MR 1's four provinces: the ARVN 2d Division in Quang Ngai and Quang Tin provinces; a U.S. Marine division and ARVN 3d Division in the Da Nang area in Quang Nam Province; and the 1st Division and an armored and a marine brigade in Quang Tri and Thua Thien provinces. Opposing these forces were five NVA main force divisions, three sapper regiments, nine infantry regiments, eight artillery regiments, three tank regiments, and twelve anti-aircraft regiments—a total of some nine divisions. The NVA's plan was to force all these ARVN units into Da Nang and destroy them.

On March 19, 1975, when Thieu ordered an elite airborne division back to Saigon it caused uneasiness among the civilians in the area around Da Nang, who began to stream into that town. At about the same time, a marine division was moved from Quang Tri Province to Quang Nam Province, which further panicked the people in Quang Tri and Thua Thien provinces, who now started a mass exodus to

LEFT: North Vietnamese T-34s maneuver around a burning ARVN tank as they force their way into Saigon, April 30, 1975.

Da Nang down Highway 1, glutting the road and preventing it from being used by the ARVN. Truong, now upset by the situation, told Thieu that he would not be responsible for the refugees, couldn't be, and requested strenuously that his forces should only be expected to defend Hue, Da Nang, and Chu Lai. Thieu assented to his demand. At this time, the Communists spread a rumor that Thieu had made a deal to cede MR 1 to them, a lie that not only demoralized the ARVN troops but unnerved the already panicky civilians. Because NVA troops had murdered thousands of civilians in Hue in 1968, the citizens' fears were well founded. The result of all this was that the roads leading to Da Nang were glutted with hundreds of thousands of civilians.

Also on March 19, the NVA, in a series of coordinated attacks, seized all of Quang Tri Province. The citizens of Hue, in Thua Thien Province, became apprehensive, so Thieu assured them in a televised address that Hue would be defended. At the same time, he ordered General Truong to defend only Da Nang. Thieu's duplicity was not lost on the people of Hue, and they began to stampede south toward possible safety at Da Nang. By March 22, the NVA had blocked the highway leading from Hue to Da Nang. Soon, the people in the two provinces south of Da Nang abandoned

their homes, too, and began moving toward Da Nang. Not long afterward, there were more than four hundred thousand refugees in Da Nang, and more were on their way. On March 24, Truong decided to move his forces out of Hue by sea. Thousands of soldiers were killed during the evacuation as the NVA showered them with artillery. The troops in Chu Lai were evacuated by sea the next day, an event equally chaotic and deadly.

By March 27, more than a million and a half refugees filled Da Nang, and the entire social order broke down, the police deserted, and pillaging became widespread. In the meantime, NVA artillery shells rained down on the town's civilians and military alike. Soldiers died by the thousands as they attempted to board boats offshore. Even General Truong was forced to swim for his life. He admitted later that "not many got out." Three days later, MR 1 was part of North Vietnam.

War's End

By April 1, 1975, the politburo was convinced that South Vietnam was on the brink of collapse. All it would take to send the country over the edge was to consolidate NVA forces

RIGHT: North Vietnamese soldiers running past Caribou transports at Saigon's Tan Son Nhut Air Base, April 30, 1975. The column of black smoke rises from other aircraft destroyed when NVA artillery shelled the air base. Several hours later, Saigon fell into the hands of the Communist troops, marking an end to the Vietnam War. Earlier shelling and the wreckage of South Vietnamese aircraft shot down over the runway had left the air base useless for operating large transport planes, and the planned removal of the last few thousand Americans from Saigon had to be scrapped in favor of an ad hoc helicopter evacuation carried out at several locations.

and mount a major assault against Saigon, using General Tra's well-conceived plan. But Tra would not be given the glory for the attack on Saigon: the politburo gave the assignment to favored general Van Tien Dung. After the collapses of MR 1 and 2, the NVA wanted to move quickly on Saigon before the ARVN could regain its balance.

Meanwhile, during all these recent events, Thieu and South Vietnam's Joint General Staff (their Joint Chiefs of Staff) did little to bolster the defenses of Saigon, making it a tempting prize waiting to be snatched. The politburo titled the final campaign the Ho Chi Minh Campaign, in honor of their late leader, who had died in September 1969. By now, almost everyone in South Vietnam knew that the war was coming to a close, that they were defeated, and that many of them were likely doomed. The collapse in the north had signaled to all the futility of the struggle. Now, the NVA, with some thirteen to twenty divisions in five corps, was approaching Saigon, supported by tanks, artillery, anti-aircraft, and even a fledgling air force. The ARVN, with only three divisions of soldiers, moved to block their way at the five main road arteries leading into Saigon. NVA

troops would move along all five routes, in accordance with their plan.

General Truong, a deputy chief of the Joint General Staff of South Vietnam's armed forces (the JGS), led the ARVN in its final defense of Saigon. Truong hoped to keep the fighting outside Saigon proper, so he set up blocking positions seventeen to thirty miles outside the city, keeping the capital beyond the range of the NVA's powerful 130-mm guns. This defense was just what the North Vietnamese had hoped for. They wished to take Saigon without damaging its infrastructure or becoming involved in a house-to-house struggle for the city. General Dung, therefore, ordered his commanders to surround the ARVN defensive positions in place. Meanwhile, other NVA units were commanded to take key targets within Saigon: the headquarters of the JGS at Tan Son Nhut Air Base; the Independence Palace, Thieu's seat of government; the Capitol Zone's headquarters; and the National Police Headquarters. Dung's thought was to destroy South Vietnam's leadership—the "head." Then, the "body"—the army and country—would collapse. He also called for a popular uprising, but that was just a sideshow.

To facilitate his attack on Saigon, Dung sought to block any ARVN reinforcements from arriving at Saigon from the east. This would be accomplished by taking Xuan Loc. Highway 4, southwest of Saigon, was another prime target. Seizing it would block ARVN reinforcements coming from the Mekong Delta area. The vastly outnumbered ARVN 18th Division at Xuan Loc, despite the odds against it, waged a valiant defense in that sector of the battlefield against four NVA divisions, holding out for thirteen days. Some twenty thousand artillery and rocket rounds were fired upon the defenders, killing 30 percent of them before they retreated on April 22, after killing five thousand NVA soldiers.

On April 21, Thieu resigned and fled the country for Taiwan, triggering the final capitulation of South Vietnam. On April 28, General Duong Van Minh ("Big Minh") became president, even though the word had leaked that he was connected with the Communists. Indeed, he was chosen for precisely that reason, but to no avail, for he failed to work out any favorable agreements with the Communists. Meanwhile, Americans and senior South Vietnamese officials were evacuated from the country in an environment of chaos. Before dawn on April 30, all Americans had been removed from Saigon, as well as selected South Vietnamese nationals. Some fifty-eight thousand South Vietnamese were flown out of the country by helicopter and military and commercial aircraft. By now, the NVA was on the outskirts of Saigon, and by midday on April 30, the Communists had run up a red flag at Independence Palace. South Vietnam was now a Communist country, and Saigon was renamed Ho Chi Minh City.

 Even Nguyen Cao Ky, a former vice president of South Vietnam and an air force general with ample prestige and influence, had to get out of South Vietnam in a makeshift manner.

But how was my family to get out? American planes, commercial and military, still flew out of Tan Son Nhut. But because we had not anticipated leaving, we had no plan, no reservation, no tickets, no papers, hardly any money. Exit visas and airline tickets were changing hands at astronomical prices; anyone with money enough for a ticket, even at regular prices, was desperate to leave. Even I could not arrange a ticket. But my wife is very resourceful, and her face was known by many Americans. I told her, "Just go to the civilian air terminal and find something." So I put them in Buddha's hands, and we said good-bye.

—Nguyen Cao Ky,
in *Buddha's Child: My Fight to Save Vietnam*

General Nguyen Cao Ky found his last hours in Saigon chaotic beyond belief.

I had not slept in days, so at nightfall, I lay down and fell at once into deep sleep. I was jolted awake by the impact of dozens of huge Soviet-made incendiary rockets raining down on the air base. These were followed by enemy artillery firing hundreds of high-explosive and antipersonnel shells that burst on and above the base. Among the first buildings hit was the hospital, which erupted in flames. The barrage went on and on, my house shaking and shuddering with each nearby concussion.

—Nguyen Cao Ky,
in *Buddha's Child: My Fight to Save Vietnam*

BELOW: Refugees flee the coastal resort village of Vung Tau, South Vietnam, during the fall of Saigon, April 21, 1975.

🎙 *Finally, General Nguyen Cao Ky was able to leave Saigon before the wolves arrived at his door. He boarded his Huey helicopter, loaded it with as many Vietnamese as he dared, and dashed out to sea. He immediately tuned his radio to the international distress channel and cried out: "Mayday! Mayday! Mayday!"*

On and on we flew; more than an hour passed, but the sea remained limitless and empty. At the point of no return, when there was not enough fuel to go back, I began to consider that I might have to ditch. I thought about the procedure, about hovering to let the others jump out, then, moving away so they would not be cut to pieces by the rotor blades, and about how long a Huey might float upright. We had neither life jackets nor rafts, and in a few hours it would be dark, but I was confident that the U.S. Navy would search for us. Well, fairly confident.

—Nguyen Cao Ky,
in *Buddha's Child: My Fight to Save Vietnam*

Abandonment of the U.S. Embassy

While the South Vietnamese military and civilians were frantically fleeing the country, American officials attempted to evacuate the U.S. Embassy. As part of this exodus, two hundred U.S. civilian and military personnel had to be airlifted from the embassy grounds to the airfield at Tan Son Nhut. The evacuation was aggravated by an influx of three thousand panicky South Vietnamese who worked with the Americans and expected to be airlifted also. Soon, a tree was toppled and cleared from the courtyard, and communications wires were severed and removed to allow large U.S. Marine CH-53 helicopters to land. Their landings and takeoffs were made difficult by the heavy loads and by their being forced to stop, hover, and then descend perpendicularly onto the confined landing area.

Wolfgang Lehmann, U.S. minister to the Republic of Vietnam and deputy chief of mission, and Colonel Jack Madison were delegated the task of supervising the evacuation, with the help of Colonels Jack Harrington and Harry G. Summers Jr., along with Master Sergeant Bill Herron, Gunnery Sergeant Ernie Pace, and Specialist 7 Bill Bell. By noon on April 29, 1975, the crowd had broken into the liquor supplies at the State Department Club and was becoming unruly. The mob was further excited by their view of helicopters shuttling in and out of the embassy grounds with the lucky early evacuees aboard. To calm them, the officials supervising the evacuation went out into the crowd and assured them that they, the organizers of the evacuation, would be the last to leave. This promise was not kept.

The evacuees were organized now into groups numbering forty Americans and seventy South Vietnamese each. The South Vietnamese were formed into larger groups because of their smaller size, which allowed more of them to be loaded aboard the helicopters. Finally, only six groups remained, but they were abandoned after the removal of twenty-six hundred people. Among the reasons offered for the cessation of the flights were that the pilots were "dead on their feet" and that the U.S. Navy was convinced there would be no end to the number of people demanding removal.

I lay down and fell at once into deep sleep. I was jolted awake by the impact of dozens of huge Soviet-made incendiary rockets raining down on the air base. . . . Among the first buildings hit was the hospital, which erupted in flames.

—Nguyen Cao Ky

Those ultimately left behind in the embassy included a South Korean CIA detachment (which faced subsequent imprisonment and death), a priest with South Vietnamese refugee children, and U.S. Embassy firemen.

While the helicopters would have been easy targets for artillery, rockets, or even automatic rifles during their landings and departures, the North Vietnamese held their fire—both at Tan Son Nhut and the embassy—for reasons only to be guessed. Finally, between 12:00 P.M. and 1:00 A.M. on April 30, the helicopter flights slowed, and the last six groups began to lose hope that they would be leaving. Their fears were not unfounded, for they were fated to stay. The supervising officials left from the embassy roof around 6:00 A.M. on April 30, to be followed by the U.S. Marine guard at

ABOVE: The identification card issued to then Lieutenant Colonel Harry G. Summers Jr. by the victorious Vietnamese Communists. From 1974 to 1975, Summers served as the chief negotiator of the Four-Party Joint Military Team's (FPJMT) small U.S. contingent. The stated purpose of the FPJMT was the resolution of the status of Americans listed as missing in action, but, as South Vietnam began to crumble, Summers found himself flying to Hanoi to negotiate the status of the U.S. diplomatic mission in Saigon instead. Several days later, Summers and the other five Americans in the delegation coordinated the evacuation of two thousand Vietnamese civilians from the U.S. Embassy grounds.

8:00 A.M. Before the Marines left the area, they locked all the doors, barricaded the stairway, then lobbed tear gas canisters behind them and boarded the last helicopter flight from the embassy roof.

Harry G. Summers Jr., chief of the Negotiations Division of the U.S. Delegation to the Four-Party Joint Military Team set up by the Paris Peace Accords, describes the scramble to get U.S. civilians and servicemen out of Saigon during the final attacks by the Communists.

It was only at noon on [April] 29th when the decision was made in Washington that all Americans would be withdrawn. So because we were there and because of the chaotic situation at the U.S. Embassy—well, essentially, the situation was that the plan called for the evacuation of about two hundred people from the embassy to Tan Son Nhut and departure from there. Instead, we had about three thousand people jammed inside the walls of the embassy, so Wolfgang Lehmann and my boss, Colonel Jack Madison, who's now retired, got together and we took over the responsibility for handling the evacuation of the embassy. By we, I mean Colonel Jack Madison, myself, Major, now Lieutenant Colonel, Stuart Harrington, who is now with the Assistant

Chief of Staff for Intelligence in Europe, and three enlisted men—Master Sergeant Bill Herron, Gunny [Gunnery] Sergeant Ernie Pace, and Specialist 7 Bill Bell. Pace, Bell, and Harrington were all Vietnamese linguists of varying abilities, and their abilities really paid off because they were able to calm the crowd, which was almost at the point of panic at noon on the 29th, for two reasons. The first was that the crowd broke into the liquor supplies at the State Department Club, and the liquor was being passed around. One of the first things that Harrington did was to lock up the liquor supply, which was a very fortuitous move. The second [reason we needed these men] was that [U.S. officials] were beginning the evacuation as planned, taking people from the roof of the embassy out to Tan Son Nhut. Air America helicopters were shuttling them back and forth—and all of the people inside the embassy walls could see this evacuation taking place. They had the feeling that they were about to be abandoned, so they were really just about to get out of hand.

So Harrington, Herron, myself, and the other two enlisted men, Bell and Pace, went through the crowd telling them that everybody was going to get out. We told them that we were going to be the last ones to leave and that everyone would get out. We convinced

them of that and then we started organizing people into seventy-person packets. In the meantime, the Marine guards had succeeded in taking the tree down in the middle of the embassy courtyard and preparing a landing zone for the Marine helicopters, the large helicopters. So when they started coming in, we fixed a load of seventy people and loaded them on each helicopter, except for Americans. When we put Americans on, we could only get about forty, but with the Vietnamese [because of their smaller size], we could get about seventy. So we worked that evacuation all that day and into the night and up until the next morning, and we finally got down to six loads left. Six loads would be about 420 people.

The ambassador's assistant, Brunson McKinley, the rotten bastard, told us that the helicopters were on the way and to hold our position on the LZ, and that everything was going to be fine. Whereupon he went back in the embassy and went up on the elevator to the roof and left with U.S. Ambassador Martin, knowing that the evacuation had been canceled. To lie about an operational matter at a time like that was absolutely unforgivable. So right after that, the head of the Marine detachment, whose name I don't recall, told us that the evacuation was over, that we had to get out immediately and that the Marines were about to secure the embassy and leave from the roof. So we

abandoned these six loads [of people]. We already had them broken down into helicopter loads, including the Korean CIA detachment, who I understand was either killed or is still in jail in Vietnam, the German priest with his refugee children, all the firemen in the embassy who volunteered to stay until the very end, and people of that ilk. And, I must say, I'm still disgusted with it. It still burns me up that we'd pull a stunt like that.

When we got out to the fleet we found out that what we were operating on was a misconception. The fleet thought they were operating with a bottomless pit [unlimited number of refugees] and that they had to cut it off someplace because the pilots were dead on their feet. They had been flying well over the safety hours they should have been flying; they didn't know that all that was left was the six loads; if they had, they would have pulled them out. I thought it was sort of the Vietnam War in microcosm: great intentions and everybody trying to do the right thing but managing to screw it up at the end because we just didn't communicate very well.

—Colonel Harry G. Summers Jr.,
U.S. Army, Retired,
in Project 82-2, "Last Days in Vietnam,"
U.S. Army War College/U.S. Army Military
History Institute's Senior Officer
Oral History Program

OPPOSITE, BOTTOM: CIA employee Oren B. Harnage ushers Vietnamese officials and their families who assisted the CIA aboard one of several agency-owned Hueys that ferried them to larger U.S. Air Force and Navy helicopters at Tan Son Nhut Air Base, April 29, 1975. This apartment building at 22 Gia Long Street, about half a mile from the U.S. Embassy, housed employees of the United States Agency for International Development, and the top floor was reserved for the CIA's deputy chief of station. Station Chief Thomas Polgar evacuated the Vietnamese by helicopter because the ground route to Tan Son Nhut was no longer considered safe.

ABOVE: A Viet Cong stands guard over ARVN soldiers and other South Vietnamese as NVA troops mill about the former presidential palace of the Republic of Vietnam, May 3, 1975. Although some ARVN soldiers attempted to avoid capture by blending in with the population, by this date, a portion of the captives were likely government supporters who had earlier been marked to be rounded up once the Communists had taken control of the city.

Boat People

Once NVA forces defeated South Vietnam on April 30, 1975, they tossed moral considerations to the wind, dropped their masks, and subjected the people of South Vietnam to a Communist dictatorship bent on revenge. Within the next few years, more than a million South Vietnamese fled their former country to avoid persecution and imprisonment. For many, this meant secretly purchasing an ordinary fishing boat—often with an underpowered engine—stashing stores of food in hidden caches, then stealing away in the night, chugging out into the open ocean and an uncertain fate. Those who chose this route came to be called boat people. For most of these people, the risks— though enormous—were considered worth it. They no longer had lives, in the ordinary sense, in Vietnam.

Major Phung Le, holder of a Bachelor of Laws degree from Saigon University, a graduate of the Military Officers School, and a division chief of litigation of military property for the Defense Department, was one of these people. Even though he had a wife and six children to support, he was sent to a remote "reeducation camp" for nine years. As a former ARVN officer, he was considered to be a threat. This was done without a trial and was meant to force him to conform. Higher-ranking officers were simply executed. Once freed from the camp, Phung Le became a "non-citizen," under continuous surveillance by the police and forced into the lowest laboring class. In the new Communist order, people were classified from 1 to 14. Phung Le and his children were now in position 13. Classification 1 people were the

ABOVE: Vietnamese boat people secure their rickety craft to the side of the combat-stores ship USS *White Plains* before climbing up a cargo net to the deck, August 8, 1979. For safety, women and children were routinely hoisted aboard U.S. ships or lifted to the deck by rescue helicopters. Some twenty-eight people were packed onto this thirty-five-foot wooden boat, found out of gas and adrift in the South China Sea.

children of dead NVA soldiers or Viet Cong and were given many rewards and advantages. Nearly all qualified, for instance, to go to the universities. The only people lower in status than Phung Le's Classification 13, however, were the children of traitors.

Many former South Vietnamese attempted to escape, often multiple times. If captured in the process, they were sentenced to prison for one or more years. Even a wife might be imprisoned for her husband's "crime" of seeking freedom. Because Phung Le's planning was superior to most, and because he had more money than some, he managed to escape Vietnam with 154 other people on his second attempt. After escaping from the

mainland, Phung Le and the boat people who accompanied him moved into open water and threw away their detested Communist flag, which they had flown only for camouflage. Most of the boat people with Phung Le stayed out of sight, inside the hull of the boat, often suffering terribly from seasickness.

Phung Le and his group managed to escape. Others were not so lucky. Invariably, their engines stalled before they got very far, leaving them to drift aimlessly in the currents, hoping for a safe landfall. Many floated toward Malaysian waters, where they found themselves easy prey for pirates, who boarded the boats, beat them unmercifully, robbed them of their valuables, and destroyed or stole any motors still operating.

Most ships that passed the boat people ignored them, but a few mercifully stopped long enough to give them directions and a few supplies. While many were ultimately rescued, others died of starvation and illness or met their fate when their boats foundered in violent storms. Those fortunate enough to be rescued usually ended up in nasty refugee camps with inadequate water supplies, poor food, and abysmal hygiene. These refugees were eventually relocated to larger camps, where there was an attempt to teach them rudimentary English and find them sponsors in various foreign countries, including the United States and Australia, often funded by Catholic, Baptist, or Methodist charities. Many of the boat people who settled in the United States went on to pursue higher educational degrees and have become model citizens and valuable assets in their communities.

Despite the chaos attendant with the evacuation of the U.S. Embassy, American officials maintained surprising order.

So anyway, they started to panic and the bottle-neck was there at the gate. Stu Harrington took it upon himself to go into this mass of people, and he was almost part of a riot. Because he had gone in, I had to go in, and then Master Sergeant Herron went in and got the people moved back and got them in lines....

One of the things that bothered me was that they brought in a Marine pathfinder team. They brought these Marines in to secure the embassy, but these guys were young kids; they had never been in combat, and they really didn't know what they were getting into. They thought, you know, they were really going to have to fight them [the NVA] off the walls. This "Gunny" Sergeant Pace, who normally was inside, came out and through his efforts he got these kids calmed down, and before long, they were carrying babies and putting them on helicopters. They really changed their attitude

about what they were doing. All this business about people storming the walls and the rest of it is pure fabrication. It just did not happen. There were people clamoring outside the walls, most of them—God, it's sad to think about this—with their certificates of service in their hands and all their papers from the U.S. in their hands, waving them and trying to get people's attention....

ABOVE: An NVA tank drives through the main gate of the presidential palace in Saigon as the city falls into the hands of Communist troops, April 30, 1975.

BELOW: The first wave of what would ultimately top 1 million refugees pulls up alongside a U.S. warship as NVA forces close in on Saigon, April 15, 1975. Nearly all would be resettled in the United States by 1980.

ABOVE: South Vietnamese soldiers, some dressed in civilian garb in an apparently futile effort to avoid capture, are marched down a Saigon street by their North Vietnamese captors, April 30, 1975.

One of the most poignant things that happened involved a Vietnamese colonel whose name I don't remember; he was a student of mine at Leavenworth when I taught there. He was in one of these Four Party Teams or Commissions, and he came down to put his family on an airplane. This was about the 20th—you know, the latter part of April—so he was, of course, broken up because he was putting his family and children all on the airplane. He was there with his driver. Captain Stu Harrington, who spoke Vietnamese, said to the colonel, "What are you doing?" He said, "I'm just sending my family out of country, and it's terrible to have to leave," and Harrington said to him, "Get on the airplane." He replied, "I can't do that. I can't abandon my country. I can't leave here. My job is here." Harrington said, "Don't be a damn fool. President Thieu has already left; all the generals have left. Get the hell out of here. Take care of your family." He practically pushed the guy onto the airplane. Well, he was lying to him, of course. The generals hadn't left, but Stu was a pessimist being an MI [military intelligence] officer. . . . [He] figured to get him out of there while he could.

—Harry G. Summers Jr.,
in "Last Days in Vietnam"

The thunder of artillery created premonitions of disaster in some soldiers and civilians awaiting evacuation from the U.S. Embassy.

You could hear the artillery in the distance. This is one of the things that unnerved people with no combat experience. You could hear the artillery in the distance. . . . You could hear the thunder in the distance and knew what it was. You knew that they [the enemy] were there; you knew they could overrun you any time they wanted; you knew they could at least shell you any time they wanted. The tension was very, very high and some people just couldn't take it. We had a couple of our own people we had to get out of the country because they just couldn't stand the pressure. But these were people

On the 17th day at sea, the woman who sat next to me began passing out from lack of food and water. The next morning she was dead. When I saw her dead body, I began to worry that in a few days I would become just like her.

—Hien Trong Nguyen

who had never been in combat before, never had any combat experience.

—Harry G. Summers Jr.,
in "Last Days in Vietnam"

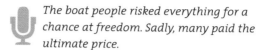 *The former South Vietnamese people sent to reeducation camps, which were in fact prisons, were forced to pretend to acquiesce to the new, oppressive regime.*

On the surface my father was a "good citizen." He did not refuse any labor, he attended reeducation meetings, and he talked with others about the "very good policy of socialism" and about the happiness it would bring the people in the future. However, my parents were living double lives. Their minds were often in a dream world where they would escape to freedom.

—Ai-Van Do,
in *Voices of Vietnamese Boat People:
Nineteen Narratives of Escape and Survival*

Nhan T. Le, who currently lives in Manchester, New Hampshire, noted how ruthless and inequitable the North Vietnamese were when they took control of South Vietnam.

Before 1975 most of the people had jobs, and after 1975, nobody had a job except for the VC and Northerners. The government didn't use Southerners or anyone who was related to the former Southern government. Every one was free now, free of having a job and free of thinking also because the government did the thinking for the people.

—Nhan T. Le,
in *Voices of Vietnamese Boat People:
Nineteen Narratives of Escape and Survival*

The boat people risked everything for a chance at freedom. Sadly, many paid the ultimate price.

On the 17th day at sea, the woman who sat next to me began passing out from lack of food and water. The next morning she was dead. When I saw her dead body, I began to worry that in a few days I would become just like her. From that point on, I began believing that my life was in the hands of God. During the next two days, two more people died from hunger.

—Hien Trong Nguyen,
in *Voices of Vietnamese Boat People:
Nineteen Narratives of Escape and Survival*

BELOW: U.S. Marines of the 2d Battalion, 9th Marine Regiment, landed by Air Force CH-53 helicopters, fan out across the Cambodian island of Koh Tang during a mission to rescue the crew of the U.S. merchant ship *Mayaguez*, captured three days earlier, on May 12, 1975. In this last, costly combat action of U.S. forces in Southeast Asia, fifteen Americans were killed in action plus twenty-three more in a related helicopter crash, with forty-nine wounded and a three-man machine-gun team missing in action and reportedly executed by the Khmer Rouge.

Afterword

Only days before the last Americans would leave Vietnam for good, Lieutenant Colonel Harry Summers flew to Hanoi aboard a C-130 with the other members of the Four-Party Joint Military Team (FPJMT) for a previously scheduled meeting with high-ranking Communist officials. But while the official agenda called for a discussion of POW/MIA issues, both sides knew that Summers's real purpose was to receive the North Vietnamese terms for the continued presence of the U.S. Embassy and FPJMT in Saigon.

Although the U.S. government would soon order all Americans out, permission was granted for the U.S. Mission, minus its Defense Attaché Office, to stay, as well as the FPJMT, which the Communists had been trying to involve in negotiations over reparations for war damage in return for information about POW/MIAs. Summers later wrote:

Hanoi, as might be imagined, was jubilant, with crowds thronging the streets. After years of struggle they had won on the battlefield what they had failed to win at the negotiating table.

"You know you never beat us on the battlefield," I said to Colonel Tu, my NVA counterpart.

"That may be so," he said, "but it is also irrelevant."

Summers would go on to write a book that greatly influenced a generation of American Army officers, *On Strategy: A Critical Analysis of the Vietnam War*. He maintained that much of the U.S. Army's combat power was squandered in ultimately futile

ABOVE: In plain language and enormous type, the May 1, 1975, edition of *Pacific Stars and Stripes* marks the end of a long, tragic war.

OPPOSITE: Members of a Viet Cong "Main Force" battalion hitch a ride with NVA troops (at left, in olive-colored uniforms) as infantry and armored units enter Saigon, April 30, 1975.

search-and-destroy operations in the South. Although frequently miscast by critics as advocating an invasion of North Vietnam and ignoring the value of unconventional operations, what Summers spells out in the last third of his book is that the United States should have established a conventional barrier—much like the Demilitarized Zone in Korea—along the border between North and South Vietnam and extending across the Communists' Ho Chi Minh Trail supply line in Laos. Summers wrote:

South Vietnam faced not only internal insurgency but also outside aggression, and counterinsurgency doctrine could only be part of the answer. . . . [T]o give credit to its originators, President Kennedy and his advisors saw counterinsurgency as first a political task to be carried out under civilian management. If it had remained at that level it could have been a valuable adjunct to U.S. military operations in Vietnam which should have been focused on protecting South Vietnam from outside aggression leaving the internal problems to the South Vietnamese themselves.

Yet important lessons were learned from the Vietnam War. The U.S. Army's—and to a great extent, America's—

political leadership gained a broad understanding that the dirty work of fighting guerrillas must be accompanied by genuine reforms if an insurgency is to be defeated rather than temporarily checked. It was also learned that if another nation's people lack the will to persevere, you cannot expect to win a war for them. Consequently, the lessons of Vietnam led to now-almost-forgotten successes on America's very doorstep, in El Salvador, Nicaragua, and Honduras. Right from the beginning of the decade-long U.S. effort to help El Salvador fight its insurgency, both

governments made—and stuck with—the wise decision not to encourage a "gringoization" of the war.

Such a policy never achieves the quick successes often demanded by an American society that has by today grown used to twenty-four-hour news cycles. More often than not, it requires almost the complete rebuilding and expansion of a host nation's military, to be accomplished in tandem with all the other unique and pressing needs of a country rent by war, a situation faced

in both Afghanistan and Iraq today and in the foreseeable future. Only time will tell just how well Americans have learned the lessons of Vietnam.

BELOW: Leathernecks place helmets on their rifles and bow their heads in tribute to the men killed in the thirty-seven operations conducted by the 9th Marines. The regiment was honored at division ceremonies, Quang Tri Combat Base, July 25, 1969.

Selected Bibliography

Braestrup, Peter. *Big Story: How the American Press and Television Reported and Interpreted the Crisis of Tet 1968 in Vietnam and Washington.* 2 vols. Boulder, CO: Westview Press, 1977.

Collins, James Lawton. *The Development and Training of the South Vietnamese Army, 1950–1972.* Vietnam Studies. Washington, DC: Department of the Army, 1975.

Davidson, Phillip B. *Vietnam at War: The History, 1946–1975.* New York: Oxford University Press, 1988.

Del Vecchio, John M. *The 13th Valley.* New York: Bantam Books, 1982.

Draper, Theodore. *Abuse of Power.* New York: Viking Press, 1967.

Duiker, William J. *The Communist Road to Power in Vietnam.* Boulder, CO: Westview Press, 1981.

Dung, Van Tien. *Our Great Spring Victory: An Account of the Liberation of South Vietnam.* New York: Monthly Review Press, 1977.

Fall, Bernard B. *The Two Vietnams, a Political and Military Analysis.* Boulder, CO: Westview Press, 1985. First published 1963 by Praeger.

Fulton, William B. *Riverine Operations, 1966–1969.* Vietnam Studies. Washington, DC: Department of the Army, 1973.

Gelb, Leslie H., and Richard K. Betts. *The Irony of Vietnam: The System Worked.* Washington, DC: Brookings Institution Press, 1979.

Giap, Vo Nguyen. *People's War, People's Army: The Viet Cong Insurrection Manual for Underdeveloped Countries.* New York: Praeger, 1962.

Goodman, Allan E. "The Dual-Track Strategy of Vietnamization and Negotiation," in *The Second Indochina War,* ed. John Schlight. Washington, DC: Center of Military History, U.S. Army, 1986.

Halberstadt, Hans. *The Wild Weasels: History of US Air Force SAM Killers, 1965 to Today.* Mil-Tech Series. Osceola, MI: Motorbooks International Publishers & Wholesalers, 1992.

Halberstam, David. *The Best and the Brightest.* Greenwich, CT: Fawcett, 1969.

———. *The Making of a Quagmire.* New York: Random House, 1965.

Hay, John H., Jr. *Tactical and Materiel Innovations.* Vietnam Studies. Washington, DC: Department of the Army, 1974.

Herring, George C. "Cold Blood: LBJ's Conduct of Limited War in Vietnam." *The Harmon Memorial Lectures in Military History,* no. 33. Colorado Springs, CO: United States Air Force Academy, 1990.

Herrington, Stuart A. *Silence Was a Weapon: The Vietnam War in the Villages.* San Francisco: Presidio Press, 1982.

Hersh, Seymour. *Mai Lai 4: A Report on the Massacre and Its Aftermath.* New York: Random House, 1970.

Hilsman, Roger. *To Move a Nation: The Politics of Foreign Policy in the Administration of John F. Kennedy.* Garden City, NY: Doubleday & Company, 1967.

Hosmer, Stephen T., et al. *The Fall of South Vietnam: Statements by Vietnamese Military and Civilian Leaders.* Santa Monica, CA: RAND Corporation, 1978.

Johnson, Sam, and Jan Winebrenner. *Captive Warriors: A Vietnam POW's Story.* Texas A&M University Military History Series, no. 23. College Station, TX: Texas A&M Press, 1992.

Kaiser, David. *American Tragedy: Kennedy, Johnson, and the Origins of the Vietnam War.* Cambridge, MA, and London: The Belknap Press of Harvard University Press, 2000.

Karnow, Stanley. *Vietnam: A History.* New York: Penguin Books, 1984.

Kinnard, Douglas. *The War Managers.* Wayne, NJ: Avery Publishing Group, Inc., 1985.

Komer, Robert W. *Impact of Pacification on Insurgency in South Vietnam.* Santa Monica, CA: RAND Corporation, 1970.

Krepinevich, Andrew F., Jr. *The Army and Vietnam.* Baltimore, MD and London: The Johns Hopkins University Press, 1988.

Le Gro, William E. *Vietnam from Cease-Fire to Capitulation.* Washington, DC: U.S. Army Center of Military History, 1981.

Lewy, Guenter. *America in Vietnam.* New York: Oxford University Press, 1978.

McNamara, Robert S. *In Retrospect: The Tragedy and Lessons of Vietnam.* New York: Times Books, 1995.

Mangold, Tom, and John Penycate. *The Tunnels of Cu Chi.* New York: Berkley Books, 1986.

Momyer, William W. *Airpower in Three Wars: World War II, Korea and Vietnam.* Washington, DC: Department of the Air Force, 1978.

Mason, Robert. *Chickenhawk.* New York: Penguin Books, 1983.

Nolan, William Keith. *Into Laos: The Story of Dewey Canyon II/Lam Son 719, Vietnam 1971.* San Francisco: Presidio Press, 1986.

Olson, James S., ed. *Dictionary of the Vietnam War.* New York, Westport, CT, and London: Greenwood Press, 1988.

Palmer, Bruce, Jr. *The 25 Year War: America's Military Role in Vietnam.* Lexington, KY: The University Press of Kentucky, 1984.

Palmer, David Richard. *Summons of the Trumpet: U.S.-Vietnam in Perspective.* San Francisco: Presidio Press, 1978.

Palmer, Gregory. *The McNamara Strategy and the Vietnam War: Program Budgeting in the Pentagon, 1960–1968.* Westport, CT: Greenwood Press, 1978.

Pape, Robert A. "Coercive Air Power in the Vietnam War." *International Security* (fall 1990).

Pearson, Willard. *The War in the Northern Provinces, 1966–1968*. Vietnam Studies. Washington, DC: Department of the Army, 1975.

Pike, Douglas Eugene. *Vietnam and the Soviet Union: Anatomy of an Alliance*. Boulder, CO: Westview Press, 1987.

———. *PAVN: People's Army of Vietnam*. San Francisco: Presidio Press, 1986.

Race, Jeffrey. *War Comes to Long An: Revolutionary Conflict in a Vietnamese Province*. Berkeley: University of California Press, 1971.

Rogers, Bernard William. *Cedar Falls-Junction City: A Turning Point*. Vietnam Studies. Washington, DC: Department of the Army, 1989.

Rosen, Stephen P. "Vietnam and the American Theory of Limited War." *International Security* (fall 1982).

Rostow, W.W. *The Diffusion of Power, 1957–1972*. New York: Macmillan, 1972.

Sharp, U.S.G., and William C. Westmoreland. *Report on the War in Vietnam*. Washington, DC: U.S. Government Printing Office, 1969.

Sheehan, Neil. *A Bright Shining Lie: John Paul Vann and America in Vietnam*. New York: Random House, 1988.

Sorley, Lewis. *A Better War: The Unexamined Victories and the Final Tragedy of America's Last Years in Vietnam*. New York: Harcourt Brace & Co., 1999.

Starry, Donn A. *Mounted Combat in Vietnam*. Vietnam Studies. Washington, DC: Department of the Army, 1978.

Summers, Harry G., Jr. *On Strategy: The Vietnam War in Context*. Carlisle Barracks, PA: Strategic Studies Institute, 1981.

Taylor, Maxwell D. *Swords and Plowshares*. New York: W.W. Norton, 1972.

Thayer, Thomas C. *War Without Fronts: The American Experience in Vietnam*. Westview Special Studies in Military Affairs. Boulder, CO: Westview Press, 1985.

Thompson, Robert Grainger Ker. *No Exit from Vietnam*. New York: David McKay, 1969.

Thompson, W. Scott, and Donaldson D. Frizzell, eds. *The Lessons of Vietnam*. Crane Russak & Co., 1977.

Thornborough, Tony, and Frank B. Mormillo. *Wild Weasels: Elite Radar Killers of the USAF*. Osprey Colour Series. London: Osprey Publishing Ltd., 1992.

Tolson, John J. *Airmobility, 1961–1971*. Vietnam Studies. Washington, DC: Department of the Army, 1973.

Turley, G.H. *The Easter Offensive: The Last American Advisors, Vietnam 1972*. San Francisco: Presidio Press, 1985.

Vien, Cao Van. *The Final Collapse*. Indochina Monographs. Washington, DC: U.S. Army Center of Military History, 1983.

———. *Reflections on the Vietnam War*. Indochina Monographs. Washington, DC: U.S. Army Center of Military History, 1980.

Westmoreland, William C. *A Soldier Reports*. New York: Doubleday, 1976.

———. *Report on the War in Vietnam*. Washington, DC: U.S. Government Printing Office, 1968.

Willbanks, James H. *Thiet Gap! The Battle of An Loc, April 1972*. Leavenworth, KS: Combat Studies Institute, U.S. Army Command and General Staff College, 1993.

ABOUT THE INTERVIEWS

The preponderance of the interviews in this book were conducted by First Person Productions for the Library of Congress' Veterans Oral History Project. The remaining interviews or excerpts in the book, reprinted gratefully with permission from the original publishers, are the exceptions, and are credited here:

Ai-Van Do, Nhan T. Le, Minh Nguyen, Hien Trong Nguyen in *Voices of Vietnamese Boat People: Nineteen Narratives of Escape and Survival*, ed., Mary Terrell Cargill and Jade Quang Huynh (Jefferson, North Carolina: McFarland, 2000); Phillip B. Davidson in *Vietnam at War: The History, 1946-1975* (New York, Oxford: Oxford University Press, 1988); Bernard Jones; Andrew F. Krepinevich in *The Army and Vietnam* (Baltimore: The Johns Hopkins University Press, 1986); Nguyen Cao Ky in *Buddha's Child: My Fight to Save Vietnam* (New York: St. Martin's Press, 2002); Harold G. Moore in *We Were Soldiers Once...and Young* (New York: Random House, 1992); Jerry D. Morelock; Bruce Palmer, Jr. in *The 25-Year War: America's Military Role in Vietnam* (Lexington: The University Press of Kentucky, 1984); Walter L. Sudol; Harry G. Summers, Jr. in "Last Days in Vietnam," *Project 82-2* (Carlisle Barracks, Pennsylvania: U.S. Army War College, 1982); Cao Van Vien and Dong Van Khuyen in *Reflections on the Vietnam War*, Indochina Monographs (Washington, DC: U.S. Army Center of Military History, 1980); James H. Willbanks in *The Battle of An Loc* (Bloomington: Indiana University Press, 2005).

Index

Photo Credits